Walt Whitman's Civil War

Walt Whitman's Civil War

Compiled & Edited from Published & Unpublished Sources

by WALTER LOWENFELS

with the assistance of Nan Braymer

Civil War drawings by Winslow Homer

A DA CAPO PAPERBACK

Library of Congress Cataloging in Publication Data

Whitman, Walt, 1819-1892.
  Walt Whitman's Civil War / compiled & edited from published
  & unpublished sources by Walter Lowenfels with the assistance of
  Nan Braymer; Civil War drawings by Winslow Homer.
      p.   cm. —(A Da Capo paperback)
  Reprint. Originally published: New York: Knopf, 1961, c1960.
  Includes index.
  ISBN 0-306-80355-0
  1. Whitman, Walt, 1819-1892—Quotations. 2. Whitman, Walt,
1819-1892—Political and social views. 3. United States—History-
Civil War, 1861-1865—Literary collections. 4. United States-
History—Civil War, 1861-1865—Literature and the war. I.
Lowenfels, Walter, 1897-1976. II. Braymer, Nan. III. Title.
PS3204.L6   1989   88-37013
818'.302—dc19   CIP

This Da Capo Press reprint edition of *Walt Whitman's Civil War* is
an unabridged republication of the edition published in New York
in 1961. It is reprinted by arrangement with the Estate of
Walter Lowenfels.

Published by Da Capo Press, Inc.
A Subsidiary of Plenum Publishing Corporation
233 Spring Street, New York, N.Y. 10013

"*Will the America of the future—will this vast,
rich Union ever realize what itself cost
back there, after all?—those hecatombs of
battle-deaths—Those times of which, O far-
off reader, this whole book is indeed finally
but a reminiscent memorial from thence
by me to you?*"

Editor's Foreword

Walt Whitman's Civil War is not a book about Whitman; it is a new book by him, composed of his own writings gathered from many sources and rearranged in new form. The record of the poet's ministrations to the wounded and his varied responses to the war were dispersed through dozens of notebooks, newspaper dispatches, letters, published and unpublished works. They are here brought together for the first time.

Whitman's writings on the Civil War were eyewitness accounts, arising out of personal experiences. For three years he served as a voluntary visitor and "consolant" to the wounded soldiers in Washington hospitals, with occasional trips to the battlefront.

"The real war will never get in the books," he wrote, ten years after Appomattox. What *was* the real war to Whitman?

Not primarily the generals nor planners nor politicians; not even Lincoln, whom he loved; not the story of battles and campaigns, but the "divine average"; and not only their courage, devotion, sacrifice, and suffering, but their personalities, their emotional upheavals, and their reactions to the war; the way they survived or died; the millions of personal histories; the young soldiers as he knew them in their critical moments—wounded, friendless, alone. This book reveals how much they were the heart of the war for Whitman.

"The dear love of comrades" he had proclaimed in the *Calamus* poems was realized during the war—on a grand scale. He became the loving comrade not of one or two but thousands of young men who looked upon him as "father, mother, brother, friend."

"How one gets to love them!" he wrote to Abby Price, a family friend, in 1863. "There is little petting in the soldier's life in the field; but, Abby, I know what is in their hearts. . . . What mutual attachments and how passing deep and tender these boys . . . love for them lives as long as I draw breath. . . . These soldiers know how to love, too, when they have the right person and the right love offered them. . . ."

Many letters exist in manuscript form showing how the soldiers responded to Whitman's love. He valued these letters so highly that he kept them all his life. Ten years after the war, one veteran wrote: "We have had a son borned since we heard from you. We call him Walter Whitman in honor to you, for love of you."

* * *

Whitman had hoped to create a book based on his war experiences. In a letter written in 1863 to his friend, the publisher John Redpath, he proposed: ". . . a book of handy size and form" containing his Civil War experiences: ". . . a book full enough of mosaic, but all fused into one comprehensive theory. . . ."

Whitman's closest friend, William O'Connor, author of *The Good Gray Poet*, on reading one of the poet's *New York Times* dispatches, wrote him: "It fills me with infinite regret that there is not a book from you embodying these rich and sad experiences. It would be sure of immortality. . . . No history of our times would ever be written without it . . . indeed, it would itself be history."

"I have entertained a brief ambition," Whitman observed

in 1875, "of writing and compiling at my leisure the history of the Civil War in one volume. . . ."

The "comprehensive theory," the grand history, did not materialize. Nor did Whitman write the history of his brother George's regiment, the 51st New York, which he had also contemplated. On December 26, 1864, while reading his brother's diary, he had noted: ". . . Even a tithe of the myriads of living and actual facts which go along and fill up this dry list of times and places . . . would outvie all the romances of the world. . . . In such a record lies folded . . . a perfect poem of the war. . . ."

For years after the Union victory, Whitman still hoped to write his war book. In 1882 he finally laid the project aside. In the opening paragraph of *Specimen Days,* he writes:

If I do it at all I must delay no longer. Incongruous and full of skips and jumps as is this huddle of diary jottings, war memoranda of 1862–65, nature notes, with Western and Canadian observations afterwards, all bundled and tied with a big string, the resolution and indeed the mandate comes to me this day, this hour . . . to go home, to untie the bundles, reel out the diary scraps and memoranda, just as they are, large or small, one after another, into print pages, and let the mélange's lackings and want of connection take care of themselves."

The "mélange's lackings" could perhaps have been more easily filled in by Whitman's contemporaries, who lived through the Civil War, than by the reader of today.

In the present book, the editor's task has been to piece together material from various parts of separate writings in such a way as to make integrated chapters and an integrated volume. Every word is Whitman's own—the changes are only in form.[1]

Along with his sometimes "convulsive" prose, I have

[1] The editor also takes the responsibility for changes in punctuation, paragraphing, and archaic spellings.

ix

placed some of the poet's most carefully wrought verse. The responsibility for choice and location of poems is mine. Incorporating them here with his prose seemed a way of presenting the totality of Whitman's response to the war—taking into account his complicated personality and the way in which he lived, often simultaneously, on different levels of experience.

"The merit of the war pieces," Whitman remarked to his friend Traubel in 1888, "is not chiefly literary—if they have merit, it is chiefly human; it is a presence-statement reduced to its last simplicity—sometimes a mere recital of names, dates, incidents—no dress put on anywhere to complicate and beautify it."

This attitude toward his war prose can be examined in relation to what he wrote O'Connor in 1865 as to why he was "mainly satisfied" with *Drum Taps* (later incorporated in *Leaves of Grass*).

"It delivers my ambition of the task that has haunted me, namely, to express in a poem (and in the way I like, which is not at all by directly stating it) the pending action of this *Time and Land we swim in,* with all their large conflicting fluctuations of despair and hope, the shiftings, masses and whirl and deafening din (yet over all as by invisible hand a definite support and idea), with the unprecedented anguish of wounded and suffering, the beautiful young men in wholesale death and agony, everything sometimes as if blood color and dripping blood. . . ."

It was not through his prose that Whitman was able to claim "my book and the war are one." "I look upon *Leaves of Grass*," he wrote in 1888, "as my definitive *carte [de] visite* to the coming generations. . . . Given the Nineteenth Century with the United States . . . *Leaves of Grass* is, or seeks to be, simply a faithful and doubtless self-willed record."

Throughout his life he struggled with the problem of integrating the poems into one work, continually reorganizing, adding, subtracting, revising. He resisted the advice of Emerson and others to eliminate some of the poems. Shortly before he died, he commented: "In the long run, the world will do as it pleases with the book. I am determined to have the world know what I was pleased to do."

He never produced a similar integration of his prose— nor of the prose together with the poems. He had made a beginning in this direction when he included his introduction to *Leaves* in the first edition. Any design he had later for producing the work that would express a "comprehensive theory" of America in both prose and verse was not accomplished. What he did give the world before his death —in addition to *Leaves*—was the "mélange" of paragraphs, speeches, and a scattering of other material that he published as *Collected Prose*.

Why did Whitman refer to the Civil War as "pivotal" to *Leaves*, when 156 of his poems had already appeared in the edition of 1860? Even those familiar with the poems in *Drum Taps* and the war notes in *Specimen Days* have been prevented by the fragmented nature of the war material (and the inaccessibility of some of it) from grasping the impact the war had on *Leaves*. The present volume should help to supply some of the answers to this and other questions about the relationship between the war and Whitman's poetry.

Toward the end of his life, in his final preface to *Leaves*, Whitman said: "It gives one man's—the author's—identity, ardors, observations." This identification of himself with the subject matter of the poems carries over into his observations of the Civil War—so that the book becomes to some degree autobiographical, giving additional insights into the contradictory nature of Whitman's personality. "Do I contradict myself? Very well then, I contradict myself. . . ."

Ten years after the war ended, Whitman noted, in a

manuscript hitherto unpublished (quoted in full in Chapter One), that his ambition to write a history—in the usual sense—would be futile because he had "become accustomed to think of the whole Secession War in its emotional, artistic and literary relations."

If the time sequence in *Walt Whitman's Civil War* moves backward and forward like Homer's story of Troy rather than Gibbon's story of Rome, it is because Whitman deals with events in their "emotional and artistic relations" rather than by chronology.

> "I have heard . . . the talk of the beginning
> and the end,
> But I do not talk of the beginning or the end.
> There never was more inception than there is now."

Thus, the book's continuity was determined by Whitman's nature and the character of the material itself—ranging from his Lincoln speech, a complete essay carefully put together by Whitman, to "episodic insights . . . convulsively written reminiscences . . . a part of the actual distraction, heat, smoke, and excitement of these times."

Soldiers, journalists, statesmen, politicians, historians, and novelists have produced thousands of volumes on the Civil War. This book is unique in that it reveals the eyewitness response of America's national poet to our country's greatest trial—"leaving it to you to prove and define it, expecting the main thing of you."

Acknowledgments

If an editor's job were something that should be dedicated, this volume would be inscribed to Nan Braymer, who worked with me at every stage of the book's final year. Without her collaboration, *Walt Whitman's Civil War* could not have been completed.

My debt to Whitman scholars and critics is acknowledged in "Sources" and the "Selected Bibliography"—to which I gratefully refer the reader.

Whitman's spoken words and certain of his letters are quoted from the four published volumes of *With Walt Whitman in Camden*, by Horace Traubel. I am indebted to his daughter, Gertrude Traubel, for permission to use passages from her father's work.

My thanks to Charles E. Feinberg of Detroit for reading the book in typescript, for valuable suggestions, and for his permission to use Whitman manuscripts in his remarkable collection.

To the following libraries who made their facilities available and gave me permission to use and quote from Whitman manuscripts in their collections, my appreciation and thanks: New York Public Library, Pierpont Morgan Library, Duke University Library, the Alderman Library (University of Virginia), Yale University Library, the Library of Congress, and the University of Pennsylvania Library.

My thanks go to Miriam Crawford and Marion Klugman

for their patience in typing parts of this book, and to Michal and Norman Kane for their many valuable suggestions. To my wife, Lillian, whose Whitman studies with Scully Bradley at the University of Pennsylvania helped instruct and inspire our whole family, and whose work with me in the libraries was so helpful—my loving thanks.
I wish also to acknowledge my debt to the Cooper Union Museum for their courtesy in making available the Winslow Homer illustrations.

*   *   *

The editor has omitted from the text footnotes and symbols referring to sources and notes in order to avoid interrupting Whitman's narrative and commentary. The reader is referred to the "Notes" section at the end of the book for the sources of each chapter, identification of Whitman's family and friends, and explanation of certain references—as well as additional material of documentary interest. No attempt has been made, however, to include notes on all of the many public figures mentioned in the text.

Contents

Chapter One

'Pivotal to the Rest'

An introductory section in which Whitman discusses the general character of the Civil War, the nature of his own contacts with the war and with the wounded, and his hopes for a book based on the countless notes he has made.

TO A CERTAIN CIVILIAN

Did you ask dulcet rhymes from me?
Did you seek the civilian's peaceful and languishing rhymes?
Did you find what I sang erewhile so hard to follow?
Why I was not singing erewhile for you to follow, to understand
    —nor am I now;
(I have been born of the same as the war was born,
The drum-corps' rattle is ever to me sweet music, I love well the
    martial dirge,
With slow wail and convulsive throb leading the officer's funeral;)
What to such as you anyhow such a poet as I? therefore leave my
    works,
And go lull yourself with what you can understand, and with
    piano-tunes,
For I lull nobody, and you will never understand me.

'Pivotal to the Rest'

The War of Attempted Secession has, of course, been the distinguishing event of my time. I commenced at the close of 1862, and continued steadily through '63, '64, and '65, to visit the sick and wounded of the army, both on the field and in the hospitals in and around Washington City.

From the first I kept little notebooks for impromptu jottings in pencil to refresh my memory of names and circumstances and what was especially wanted, etc. In these I briefed cases, persons, sights, occurrences in camp, by the bedside, and not seldom by the corpses of the dead.

Some were scratched down from narratives I heard and itemized while watching or waiting or tending somebody amid those scenes. I have dozens of such little notebooks left, forming a special history of those years for myself alone, full of associations never to be possibly said or sung. I wish I could convey to the reader the associations that attach to these soiled and creased livraisons, each composed of a sheet or two of paper folded small enough to carry in the pocket and fastened with a pin.

I leave them just as I threw them by after the war, blotched here and there with more than one bloodstain, hurriedly written—sometimes at the clinique, not seldom amid the excitement of uncertainty or defeat, or of action or getting ready for it, or a march.

I carried sometimes half a dozen such books in my pocket at one time; never was without one of them; I took notes as I went along, often as I sat talking, maybe, . . . I writing while the other fellow told his story. I would take the best paper (you can see, the best I could find) and make it up into these books, tying with string or tape or getting someone (often it was Nellie O'Connor) to stitch them for me.

My little books were beginnings—they were the ground into which I dropped the seed. See, here is a little poem itself . . . probably it is included in the *Leaves* somewhere. I would work in this way when I was out in the crowds, then put the stuff together at home. *Drum Taps* was all written in that manner—all of it put together by fits and starts, on the field, in the hospitals, as I worked with the soldier boys. Some days I was more emotional than others; then I would suffer all the extra horrors of my experience; I would try to write blind, blind with my own tears.

O Horace! Horace! Horace! Should I ever go to Washington again, I must look up my old cherry tree there—the great old tree under which I used to sit and write, write long, write. I want to give you one, several, of these books, if you would like to have them from me. They are more than precious—precious because they recall the old years, bring back the pictures of agony and death, reassociate me with the scenes and human actors of that tragic period. . . .

. . . During those three years in hospital, camp or field, I made over six hundred visits or tours and went, as I estimate, counting all, among from eighty thousand to one hundred thousand of the wounded and sick, as sustainer of spirit and body in some degree in time of need. These visits varied from an hour or two to all day or night, for with dear or critical cases I generally watched all night. Sometimes I took up my quarters in the hospital and slept or watched there several nights in succession.

Those three years I consider the greatest privilege and satisfaction (with all their feverish excitements and physical deprivations and lamentable sights) and, of course, the most profound lesson of my life. I can say that in my ministerings I comprehended all, whoever came in my way, Northern or Southern, and slighted none. It aroused and brought out and decided undreamed-of depths of emotion. It has given me my most fervent view of the true ensemble and extent of these States.

While I was with wounded and sick in thousands of cases from the New England States and from New York, New Jersey and Pennsylvania, and from Michigan, Wisconsin, Ohio, Indiana, Illinois, and all the Western States— I was with more or less from all the states, North and South, without exception. I was with many of the border states—especially from Maryland and Virginia—and found, during those lurid years 1862–'63, far more Union Southerners, especially Tennesseans, than is supposed. I was with many Rebel officers and men among our wounded and gave them always what I had and tried to cheer them the same as any. I was among the army teamsters considerably and, indeed, found myself drawn to them; among the black soldiers, wounded or sick; and in the contraband camps. I also took my way whenever in their neighbourhood and did what I could for them.

The Million Dead, Too, Summed Up.

The dead in this war—there they lie, strewing the fields and woods and valleys and battlefields of the South—Virginia, the Peninsula, Malvern Hill and Fair Oaks, the banks of the Chickahominy, the terraces of Fredericksburg, Antietam Bridge, the grisly ravines of Manassas, the bloody promenade of the Wilderness; the varieties of the *strayed* dead

5

(the estimate of the War Department is twenty-five thousand national soldiers killed in battle and never buried at all; three thousand drowned; fifteen thousand inhumed by strangers or on the march in haste, in hitherto unfound localities; two thousand graves covered by sand and mud, by Mississippi freshets; three thousand carried away by caving-in of banks, etc.; Gettysburg, the West, Southwest, Vicksburg, Chattanooga, the trenches of Petersburg; the numberless battles, camps, hospitals everywhere; the crop reaped by the mighty reapers—typhoid, dysentery, inflammations; and—blackest and loathsomest of all—the dead and living burial pits—the prison pens of Andersonville, Salisbury, Belle Isle, etc. (Not Dante's pictured hell and all its woes, its degradations, filthy torments excelled these prisons.)

The dead, the dead, the dead, our dead—or South or North—ours all (all, all, all finally dear to me), or East or West, Atlantic Coast or Mississippi Valley—somewhere they crawled to die alone—in bushes, low gullies, or on the sides of hills. (There, in secluded spots, their skeletons, bleached bones, tufts of hair, buttons, fragments of clothing are occasionally found yet.)

Our young men, once so handsome and so joyous, taken from us—the son from the mother, the husband from the wife, the dear friend from the dear friend—the clusters of many graves in Georgia, the Carolinas and in Tennessee; the single graves left in the woods or by the roadside (hundreds, thousands, obliterated); the corpses floated down the rivers and caught and lodged (dozens, scores, floated down the upper Potomac after the cavalry engagements, the pursuit of Lee, following Gettysburg).

Some lie at the bottom of the sea—the general million—and the special cemeteries in almost all the states; the infinite dead (the land entire saturated, perfumed with their impalpable ashes' exhalation in Nature's chemistry distilled

—and shall be so forever—in every future grain of wheat and ear of corn and every flower that grows and every breath we draw); not only Northern dead leavening Southern soil—thousands, aye tens of thousands, of Southerners crumble today in Northern earth.

And everywhere among these countless graves—everywhere in the many soldiers' cemeteries of the nation (there are now, I believe, over seventy of them)—as at the time in the vast trenches, the depositories of slain, Northern and Southern, after the great battles—not only where the scathing trail passed those years, but radiating since in all the peaceful quarters of the land—we see, and ages yet may see, on monuments and gravestones, singly or in masses to thousands or tens of thousands, the significant word UNKNOWN.

(In some of the cemeteries nearly *all* the dead are unknown. At Salisbury, N.C., for instance, the known are only 85, while the unknown are 12,027, and 11,700 of these are buried in trenches. A national monument has been put up here, by order of Congress, to mark the spot—but what visible, material monument can ever fittingly commemorate that spot?)

A Word for Dead Soldiers.

Under the southern sun—those clustering, green-roofed, grassy camps of silent warriors. Silent? O no, no, no! America has already borne proud speakers—in times to come haply the grandest orators the world has known may peal their voices in her halls—but where the eloquence, as time goes on, to tally those green mounds? Two hundred thousand graves! They say we have no monument. Travelers wending hither tell of Palmyra and Thebes, of India's temples, the Italian great cathedrals. . . . These and the like of those, we have not. Let them be our fame, our monument. Has the earth clearer, tenderer, more suggestive,

7

prouder? Not that our States monopolize such things; all times, all lands, thank God!, [have] brave, brave men— brave buried and precious dead. But where else, what nation else has planted in her soil three hundred thousand graves for an abstract passionate idea—the Democratic idea —aye, would have planted three hundred thousand more, and still continued, before that Idea, before this Union should be lost? . . .

Of reminiscences of the Secession War, after the rest is said, I have thought it remains to give a few special words —in some respects at the time the typical words of all, and most definite—of the samples of the killed and wounded in action and of soldiers who lingered afterward from these wounds or were laid up by obstinate disease or prostration. The general statistics have been printed already, but can bear to be briefly stated again. There were over three million men (for all periods of enlistment, large and small) furnished to the Union Army during the war, New York State furnishing over five hundred thousand, which was the greatest number of any one state. The losses by disease, wounded, killed in action, accidents, etc. were altogether about six hundred thousand, or approximating to that number. Over four million cases were treated in the main and adjudicatory army hospitals.

The number sounds strange, but it is true. More than two thirds of the deaths were from prostration or disease. Today there lie buried over three hundred thousand soldiers in the various national army cemeteries—more than half of them (and that is really the most eloquent bequest of the war) marked "unknown." In full mortuary statistics of the war, the greatest deficiency arises from our not having the rolls—even as far as they were kept—of most of the Southern military prisons, a gap which probably both adds to, and helps conceal, the indescribable horrors of those places. It is, however (restricting one vivid point only), certain that over thirty thousand Union soldiers died—largely of actual starvation—in them.

And now, leaving all figures and their "sum totals," I feel sure a few genuine memoranda of such things—some cases jotted down '64, '65, and '66, made at the time and on the spot, with all the associations of those scenes and places brought back, will not only go directest to the right spot, but give a clearer and more actual sight of that period than anything else. . . .

Brooklyn, N.Y., December 26, 1864.

Looking over George's[1] diary, merely a skeleton of dates, voyages, and places camped in or marched through, battles fought, etc., . . . I can realize clearly that by calling upon even half, even a tithe, of the myriads of living and actual facts which go along with and fill up this dry list of times and places, it would outvie all the romances in the world and most of the famous histories and biographies, to boot.

It does not need calling in play the imagination to see that in such a record as this lies folded a perfect poem of the war, comprehending all its phases, its passions, the fierce tug of the Secessionists, the interminable fibre of the National Union, and all the special hues and characteristic forms and pictures of the actual battles—rifles snapping, cannon thundering, grape whirling, armies struggling, ships at sea or bombarding shore batteries, skirmishes in woods, great pitched battles—all the profound scenes of individual death, courage, endurance, and superbest hardihood, and splendid muscular wrestle of a newer, larger race of human giants—with all furious passions aroused on one side and unalterable determination on the other. . . .

---

[1] Whitman's brother, Captain George Whitman

The way to bring the severest wipe to the bevy of American "poets" is to draw a strong picture of the splendor, variety, amplitude, etc. of America, with her noble, heroic masses of young and other men; also fill up the picture with her great distances, the unparalleled and unprecedented points (locale), and then scornfully add (or make precede), as if the stuff—the silly little tinkling and tepid, sentimental, warm water that is called the works of the American poets—has any reference here or any foothold in the future.

To James Redpath, Washington, October 21, 1863.

Dear friend: My idea of a book of the time, worthy the time—something considerably beyond mere hospital sketches—a book for sale perhaps in a larger American market—the premises or skeleton memoranda of incidents, persons, places, sights the past year (mostly jotted down either on the spot or in the spirit of what is narrated); seeing or hearing (I left New York last December and have been around in the front or here ever since); full of interest, I surely think—in some respects somewhat a combination in handling of the old French memoirs and my own personality (things seen through my eyes and what my vision brings); a book full enough of mosaic but all fused in one comprehensive theory. One of the main drifts is to push forward the very big and needed truths that our national military system needs shifting, revolutionizing, and made to tally with democracy, the people. The officers should almost invariably rise from the ranks (there is an absolute want of democratic spirit in the present system and officers; it is the feudal spirit exclusively). Nearly the entire capacity, keenness, and courage of our army are in the ranks; what has been done has been unavoidable so far, but the time has come to discuss the change.

Have much to say of the hospitals, the immense national hospitals—in them, too, most radical changes of premises are demanded (the air, the spirit of a thing is everything; the details follow and adjust themselves).

I have many hospital incidents that will take the general reader; I ventilate my general democracy with details very largely and with reference to the future, bringing in persons—the President, Seward, Congress, the Capitol, Washington City, many of the actors of the drama; have something to say of the great trunk America, the West, etc., etc.; do not hesitate to diffuse *myself;* the book is very rapid; is a book that can be read by the five or ten minutes (as being full of small parts, pieces, paragraphs, with their dates, incidents, etc.); I should think two or three thousand sale ought to be certainly depended on here, in hospitals, in Washington departments, etc.

My idea is a book of handy size and form—16 mo or smallish 12 mo, *first-rate paper* (this last indispensable); ordinary binding, strongly stitched; to cost, including copyright, not more than thirty-five cents or thereabouts to make; to retail for a dollar. It should be put out *immediately.* I think an edition, elegantly bound, might be pushed off for books for presents, etc. for the holidays, if advertised for that purpose. It would be very appropriate. I think it is a book that would please women. I should expect it to be popular with the trade.

Of course, I propose the affair to you publisherially as something to invest in, to make out of (for both of us); I take it it would be a very handsome speculation. Only it is to be done while the thing is warm, namely, *at once.* I have been, and am, in the midst of these things; feel myself full of them; and I know the people generally now are, too (far more than they know), and would readily absorb and understand my mem. —Wherefore, let us make and publish the book and out with it, so as to have it for sale by the middle or twentieth of November.

It is certain, I say, that, although I had made a start before —only from the occurrence of the Secession War and what it showed me as by flashes of lightning . . . with the emotional depths it sounded and aroused (of course, I don't mean in my own heart only—I saw it just as plainly in others, in millions)—that only from the strong flare and provocation of that war's sights and scenes, the final reasons-for-being of an autochthonic and passionate song definitely came forth.

I went down to the fields in Virginia (end of '62); lived thenceforward in camp; saw great battles and the days and nights afterward; partook of all the fluctuations, gloom, despair, hopes again aroused, courage evoked, death readily risked—the *cause*, too, along and filling those agonistic and lurid following years, 1863, '64, '65, the real parturition years (more than 1776–'83) of this henceforth homogeneous Union. Without those three or four years and the experiences they gave, *Leaves of Grass* would not now be existing.

I have entertained a brief ambition of writing and compiling at my leisure (with what I thought the many advantages of having been on the entire scene, sufficiently in the midst of, and previous to, it, and feeling that I could do justice in spirit to both sides, and now that ten years have passed away, and compiling about as much as is known of the onus of it all as ever will be known) the History of the War in a great volume or several volumes. . . .

But a very few attempts and reflections thoroughly convince me how futile (from a high point of view) are all efforts either at a full statement of the war in its origins or for writing its history—not only its military history, but what may be, with its vast complications, civil and domestic, diplomatic and social byplay, not less important than its military history . . . with results of greatest importance for scores, centuries of years to come. But I have become accustomed to think of the whole of the Secession War in its emotional, artistic and literary relations. . . .

The long, long solemn trenches,
Has anyone thought who has stood in one of those trenches,
    what a measureless history it held?
What a stately poem and mighty and awful hymn it held?
What a history there holds in the crumbling contents of trenches?
What a poem beyond all ever written or chanted? [1]

. . . And was there not something grand and an inside proof of perennial grandeur in that war? We talk about [the] ages and the States' materialism, and it is true. But how amid the whole sordidness—the entire devotion of America, at any price, to pecuniary success, merchandise, disregarding all but business and profit—this war for a bare idea and abstraction? A mere, at bottom, heroic dream and reminiscence burst forth in its great devouring flame and conflagration, quickly and fiercely spreading and raging and enveloping all; defining in two conflicting issues—first, the Union cause; second, the other; a strange, deadly interrogation point, hard to define—can we not now safely confess it?—with magnificent rays, streaks of noblest heroism, fortitude, perseverance, and ever conscientiousness through its pervadingly malignant darkness.

What an area and rounded field upon the whole—the spirit, arrogance, grim tenacity of the South; the long stretches of murky gloom; the general national will below and behind and comprehending all, not once really wavering—not a day, not an hour. What could be, or ever can be, grander?

[1] From an unpublished poem.

13

. . . As the period of the war recedes, I am more than ever convinced that it is important for those of us who were on the scene to put our experiences on record. There is infinite treasure—O inestimable riches in that mine! . . . I took the first scrap of paper, the first doorstep, the first desk, and wrote, wrote, wrote. No prepared picture, no elaborated poem, no after-narrative could be what the thing itself was. . . . You want to catch the first spirit, to tally its birth. By writing at the instant, the very heartbeat of life is caught.

My place in Washington was a peculiar one; my reasons for being there; my doing there what I did do. I do not think I quite had my match. People went there for all sorts of reasons, none of which were my reasons: went to convert, to proselyte, to observe, to do good, to sentimentalize —from a sense of duty, from philanthropic motives; women, preachers, emotionalists, gushing girls—and I honor them all, all. I knew them, hundreds of them, well, and in some cases came to love them.

But no one—at least no one I met—went just from my own reasons, from a profound conviction of necessity, affinity, coming into closest relations—relations O so close and dear!—with the whole strange welter of life gathered to that mad focus. I could not expect to do more for my own part at this late day than collect a little of the driftwood of that epoch and pass it down to the future. . . .

I was always between two loves at that time—I wanted to be in New York; I had to be in Washington. I was never in the one place but I was restless for the other. My heart was distracted; yet it never occurred to me for a minute that there were two things to do—that I had any right or call to abandon my work. It was a religion with me. A religion? Well, every man has a religion; has something in heaven or earth which he will give up everything else for—

something which absorbs him, possesses itself of him, makes him over in its image—something. It may be something regarded by others as being very paltry, inadequate, useless, yet it is his dream; it is his lodestar; it is his master. That, whatever it is, seized upon me, made me its servant, slave; induced me to set aside other ambitions—a trail of glory in the heavens, which I followed, followed with a full heart.

The critical factors of the national life in those years lay not in the South alone, but North here, too—here more insidiously. I was bred in Brooklyn; initiated to all the mysteries of city life—population, perturbations; knew the rough elements—what they stood for; what might be apprehended from them. There in Brooklyn, New York, through many, many years; tasted its familiar life. When the war came on, I quite well recognized the powers to be feared, understood—and not alone in New York, Brooklyn—in Boston as well—the great cities West, Northwest, the very hotbeds of dissent.

It was in such an experience as of the war that my heart needed to be fully thrown—thrown without reserve. I do not regret it—could not regret it. What was a man to do? The war had much to give—there were thousands, tens of thousands, hundreds of thousands needing me—needing all who might come. What could I do?

. . . I never once questioned the decision that led me into the war; whatever the years have brought—whatever sickness, what not—I have accepted the result as inevitable and right. This is the very centre, circumference, umbilicus, of my whole career. You remember Homer—the divine horses: "Now, Achilles, we'll take you there, see you safely back again, but only on condition that you will not do this thing again—act unwisely; will be steady peaceful, quiet—

15

cut up no capers." But you know Achilles said: "No, let what must, come; I must cut up my capers." So it was with me—I had to cut up my capers. Why, I would not for all the rest have missed those three or four years.

. . . When once I am convinced, I never let go; after I first took hold of this thing, I never let go. I had to pay much for what I got; but what I got made what I paid for it —much as it was—seem cheap. I had to give up health for it, my body, the vitality of my physical self, O so much had to go! Much that was inestimable, that no man should give up until there is no longer any help for it; had to give that up—all that—and what did I get for it? I never weighed what I gave for what I got, but I am satisfied with what I got.

What did I get? Well, I got the boys, for one thing—the boys, thousands of them—they were, they are, they will be, mine. I gave myself for them—myself. I got the boys; then I got *Leaves of Grass*—but for this I never would have had *Leaves of Grass*—the consummated book (the last confirming word); I got that—the boys, the *Leaves*—I got them. . . .

Then, behind all, the deep-down consolation (it is a glum one, but I dare not be sorry for the fact of it in the past nor refrain from dwelling, even vaunting, here at the end) that this late-years, palsied, old shorn and shell-fish condition of me is the indubitable outcome and growth—now near for twenty years along—of the overzealous, overcontinued bodily and emotional excitement through the years of 1862, '63, '64, and '65, visiting and waiting on wounded and sick army volunteers, both sides, in campaigns or contests or after them, or on hospitals or fields south of Washington City, or in that place and elsewhere.

Those hot, sad, wrenching times—the army volunteers,

all states, or North or South; the wounded, suffering, dying; the exhausting, sweating summers; marches, battles' carnage; those trenches hurriedly heaped by the corpses, thousands, mainly unknown—will the America of the future, will this vast, rich Union ever realize what itself cost back there, after all?—those hecatombs of battle deaths; those times of which, O far-off reader, this whole book is indeed finally but a reminiscent memorial from thence by me to you?

ASHES OF SOLDIERS

Ashes of soldiers South or North,
As I muse retrospective murmuring a chant in thought,
The war resumes, again to my sense your shapes,
And again the advance of the armies.

Noiseless as mists and vapors,
From their graves in the trenches ascending,
From cemeteries all through Virginia and Tennessee,
From every point of the compass out of the countless graves,
In wafted clouds, in myriads large, or squads of twos or threes
    or single ones they come,
And silently gather round me.

Now sound no note O trumpeters,
Not at the head of my cavalry parading on spirited horses,
With sabres drawn and glistening, and carbines by their thighs,
    (ah my brave horsemen!
My handsome tan-faced horsemen! what life, what joy and pride,
With all the perils were yours.)

Nor you drummers, neither at reveillé at dawn,
Nor the long roll alarming the camp, nor even the muffled beat for
    a burial,
Nothing from you this time O drummers bearing my warlike
    drums.

But aside from these and the marts of wealth and the crowded
  promenade,
Admitting around me comrades close unseen by the rest and voice-
  less,
The slain elate and alive again, the dust and debris alive,
I chant this chant of my silent soul in the name of all dead soldiers.

Faces so pale with wondrous eyes, very dear, gather closer yet,
Draw close, but speak not.

Phantoms of countless lost,
Invisible to the rest henceforth become my companions,
Follow me ever—desert me not while I live.

Sweet are the blooming cheeks of the living—sweet are the musical
  voices sounding,
But sweet, ah sweet, are the dead with their silent eyes.

Dearest comrades, all is over and long gone,
But love is not over—and what love, O comrades
Perfume from battle-fields rising, up from the foetor arising.

Perfume therefore my chant, O love, immortal love,
Give me to bathe the memories of all dead soldiers,
Shroud them, embalm them, cover them all over with tender pride.

Perfume all—make all wholesome,
Make these ashes to nourish and blossom,
O love, solve all, fructify all with the last chemistry.

Give me exhaustless, make me a fountain,
That I exhale love from me wherever I go like a moist perennial
  dew,
For the ashes of all dead soldiers South or North.

Chapter Two

'Beat! Beat! Drums!'

(At the outbreak of the war.)

Whitman in New York City hears the news of the firing on Fort
Sumter; describes the reactions of the people; analyzes the state of
the nation's mind at that time; and then, in Washington, tells how
the defeated soldiers return after the First Battle of Bull Run.

Arm'd year—year of the struggle,

No dainty rhymes or sentimental love verses for you terrible year,

Not you as some pale poetling seated at a desk lisping cadenzas
piano,

But as a strong man erect, clothed in blue clothes, advancing, carry-
ing a rifle on your shoulder,

With well-gristled body and sunburnt face and hands, with a knife
in the belt at your side,

As I heard you shouting loud, your sonorous voice ringing across
the continent,

Your masculine voice O year, as rising amid the great cities,

Amid the men of Manhattan I saw you as one of the workmen, the
dwellers in Manhattan,

Or with large steps crossing the prairies out of Illinois and Indiana,

Rapidly crossing the West with springy gait and descending the
Alleghanies,

Or down from the great lakes or in Pennsylvania, or on deck along
the Ohio river,

Or southward along the Tennessee or Cumberland rivers, or at
Chattanooga on the mountain top,

Saw I your gait and saw I your sinewy limbs clothed in blue, bearing
weapons, robust year,

Heard your determin'd voice launch'd forth again and again,

Year that suddenly sang by the mouths of the round-lipp'd cannon.

I repeat you, hurrying, crashing, sad, distracted year.

'Beat! Beat! Drums!'

News of the attack on Fort Sumter and *the flag* at Charleston Harbor, South Carolina, was received in New York City late at night (13th April 1861) and was immediately sent out in extras of the newspapers.

I had been to the opera in Fourteenth Street that night, and after the performance was walking down Broadway around twelve o'clock on my way to Brooklyn, when I heard in the distance the loud cries of the newsboys, who came presently tearing and yelling up the street, rushing from side to side more furiously than usual.

I bought an extra and crossed to the Metropolitan Hotel [Niblo's], where the great lamps were still brightly blazing, and, with a crowd of others who gathered impromptu, read the news—which was evidently authentic.

For the benefit of some who had no papers, one of us read the telegram aloud, while all listened silently and intently.

No remark was made by any of the crowd, which had increased to thirty or forty, but all stood a moment or two, I remember, before they dispersed. I can almost see them there now, under the lamps of midnight again. . . .

Even after the bombardment of Sumter, however, the gravity of the revolt, and the power and will of the Slave States for a strong and continued military resistance to national authority were not at all realized at the North, except by a few. Nine tenths of the people of the Free States looked upon the rebellion as started in South Carolina from a feeling one half of contempt and the other half composed of anger and incredulity. It was not thought it would be joined in by Virginia, North Carolina, or Georgia. A great and cautious national official predicted that it would blow over "in sixty days," and folks generally believed the prediction.

I remember talking about it on a Fulton ferryboat with the Brooklyn mayor, who said he only "hoped the Southern fire-eaters would commit some overt act of resistance, as they would then be at once so effectually squelched, we would never hear of secession again—but he was afraid they never would have the pluck to really do anything."

I remember, too, that a couple of companies of the Thirteenth Brooklyn, who rendez-vous'd at the city armory and started thence as thirty-days' men, were all provided with pieces of rope, conspicuously tied to their musket barrels, with which to bring back each man a prisoner from the audacious South, to be led in a noose, on our men's early and triumphant return!

All this sort of feeling was destined to be arrested and reversed by a terrible shock—the Battle of First Bull Run—certainly, as we now know it, one of the most singular fights on record. (All battles, and their results, are far more matters of accident than is generally thought; but this was throughout a casualty, a chance. One [side] had, in point of fact, just the same right to be routed as the other. By a fiction, or series of fictions, the national forces at the last moment exploded in a panic and fled from the field.) The defeated troops commenced pouring into Washington over the Long Bridge at daylight on Monday, 22nd—day drizzling all through with rain.

The Saturday and Sunday of the battle (20th, 21st) had been parched and hot to an extreme—the dust, the grime, and smoke in layers, sweated in, followed by other layers again sweated in, absorbed by those excited souls—their clothes all saturated with the clay-powder filling the air, stirred up everywhere on the dry roads and trodden fields by the regiments, swarming wagons, artillery, etc.—all the men with this coating of murk and sweat and rain, now re-coiling back, pouring over the Long Bridge—a horrible march of twenty miles—returning to Washington, baffled, humiliated, panic-struck.

Where are your banners and your bands of music and your ropes to bring back your prisoners? Well, there isn't a band playing, and there isn't a flag but clings ashamed and lank to its staff.

The sun rises but shines not. The men appear, at first sparsely and shamefaced enough, then thicker, in the streets of Washington; appear in Pennsylvania Avenue and on the steps and basement entrances. They come along in disor-derly mobs; some in squads, stragglers, companies. Occa-sionally a rare regiment, in perfect order, with its officers (some gaps, dead—the true braves), marching in silence, with lowering faces—stern, weary to sinking, all black and dirty, but every man with a big musket and stepping alive; but these are the exceptions.

Sidewalks of Pennsylvania Avenue, Fourteenth Street, etc. crowded, jammed with citizens, darkies, clerks, every-body, lookers-on; women in the windows; curious expres-sions from faces, as those swarms of dirt-covered returned soldiers there (will they never end?) move by; but nothing said, no comments; (half our lookers-on Secesh of the most venomous kind—they say nothing, but the devil snickers in their faces). During the forenoon Washington gets all over motley with these defeated soldiers—queer-looking objects —strange eyes and faces, drenched (the steady rain drizzles all day) and fearfully worn, hungry, haggard, blistered in the feet.

Good people (but not over-many of them either) hurry up something for their grub. They put wash-kettles on the fire for soup, for coffee. They set tables on the sidewalks, wagonloads of bread are purchased, swiftly cut in stout chunks. Here are two aged ladies, beautiful, the first in the city for culture and charm—they stand with store of eating and drink at an improvised table of rough plank, and give food and have the store replenished from their house every half-hour all that day; and there in the rain they stand, active, silent, white-haired, and give food, though the tears stream down their cheeks almost without intermission the whole time.

Amid the deep excitement, crowds and motion and desperate eagerness, it seems strange to see many, very many of the soldiers sleeping—in the midst of all—sleeping sound. They drop down anywhere—on the steps of houses, up close by the basements or fences, on the sidewalk, aside on some vacant lot—and deeply sleep. A poor seventeen- or eighteen-year-old boy lies there on the stoop of a grand house; he sleeps so calmly, so profoundly. Some clutch their muskets firmly even in sleep. Some in squads—comrades, brothers, close together—and on them, as they lay, sulkily drips the rain.

As afternoon passed and evening came, the streets, the barrooms, knots everywhere—listeners, questioners, terrible yarns, bugaboo, masked batteries, "our regiment all cut up," and so on—stories and storytellers, windy, bragging, vain centers of street crowds. Resolution, manliness, seem to have abandoned Washington.

The principal hotel, Willard's, is full of shoulder-straps. (I see them and must have a word with them. There you are, shoulder straps!—But where are your companies? Where are your men? Incompetents! Never tell me of chance of battle, of getting strayed, and the like. I think this is your work, this retreat, after all. Sneak, blow, put on airs there in Willard's sumptuous parlors and barrooms or anywhere—no explanation shall save you. Bull Run is your work; had you been half or one-tenth worthy your men, this never would have happened.)

Meantime in Washington, among the great persons and their entourage, a mixture of awful consternation, uncertainty, rage, shame, helplessness, and stupefying disappointment. The worst is not only imminent but already there. In a few hours—perhaps before the next meal—the Secesh generals, with their victorious hordes, will be upon us. The dream of humanity, the vaunted Union we thought so strong, so impregnable—lo! it seems already smashed like a china plate.

One bitter, bitter hour—perhaps proud America will never again know such an hour. She must pack and fly—no time to spare. Those white palaces, the dome-crowned Capitol there on the hill, so stately over the trees—shall they be left, or destroyed first? For it is certain that talk among certain of the magnates and officers and clerks and officials everywhere for twenty-four hours in and around Washington after Bull Run was loud and undisguised for yielding out and out and substituting the Southern rule and Lincoln promptly abdicating and departing.

If the Secesh officers and forces had immediately followed, and by a bold Napoleonic movement had entered Washington the first day (or even the second), they could have had things their own way and a powerful faction North to back them. One of our returning colonels expressed in public that night, amid a swarm of officers and gentlemen in a crowded room, the opinion that it was useless to fight, that the Southerners had made their title clear, and that the best course for the National Government to pursue was to desist from any further attempt at stopping them and admit them again in the lead, on the best terms they were willing to grant. Not a voice was raised against this judgment amid that large crowd of officers and gentlemen.

(The fact is, the hour was one of the three or four of those crises we had then and afterward, during the fluctuations of four years, when human eyes appeared at least just as likely to see the last breath of the Union as to see it continue.)

BEAT! BEAT! DRUMS!

Beat! beat! drums—blow! bugles, blow!
Through the windows—through doors—burst like a ruthless force,
Into the solemn church, and scatter the congregation,
Into the school where the scholar is studying;
Leave not the bridegroom quiet—no happiness must he have now with his bride,
Nor the peaceful farmer any peace, ploughing his field or gathering his grain,
So fierce you whirr and pound you drums—so shrill you bugles blow.

Beat! beat! drums—blow! bugles! blow!
Over the traffic of cities—over the rumble of wheels in the streets;
Are beds prepared for sleepers at night in the houses? no sleepers must sleep in those beds,
No bargainers' bargains by day—no brokers or speculators—would they continue?
Would the talkers be talking? would the singer attempt to sing?
Would the lawyers rise in the court to state his case before the judge?
Then rattle quicker, heavier drums—you bugles wilder blow.

Beat! beat! drums!—blow! bugles! blow!
Make no parley—stop for no expostulation,
Mind not the timid—mind not the weeper or prayer,
Mind not the old man beseeching the young man,
Let not the child's voice be heard, nor the mother's entreaties,
Make even the trestles to shake the dead where they lie awaiting the hearses,
So strong you thump O terrible drums—so loud you bugles blow.

Chapter Three

'The Dense Brigades Press On'

(Down at the front.)

Whitman goes to the battle front in Virginia in search of his wounded brother; descriptions of "war's hell scenes" as he observes them; descriptions of battles of Fredericksburg, Antietam, Chancellorsville.

AN ARMY CORPS ON THE MARCH

With its cloud of skirmishers in advance,
With now the sound of a single shot snapping like a whip, and now
    an irregular volley,
The swarming ranks press on and on, the dense brigades press on,
Glittering dimly, toiling under the sun—the dust-cover'd men,
In columns rise and fall to the undulations of the ground,
With artillery interspers'd—the wheels rumble, the horses sweat,
As the army corps advances.

'The Dense Brigades Press On'

In 1862, startled by news that my brother George, an officer in the 51st New York Volunteers, had been seriously wounded (First Fredericksburg Battle, December 13th), I hurriedly went down to the field of war in Virginia. . . .

Falmouth, Va., opposite Fredericksburg,
December 21, 1862.

Began my visits among the camp hospitals in the Army of the Potomac. Spend a good part of the day in a large brick mansion on the banks of the Rappahannock, used as a hospital since the battle; seems to have received only the worst cases. . . . Outdoors, at the foot of a tree, within ten yards of the front of the house, I notice a heap of amputated feet, legs, arms, hands, etc.—a full load for a one-horse cart. Several dead bodies lie near, each covered with its brown woolen blanket. In the dooryard, towards the river, are fresh graves, mostly of officers, their names on pieces of barrel staves or broken boards stuck in the dirt. (Most of these bodies were subsequently taken up and transported north to their friends.)

The large mansion is quite crowded upstairs and down —everything impromptu, no system, all bad enough—but I have no doubt the best that can be done; all the wounds pretty bad, some frightful; the men in their old clothes, unclean and bloody.

Some of the wounded are rebel soldiers and officers, prisoners. One, a Mississippian, a captain, hit badly in leg, I talked with some time; he asked me for papers, which I gave him. (I saw him three months afterward in Washington, with his leg amputated, doing well.) I went through the rooms, downstairs and up. Some of the men were dying. I had nothing to give at that visit, but wrote a few letters to folks home, mothers, etc. Also talked to three or four who seemed most susceptible to it and needing it. . . .

Washington, Monday forenoon, December 29, 1862.

Dear, dear Mother: Friday, the 19th inst., I succeeded in reaching the camp of the 51st New York and found George alive and well. In order to make sure that you would get the good news, I sent back by messenger to Washington a telegraphic dispatch (I daresay you did not get it for some time) as well as a letter—and the same to Hanna[1] at Burlington.

I have stayed in camp with George ever since, till yesterday when I came back to Washington (about the 24th). George got Jeff's[2] letter of the 20th.

Mother, how much you must have suffered all that week till George's letter came—and all the rest must too. As to me, I know I put in about three days of the greatest suffering I ever experienced in my life. I wrote to Jeff how I had my pocket picked in a jam and hurry, changing cars at Philadelphia—so that I landed here without a dime.

The next two days I spent hunting through the hospitals, walking day and night, unable to ride, trying to get information, trying to get access to big people, etc. I could not get the least clue to anything. Odell would not see me at all. But Thursday afternoon I lit on a way to get down on the government boat that runs to Aquia Creek, and so by

[1] Whitman's sister
[2] Whitman's brother

railroad to the neighborhood of Falmouth, opposite Fredericksburg. So by degrees I worked my way to Ferrero's Brigade, which I found Friday afternoon without much trouble after I got in camp.

When I found dear brother George and found that he was alive and well, O you may imagine how trifling all my little cares and difficulties seemed—they vanished into nothing. And now that I have lived for eight or nine days amid such scenes as the camps furnish, and had a practical part in it all, and realize the way that hundreds of thousands of good men are now living—and have had to live for a year or more—not only without any of the comforts, but with sickness and death and hard marching and hard fighting (and no success at that) for their continual experience—really nothing we call trouble seems worth talking about. . . .

George is very well in health, has a good appetite; I think he is at times more wearied out and homesick than he shows, but stands it upon the whole very well. Everyone of the soldiers, to a man, wants to get home.

I suppose Jeff got quite a long letter I wrote from camp about a week ago. I told you our George had been promoted to captain; his commission arrived while I was there. When you write, address Cap. George W. Whitman, Co. K., 51st New York Volunteers, Ferrero's Brigade, near Falmouth, Va. Jeff must write oftener and put in a few lines from mother, even if it is only two lines; then in the next letter a few lines from Mat,[1] and so on. You have no idea how letters from home cheer one up in camp and dissipate homesickness.

While I was there, George still lived in Captain Francis's tent. There were five of us altogether to eat, sleep, write, etc. in a space twelve feet square, but we got along very well. The weather all along was very fine, and [we]

[1] Whitman's sister-in-law

31

would have got along to perfection, but Captain Francis is not a man I could like much; I had very little to say to him.

George is about building a place, half hut and half tent, for himself (he is probably about it this very day), and then he will be better off, I think. Every captain has a tent in which he lives, transacts company business, etc., has a cook (or a man of all work); and in the same tent mess and sleep his lieutenants and perhaps the first sergeant. They have a kind of fireplace, and the cook's fire is outside on the open ground.

George had very good times while Francis was away. The cook, a young disabled soldier, Tom, is an excellent fellow and a first-rate cook; and the second lieutenant, Pooley, is a tiptop young Pennsylvanian. Tom thinks all the world of George. When he heard he was wounded, on the day of the battle he left everything, got across the river, and went hunting for George across the river, through the field, through thick and thin.

I wrote to Jeff that George was wounded by a shell, a gash in the cheek you could stick a splint through into the mouth, but it has healed up without difficulty already.

Everything is uncertain about the army, whether it moves or stays where it is. There are no furloughs granted at present. I will stay here for the present, at any rate long enough to see if I can get any employment at anything, and shall write what luck I have. Of course, I am unsettled at present. . . .

BY THE BIVOUAC'S FITFUL FLAME

By the bivouac's fitful flame,
A procession winding around me, solemn and sweet and slow—but first I note,
The tents of the sleeping army, the fields' and woods' dim outline,
The darkness lit by spots of kindled fire, the silence,
Like a phantom far or near an occasional figure moving,

The shrubs and trees, (as I lift my eyes they seem to be stealthily
watching me,)
While wind in procession thoughts, O tender and wondrous
thoughts,
Of life and death, of home and the past and loved, and of those
that are far away;
A solemn and slow procession there as I sit on the ground,
By the bivouac's fitful flame.

* * *

BIVOUAC ON A MOUNTAIN SIDE

I see before me now a traveling army halting,
Below a fertile valley spread, with barns and the orchards of sum-
mer,
Behind, the terraced sides of a mountain, abrupt, in places rising
high,
Broken, with rocks, with clinging cedars, with tall shapes dingily
seen,
The numerous camp-fires scatter'd near and far, some away up on
the mountain,
The shadowy forms of men and horses, looming, large-sized, flicker-
ing,
And over all the sky—the sky! far, far out of reach, studded,
breaking out, the eternal stars.

*Antietam—the Fight at the Bridge.
17th September, 1862.*

This was a stone bridge over Antietam Creek, in a position
naturally almost impregnable and fortified by the rebels.
Orders were given to carry this point at all hazards, and
the work was deputed to the 51st New York and the 51st
Pennsylvania. At 1 o'clock these regiments made a charge
with the bayonet, carrying this through with a determina-
tion and courage never surpassed. They cleared the bridge,
gained the opposite side and held it, in the contest losing a

33

large number of officers and men, the 51st going on picket on the hill in advance.

On the Battlefield of Fredericksburg.

Sunday, 14th December, 1862, the day after the engagement.—The general engagement was Saturday 13th. Sunday was comparatively quiet, with occasional picket firing. On Sunday night, the 51st was ordered on a picket in force, to relieve the men holding a hill in advance of our line, south of Fredericksburg, perhaps two miles beyond the river. The 51st men went on this duty about 9 o'clock Sunday night. Any member of the regiment will recollect till his dying day the circumstances of this night and the following day—up to 12 o'clock Monday night—the regiment being on continuous duty in a most dangerous position about twenty-seven hours.

During the whole of that time, everyone, from the Colonel down, was compelled to lie at full length on his back or belly in the mud, which was deep and tenacious. The surface of the ground, slightly elevated just south of them, served as a natural bulwark and protection against the Rebel batteries and sharpshooters, as long as the men lay in this manner. But the moment the men raised their heads or a limb, even if only a few inches—snap and o-s-st went the weapons of Secesh! In this manner, the 51st remained spread out in the mud all Sunday night, all Monday, and Monday night till after midnight. Although the troops could plainly hear the Rebels whistling, etc., the latter did not dare advance upon them.

Altogether this was a night to be remembered. Soon after midnight, the 51st (as a blind) took up their march (the relief soon followed) through Fredericksburg, over the pontoon bridge to Falmouth, where they halted and took their old camping ground. The 51st was relieved Tuesday morning, 16th, about 3 o'clock, after four days' absence.

Just After Candlelight—Papers! Papers!

At dark a horseman will come galloping through the camp, with something white thrown across the pommel of the saddle in front of him, and you will hear the cry, papers! papers! Then quite a rush out of the tents, and the shin-plasters fly around lively—the New York papers are ten cents and the Washington and Philadelphia ones, five.

Falmouth, Tuesday Morning, December 23, 1862.

I write this standing on a high slope between General Sumner's headquarters and the railroad terminus down towards the river. The day is soft, brightly beautiful. Down below is spread out a picturesque scene—the countless baggage wagons with their white roofs, the numerous strings of mules, the railroad locomotives, the broad spread of slopes and hills. Winding their way over the railroad track and making a huge *S* towards the river—which is only a few hundred yards distant—are the whole of the 51st New York, 51st Pennsylvania, and one hundred men of the 11th New York going on picket duty along the shore.

Virginia, on the Falmouth Side, Friday,
December 26, 1862.

Early this morning I walked out in the open fields one side of the camp. I found some of the soldiers digging graves; they were for the 51st New York, and the 11th New Hampshire. There was a row of graves there already, each with a slat of board—generally a piece of barrelhead—on which was inscribed the name of the soldier.

Death is nothing here. As you step out in the morning from your tent to wash your face, you see before you on a stretcher a shapeless, extended object, and over it is thrown a dark gray blanket. It is the corpse of some wounded or sick soldier of the regiment who died in the hospital tent

35

during the night; perhaps there is a row of three or four of these corpses lying covered over. No one makes an ado. There is a detail of men to bury them; all useless ceremony is omitted. (The stern realities of the marches and many battles of a long campaign make the old etiquets a cumber and a nuisance.)

I walked on over to a camp of teamsters in the woods—or rather what had been the woods but was now pretty well cut down—a few trees standing at intervals, stumps all over, and plenty of boughs and branches strewing the ground. The teamsters were in groups around here and there, mostly squatted by the fires, idling or cooking breakfast, etc.

Nearby was the camp of the 26th Pennsylvania, who have been out since the commencement of the war. I talked with a couple of the men, part of a squad around a fire, in the usual enclosure of green branches fencing three sides of a space perhaps twenty feet square—breaking the wind from north and east. Where there are boughs to be had, these sylvan corrals are to be met with in all the camps, some of them built very finely and making a picturesque appearance for a camp. They serve as the company kitchens and the same purpose of rendezvous of an evening that the public house, the reading room, or the engine house did at home. . . .

The men I talked with in the 26th Pennsylvania appeared to be in the best spirits and less growling than any I had met with yet. To a stranger, the men in the ranks appear great growlers. By and by you learn this is nothing; a large proportion of men in the world, even the good fellows, would burst if they couldn't grumble.

The tents of this camp were quite comfortable, such moderate weather as we are having now. One of the men came out of a tent close by, with a couple of slices of beef and some crackers, and commenced cooking the mess in a frying pan for his breakfast. It looked very good. Another man was waiting with similar articles to have the use of the frying pan.

As I examined the little shelter tent through the open entrance—the ground strewn with pine twigs and protected on each side with a pine log for an entrance; the knapsacks piled at one end for pillows (three men asleep in one of the tents), I thought, rough as it was, that men in health might endure it and get along with more comfort than most outsiders would suppose—as indeed the condition of the men around me was a tolerable proof.

The mass of our men in our army are young; it is an impressive sight to me to see the countless number of youths and boys. There is only a sprinkling of elderly men. On a parade at evening there you see them, poor lads, many of them already with the experience of the oldest veterans.

Christmas Afternoon, 1862. In Virginia, near Rappahannock, Army of the Potomac.

I write this paragraph in the midst of a large deserted camp ground, with the remains of hundreds of mud huts and the debris of an old brigade or division of soldiers all around me. On a road near at hand successive caravans of army wagons, some of them apparently interminable, with their six-mule teams, are passing and passing, with only slight intervals, nearly all the time. Not far off is a camp of several hundred teamsters, with rows and half-moons of wagons ranged around and heaps of forage, hay, temporary stables, etc. In sight, as I sweep my eye over the open ground (for I can see without obstruction from two to four miles every way), I behold several other such teamsters' camps. Off outside, I see the carcasses of dead horses and mules. The wooded parts of the surface have been cleared for fuel and building purposes for a hundred thousand soldiers.

I hear plainly the music of a good band at some Brigadier's quarters a mile and a half away; it is a beautiful, soft, sunny Christmas day, with a thin haze in the air. Then the drum tap from one direction or other comes constantly breaking in.

Where I sit, I am not within many hundred rods of any soldiers' quarters, but I can see them—regiments, brigades and divisions—spread out in the distance, at every point of the compass. All is open ground, not a particle of fence anywhere. Squads of soldiers are wandering, crossing the space, the roads, etc. at a distance, but where I sit, a couple of hundred feet off the road, I am quite solitary.

I am sitting on a remnant of pine log—the old ground site of what was probably a large camp hut. I can see to the southeast the depression in the landscape where the Rappahannock runs, and one or two signs of Fredericksburg (a battery could easily shell it from where I sit). I hear the sound of bugle calls, very martial, at this distance; a fine, large troop of cavalry is just passing; the hoofs of the horses shake the ground, and I hear the clatter of sabres. Amid all this pleasant scene, under the sweet sky and warm sun, I sit and think over the battle of last Saturday week.

The Old Flag of the 51st.

Old flag, all shot through with fragments of shell, bullets, etc., its staff shattered, carried sternly into seven engagements and into the thickest of the fight, and safely brought out again—all full of shreds, fringed as with the sword, the silk stained with blood.

The Fighting at Fredericksburg.

Taking the army as a whole, it is almost certain that never did mortal man in an aggregate fight better than our troops at Fredericksburg. In the highest sense, it was no failure.

38

The main body troops descending the hills on the Falmouth side to cross the pontoon bridge could plainly see, over back of Fredericksburg, the Secesh batteries rising in tremendous force and plenty on the terrace required to our men's crossing exposed stretches of land—which were fearfully commanded by their batteries—and also the flats thick with their rifle pits. Yet all the brigade went forward unflinchingly.

Nearer view on Saturday, the day of the fight, made everything still more ominous to our side. But still the men advance with unsurpassed gallantry—and would have gone again further, if ordered.

After First Fredericksburg, December 23 to 31, 1862.

The results of the late battle are exhibited everywhere about here in thousands of cases (hundreds die every day) in the camp, brigade, and division hospitals. These are merely tents—and sometimes very poor ones—the wounded lying on the ground, lucky if their blankets are spread on layers of pine or hemlock twigs or small leaves. No cots; seldom even a mattress. It is pretty cold. The ground is frozen hard, and there is occasional snow. . . .

Besides the hospitals, I also go occasionally on long tours through the camps talking with the men, etc., sometimes at night among the groups around the fires, in their shebang enclosures of bushes. These are curious shows, full of characters and groups. I soon get acquainted anywhere in camp with officers or men, and am always well used. Sometimes I go down on picket with the regiment I know best.

As to rations, the army here at present seems to be tolerably well supplied, and the men have enough, such as it is —mainly salt pork and hard tack. Most of the regiments lodge in the flimsy little shelter tents. A few have built themselves huts of logs and mud with fireplaces.

39

Back to Washington, January, 1863.

Left camp at Falmouth with some wounded a few days since and came here by Aquia Creek railroad, and so on government steamer up the Potomac. Many wounded were with us on the cars and boat; the cars were just common platform ones. The railroad journey of ten or twelve miles was made mostly before sunrise. The soldiers guarding the road came out from their tents or shebangs of bushes, with rumpled hair and half-awake look. Those on duty walked their posts—some on banks over us; others down far below the level of the track. I saw large cavalry camps off the road.

At Aquia Creek landing were numbers of wounded going north. While I waited some three hours, I went around among them. Several wanted word sent home to parents, brothers, wives, etc.—which I did for them (by mail the next day from Washington). On the boat I had my hands full. One poor fellow died going up.

Virginia.

Dilapidated, fenceless, and trodden with war as Virginia is, wherever I move across her surface I find myself roused to surprise and admiration. What capacity for products, improvements, human life, nourishment, and expansion! Everywhere that I have been in the Old Dominion (the subtle mockery of that title now!) such thoughts have filled me. The soil is yet far above the average of any of the northern states. And how full of breadth the scenery—everywhere convenient rivers, everywhere distant mountains! Even yet prodigal in forest woods and surely eligible for all the fruits, orchards, and flowers; the skies and atmosphere most luscious, as I feel certain from more than a year's residence in the state and movements hither and yon. I should say very healthy, as a general thing. The sun rejoices in his strength, dazzling and burning and yet, to me, never unpleasantly weakening. It is not the panting tropical heat, but invigorates. The north tempers it. The nights are often unsurpassable.

Last evening (February 8, 1863), I saw the first of the new moon, the outlined old moon clear along with it; the sky and air so clear, such transparent hues of color, it seemed to me I had never really seen the new moon before. It was the thinnest-cut crescent possible. It hung delicate just above the sulky shadow of the Blue Mountains. Ah, if it might prove an omen and a good prophecy for this unhappy state!

A Glimpse of War's Hell-Scenes.

In one of the late movements of our troops in the valley (near Upperville, I think), a strong force of Mosby's guerrillas attacked a train of wounded and the guard of cavalry convoying them. The ambulances contained about sixty wounded, quite a number of them officers of rank. The Rebels were in strength, and the capture of the train and its partial guard after a short snap was effectually accomplished. No sooner had our men surrendered, the Rebels instantly commenced robbing the train and murdering their prisoners, even the wounded. Here is the scene or a sample of it—ten minutes after.

Among the wounded officers in the ambulances were one, a lieutenant of regulars, and another, of higher rank. These two were dragged out on the ground on their backs and were now surrounded by the guerrillas, a demoniac crowd, each member of which was stabbing them in different parts of their bodies. One of the officers had his feet pinned firmly to the ground by bayonets stuck through them and thrust into the ground. These two officers, as afterwards found on examination, had received about twenty such

41

thrusts, some of them through the mouth, face, etc. The wounded had all been dragged (to give a better chance for plunder) out of their wagons; some had been effectually dispatched, and their bodies were lying there lifeless and bloody. Others, not yet dead but horribly mutilated, were moaning or groaning. Of our men who surrendered, most had been thus maimed or slaughtered.

At this instant, a force of our cavalry, who had been following the train at some interval, charged suddenly upon the Secesh captors, who proceeded at once to make the best escape they could. Most of them got away, but we gobbled two officers and seventeen men in the very acts just described. The sight was one which admitted of little discussion, as may be imagined. The seventeen captured men and two officers were put under guard for the night, but it was decided there and then that they should die.

The next morning the two officers were taken in the town—separate places—put in the centre of the street and shot. The seventeen men were taken to an open ground a little to one side. They were placed in a hollow square, half encompassed by two of our cavalry regiments, one of which regiments had three days before found the bloody corpses of three of their men hamstrung and hung up by the heels to limbs of trees by Mosby's guerrillas; and the other had not long before had twelve men, after surrendering, shot and then hung by the neck to limbs of trees, and jeering inscriptions pinned to the breast of one of the corpses, who had been a sergeant.

Those three, and those twelve, had been found, I say, by these environing regiments. Now, with revolvers, they formed the grim cordon of the seventeen prisoners. The latter were placed in the midst of the hollow square, unfastened, and the ironical remark made to them that they were now to be given "a chance for themselves." A few ran for it. But what use? From every side the deadly pills came. In a few minutes the seventeen corpses strewed the hollow square.

I was curious to know whether some of the Union soldiers, some few (some one or two at least of the youngsters), did not abstain from shooting on the helpless men. Not one. There was no exultation, very little said—almost nothing—yet every man there contributed his shot.

Multiply the above by scores, aye hundreds; verify it in all the forms that different circumstances, individuals, places could afford; light it with every lurid passion—the wolf's, the lion's lapping thirst for blood; the passionate, boiling volcanoes of human revenge for comrades, brothers slain; with the light of burning farms and heaps of smutting, smouldering black embers—and in the human heart everywhere, black, worse embers—and you have an inkling of the war.

* * *

A MARCH IN THE RANKS HARD-PREST

A march in the ranks hard-prest, and the road unknown,
A route through a heavy wood with muffled steps in the darkness,
Our army foil'd with loss severe, and the sullen remnant retreating,
Till after midnight glimmer upon us the lights of a dim-lighted
    building,
We come to an open space in the woods, and halt by the dim-
    lighted building,
'Tis a large old church at the crossing roads, now an impromptu
    hospital,
Entering but for a minute I see a sight beyond all the pictures and
    poems ever made,
Shadows of deepest, deepest black, just lit by moving candles and
    lamps,
And by one great pitchy torch stationary with wild red flame and
    clouds of smoke,
By these, crowds, groups of forms vaguely I see on the floor, some
    in the pews laid down,

43

At my feet more distinctly a soldier, a mere lad, in danger of bleed-
ing to death, (he is shot in the abdomen,)
I stanch the blood temporarily, (the youngster's face is white as a
lily,)
Then before I depart I sweep my eyes o'er the scene fain to absorb
it all,
Faces, varieties, postures beyond description, most in obscurity,
some of them dead,
Surgeons operating, attendants holding lights, the smell of ether,
the odor of blood,
The crowd, O the crowd of the bloody forms, the yard outside also
fill'd,
Some on the bare ground, some on planks or stretchers, some in the
death-spasm sweating,
An occasional scream or cry, the doctor's shouted orders or calls,
The glisten of the little steel instruments catching the glint of the
torches,
These I resume as I chant, I see again the forms, I smell the odor,
Then hear outside the orders given, *Fall in, my men, fall in;*
But first I bend to the dying lad, his eyes open, a half-smile gives
he me,
Then the eyes close, calmly close, and I speed forth to the dark-
ness,
Resuming, marching, ever in darkness marching, on in the ranks,
The unknown road still marching.

A Night Battle, Over a Week Since. May 12, 1863.

There was part of the battle at Chancellorsville (Second
Fredericksburg) a little over a week ago, Saturday, Satur-
day night, and Sunday, under General Joe Hooker, I would
like to give just a glimpse of (a moment's look in a terrible
storm at sea, of which a few suggestions are enough, and
full details impossible).

The fighting had been very hot during the day, and, after
an intermission, the latter part was resumed at night and
kept up with furious energy till three o'clock in the morn-
ing. That afternoon (Saturday), an attack sudden and

44

strong by Stonewall Jackson had gained a great advantage
to the Southern Army and broken our lines, entering us
like a wedge and leaving things in that position at dark. But
Hooker at 11 at night made a desperate push, drove the
Secesh forces back, restored his original lines, and resumed
his plans.

This night scrimmage was very exciting, and afforded
countless strange and fearful pictures. The fighting had
been general both at Chancellorsville and northeast at Fred-
ericksburg. (We hear of some poor fighting, episodes, ske-
daddling on our part—I think not of it. I think of the
fierce bravery, the general rule.)

One corps, the 6th, Sedgwick's, fights four dashing and
bloody battles in thirty-six hours, retreating in great jeop-
ardy, losing largely, but maintaining itself, fighting with
the sternest desperation under all circumstances, getting
over the Rappahannock only by the skin of its teeth, yet
getting over. It lost many, many, brave men, yet it took
vengeance, ample vengeance.

But it was the tug of Saturday evening and through the
night and Sunday morning I wanted to make a special note
of. It was largely in the woods and quite a general en-
gagement. The night was very pleasant; at times the moon
shining out full and clear, all Nature so calm in itself, the
early summer grass so rich and foliage of the trees—yet
there was the battle raging and many good fellows lying
helpless, with new accessions to them; and every minute,
amid the rattle of muskets and crash of cannon (for there
was an artillery contest, too), the red lifeblood oozing
out from heads or trunks or limbs upon that green and dewy
earth.

Patches of the woods take fire, and several of the
wounded, unable to move, are consumed; quite large
spaces are swept over, burning the dead also. Some of the
men have their hair and beards singed; some, burns on

their faces and hands; others, with holes burnt in their clothing.

The flashes of fire from the cannon, the quick-flaring flames and smoke, and the immense roar; the musketry so general; the light nearly bright enough for each side to see the other; the crashing, tramping of men; the yellow, close quarters. We hear the Secesh yells; our men cheer loudly back, especially if Hooker is in sight; hand-to-hand conflicts; each side stands up to it—brave, determined as demons, they often charge upon us; a thousand deeds are done worth to write newer, greater poems on—and still the woods on fire; still many are not only scorched; too many, unable to move, are burned to death.

Then the camps of the wounded—O heavens! what scene is this? Is this indeed *humanity*—these butchers' shambles? There are several of them. There they lie in the largest, in an open space in the woods, from two hundred to three hundred poor fellows; the groans and screams, the odor of blood mixed with the fresh scent of the night, the grass, the trees; that slaughter house!

O well is it their mothers, their sisters, cannot see them; cannot conceive and never conceived these things. One man is shot by a shell, both in the arm and leg; both are amputated—there lie the rejected members. Some of them have their legs blown off; some bullets through the breast; some indescribably horrid wounds in the face or head. All mutilated, sickening, torn, gouged out—some in the abdomen—some mere boys, many Rebels (they take their regular turns with the rest, just the same as any; the surgeons use them just the same).

Such is the camp of the wounded; such a fragment, a reflection afar off of the bloody scene; while over all the clear, large moon comes out at times softly, quietly shining. Amid the woods—that scene of flitting souls; amid the crack and crash and yelling sounds—the impalpable perfume of the woods and yet the pungent stifling smoke; the radiance of the moon looking from the heaven at intervals, so placid; the sky so heavenly; the clear-obscure up there, those buoyant upper oceans; a few large, placid stars beyond, coming silently and languidly out and then disappearing; the melancholy, draperied night above, around.

And there, upon the roads, the fields, and in those woods, that contest, never one more desperate in any age or land; both parties now in force—masses—no fancy battle, no semi-play, but fierce and savage demons fighting there; courage and scorn of death the rule, exceptions almost none.

What history, I say, can ever give—for who can know?—the mad, determined tussle of the armies in all their separate large and little squads—as this—each steeped from crown to toe in desperate, mortal purports? Who know the conflict, hand-to-hand, the many conflicts in the dark, those shadowy-tangled, flashing-moonbeamed woods, the writhing groups and squads, the cries, the din, the cracking guns and pistols, the distant cannon, the cheers and calls and threats and awful music of the oaths; the indescribable mix—the officers' orders, persuasions, encouragements—the devils fully roused in human hearts; the strong shout: "charge, men, charge," the flash of the naked sword—and rolling flame and smoke?

And still the broken clear and clouded heaven; and still again the moonlight pouring silvery soft its radiant patches over all. Who paint the scene, the sudden partial panic of the afternoon, at dusk? Who paint the irrepressible advance of the 2nd Division of the 3rd Corps, under Hooker himself, suddenly ordered up—those rapid-filing phantoms through the woods? Who show what moves there in the shadows, fluid and firm, to save (and it did save) the army's name, perhaps the nation—as there the veterans held the field? . . .

A SIGHT IN CAMP IN THE DAYBREAK GRAY AND DIM

A sight in camp in the daybreak gray and dim,
As from my tent I emerge so early sleepless,
As slow I walk in the cool fresh air the path near by the hos-
pital tent,
Three forms I see on stretchers lying, brought out there un-
tended lying,
Over each the blanket spread, ample brownish woolen blanket,
Gray and heavy blanket, folding, covering all.

Curious I halt and silent stand,
Then with light fingers I from the face of the nearest the first
just lift the blanket;
Who are you elderly man so gaunt and grim, with well-gray'd
hair, and flesh all sunken about the eyes?
Who are you my dear comrade?

Then to the second I step—and who are you my child and darling?
Who are you sweet boy with cheeks yet blooming?

Then to the third—a face nor child nor old, very calm, as of
beautiful yellow-white ivory;
Young man I think I know you—I think this face is the face
of the Christ himself,
Dead and divine and brother of all, and here again he lies.

* * *

AS TOILSOME I WANDER'D VIRGINIA'S WOODS

As toilsome I wander'd Virginia's woods,
To the music of rustling leaves kick'd by my feet, (for 'twas
autumn,)
I mark'd at the foot of a tree the grave of a soldier;
Mortally wounded he and buried on the retreat, (easily all could I
understand,)

48

The halt of a mid-day hour, when up! no time to lose—yet this
    sign left,
On a tablet scrawl'd and nail'd on the tree by the grave,
Bold, cautious, true, and my loving comrade.

Long, long I muse, then on my way go wandering,
Many a changeful season to follow, and many a scene of life,
Yet at times through changeful season and scene, abrupt, alone, or
    in the crowded street,
Comes before me the unknown soldier's grave, comes the inscription
    rude in Virginia's woods,
Bold, cautious, true, and my loving comrade.

Down at the Front, Culpepper, Va., February 1864.

Here I am, pretty well down toward the extreme front.
Three or four days ago General S. [Sedgwick], who is
now in chief command (I believe Meade is absent, sick),
moved a strong force southward from camp as if intending
business. They went to the Rapidan; there has since been
some maneuvering and a little fighting, but nothing of con-
sequence. The telegraphic accounts given Monday morn-
ing last make entirely too much of it, I should say.

What General S. intended we here know not; but we
trust in that competent commander. We were somewhat ex-
cited (but not so very much either) on Sunday, during the
day and night, as orders were sent out to pack and harness
and be ready to evacuate, to fall back towards Washing-
ton. But I was very sleepy and went to bed. Some tremen-
dous shouts arousing me during the night, I went forth and
found it was from the men above mentioned, who were re-
turning. I talked with some of the men; as usual, I found
them full of gayety, endurance, and many fine little out-
shows, the signs of the most excellent good manliness of the
world.

It was a curious sight to see those shadowy columns mov-
ing through the night. I stood unobserved in the darkness

49

and watched them long. The mud was very deep. The men had their usual burdens—overcoats, knapsacks, guns, and blankets. Along and along, they filed by me, with often a laugh, a song, a cheerful word, but never once a murmur.

It may have been odd, but I never before so realized the majesty and reality of the American people *en masse*. It fell upon me like a great awe. The strong ranks moved neither fast nor slow. They had marched seven or eight miles already through the slipping, unctuous mud. The brave 1st Corps stopped here. The equally brave 3rd Corps moved on to Brandy Station. The famous Brooklyn 14th are here, guarding the town. You see their red legs actively moving everywhere. Then they have a theatre of their own here. They give musical performances; nearly everything is done capitally. Of course, the audience is a jam. . . .

Culpepper, Virginia, Friday Night, February 12, 1864.

. . . I am still stopping down in this region. I am a good deal of the time down within half a mile of our picket lines, so that you see I can indeed call myself in the front. I stopped yesterday with an artillery camp in the 1st Corps, at the invitation of Captain Crawford, who said he knew me in Brooklyn. It is close to the lines; I asked him if he did not think it dangerous. He said, no, he could have a large force of infantry to help him there in very short metre if there was any sudden emergency.

The troops here are scattered all around, much more apart than they seemed to me to be opposite Fredericksburg last winter. They mostly have good huts and fireplaces, etc. I have been to a great many of the camps, and I must say I am astonished [how] good the houses are almost everywhere. I have not seen one regiment, nor any part of one, in the poor, uncomfortable little shelter tents that I saw so common last winter after Fredericksburg, but all the men have built huts of logs and mud. A good many of them would be comfortable enough to live in under any circumstances.

I have been in the division hospitals around here. There are not many men sick here and no wounded; they now send them on to Washington. I shall return there in a few days, as I am very clear that the real need of one's services is there, after all. There the worst cases concentrate, and probably will while the war lasts.

I suppose you know that what we call hospital here is nothing but a collection of tents on the bare ground for a floor—rather hard accommodation for a sick man. They heat them there by digging a long trough in the ground under them, covering it over with old railroad iron and earth, and then building a fire at one end and letting it draw through and go out at the other—as both ends are open. This heats the ground through the middle of the hospital quite hot. . . .

Today I have been out among some of the camps of the 2nd Division of the 1st Corps. I have been wandering around all day and have had a very good time—over woods, hills, and gullies, indeed, a real soldier's march. The weather is good and the travelling quite tolerable. I have been in the camps of some Massachusetts, Pennsylvania, and New York regiments. I have friends in them and went out to see them and see soldiering generally, as I can never cease to crave more and more knowledge of actual soldiers' life and to be among them as much as possible.

This evening I have also been in a large wagoners' camp. They had good fires and were very cheerful. I went to see a friend there, too, but did not find him in. It is curious how many I find that I know and that know me. . . . I have no difficulty at all in making myself at home among the soldiers, teamsters, or any. I most always find they like to have me very much; it seems to do them good. No doubt they soon feel that my heart and sympathies are truly with them, and it is both a novelty and pleases them and touches their feelings, and so doubtless does them good—and I am sure it does that to me.

There is more fun around here than you would think for. I told you about the theatre the 14th Brooklyn has got up; they have songs and burlesques, etc., some of the performers real good. As I write this, I have heard in one direction or another two or three good bands playing, and hear one tooting away some gay tunes now, though it is quite late at night. . . .

July 6th [1864].

A steady rain, dark and thick and warm. A train of six-mule wagons has just passed bearing pontoons, great square and flat boats, and the heavy planking for overlaying them. We hear that the Potomac above here is flooded, and are wondering whether Lee will be able to get back across again, or whether Meade will indeed break him in pieces.

The cavalry camp on the hill is a ceaseless field of observation for me. This forenoon there stand the horses tethered together, dripping, streaming, chewing their hay. The men emerge from their tents, dripping also. The fires are half quenched.

July 10 [1864].

Still the camp opposite, perhaps fifty or sixty tents. Some of the men are cleaning their sabres (pleasant today), some brushing boots, some laying off, reading, writing; some cooking; some sleeping. On long temporary cross-sticks back of the tents are cavalry accoutrements; blankets and overcoats are hung out to air; there are the squads of horses tethered, feeding, continually stamping and whisking their tails off to keep off flies. I sit long in my third-story window and look at the scene—a hundred little things going on— peculiar objects connected with the camp that could not be described, any one of them, justly, without much minute drawing and coloring in words.

Central Virginia in 1864.

Culpepper, where I am stopping, looks like a place of two or three thousand inhabitants. Must be one of the pleasantest towns in Virginia. Even now—dilapidated fences, all broken down, windows out—it has the remains of much beauty. I am standing on an eminence overlooking the town, though within its limits. To the west, the long Blue Mountain range is very plain; looks quite near, though from thirty to fifty miles distant, with some gray splashes of snow yet visible. The show is varied and fascinating. I see a great eagle up there in the air, sailing with poised wings, quite low. Squads of red-legged soldiers are drilling, I suppose some of the new men of the Brooklyn 14th; they march off presently with muskets on their shoulders.

In another place, just below me, are some soldiers squaring off logs to build a shanty—chopping away, and the noise of the axes sounding sharp. I hear the bellowing, unmusical screech of the mule. I mark the thin, blue smoke rising from campfires.

Just below me is a collection of hospital tents, with a yellow flag elevated on a stick and moving languidly in the breeze. The discharged men (I know them both) are just leaving. One is so weak he can hardly walk; the other is stronger and carries his comrade's musket. They move slowly along the muddy road toward the depot. The scenery is full of breadth, and spread on the most generous scale (everywhere in Virginia this thought filled me). The sights, the scenes, the groups have been varied and picturesque here beyond description, and remain so.

I heard the men return in force the other night; heard the shouting, and got up and went out to hear what was the

53

matter. That night scene of so many hundred tramping steadily by through the mud (some big flaring torches of pine knots), I shall never forget.

I like to go to the paymaster's tent and watch the men getting paid off. Some have furloughs and start at once for home, sometimes amid great chaffing and blarneying.

There is every day the sound of the wood-chopping axe and the plentiful sight of Negroes, crows, and mud. I note large droves and pens of cattle. The teamsters have camps of their own, and I go often among them. The officers occasionally invite me to dinner or supper at headquarters. The fare is plain, but you get something good to drink and plenty of it. General Meade is absent; Sedgwick is in command.

March 27, 1865.

Sergeant Calvin F. Harlowe, Company C, 29th Massachusetts, 3rd Brigade, 1st Division, 9th Corps, a marked sample of *heroism*, of grandest, oldest order, in the late attack by the Rebel troops and temporary capture by them of Fort Steadman at night. The fort was surprised at dead of night. Suddenly awakened from sleep and rushing from their tents, Harlowe, with others, found himself in the hands of the Secesh; they demanded his surrender; he answered: *"Never while I live."* (Of course, it was useless. The others surrendered; the odds were too great.) Again he was asked to yield, this time by a Rebel captain. Though surrounded and quite calm, he again refused, called sternly to his comrades to fight on, and himself attempted to do so. The Rebel captain then shot him—but at the same instant he shot the captain. Both fell together, mortally wounded. Harlowe died almost instantly.

The Rebels were driven out in a very short time. The body was buried next day, but soon taken up and sent home (Plymouth County, Mass.). Harlowe was only 22 years of age—was a tall, slim, dark-haired, blue-eyed young man; had come originally with the 29th; and that is the way he met his death, after four years' campaign.

He was in the Seven Days' Fight before Richmond, in Second Bull Run, Antietam, First Fredericksburg, Vicksburg, Jackson, Wilderness, and the campaigns following; was as good a soldier as ever wore the blue, and every old officer in the regiment will bear that testimony. Though so young and in a common rank, he had a spirit as resolute and brave as any here in the books, ancient or modern; it was too great to say the words "I surrender," and so he died.

When I think of such things, knowing them well, all the vast and complicated events of the war, on which history dwells and makes its volumes, fall aside; and for the moment at any rate I see nothing but young Calvin Harlowe's figure in the night, disdaining to surrender.

Unnamed Remains the Bravest Soldier.

Of scenes like these, I say, who writes—whoe'er can write the story? Of many a score, aye, thousands, north and south; of unwrit heroes, unknown heroisms, incredible, impromptu, first-class desperations—who tells? No history ever, no poem sings, no music sounds those bravest men of all—those deeds. No formal general's report, nor book in the library, nor column in the paper, embalms the bravest, North or South, East or West.

Unnamed, unknown, remain and still remain the bravest soldiers. Our manliest, our boys, our hardy darlings: no picture gives them. Likely, the typic one of them (standing, no doubt, for hundreds, thousands) crawls aside to some bush-clump or ferny tuft on receiving his death-shot; there, sheltering a little while, soaking roots, grass, and soil with red blood; the battle advances, retreats, flits from the scene, sweeps by; and there, haply with pain and suffering (yet less, far less than is supposed), the last lethargy winds like a serpent round him; the eyes glaze in death; none recks——perhaps the burial squads (in truce, a week afterwards) search not the secluded spot; and there, at last, the Bravest Soldier, crumbles in Mother Earth, unburied and unknown.

VIGIL STRANGE I KEPT ON THE FIELD ONE NIGHT

Vigil strange I kept on the field one night;
When you my son and my comrade dropt at my side that day,
One look I but gave which your dear eyes return'd with a look
    I shall never forget,
One touch of your hand to mine O boy, reach'd up as you lay on
    the ground,
Then onward I sped in the battle, the even-contested battle,
Till late in the night reliev'd to the place at last again I made my
    way,
Found you in death so cold dear comrade, found your body son of
    responding kisses, (never again on earth responding,)
Bared your face in the starlight, curious the scene, cool blew the
    moderate night-wind,
Long there and then in vigil I stood, dimly around me the battle-
    field spreading,
Vigil wondrous and vigil sweet there in the fragrant silent night,
But not a tear fell, not even a long-drawn sigh, long, long I gazed,
Then on the earth partially reclining sat by your side leaning my
    chin in my hands,
Passing sweet hours, immortal and mystic hours with you dearest
    comrade—not a tear, not a word,
Vigil of silence, love and death, vigil for you my son and my soldier,
As onward silently stars aloft, eastward new ones upward stole,
Vigil final for you brave boy, (I could not save you, swift was your
    death,
I faithfully loved you and cared for you living, I think we shall
    surely meet again,)
Till at latest lingering of the night, indeed just as the dawn appear'd,
My comrade I wrapt in his blanket, envelop'd well his form,

Folded the blanket well, tucking it carefully over head and carefully
  under feet,
And there and then and bathed by the rising sun, my son in his
  grave, in his rude-dug grave I deposited,
Ending my vigil strange with that, vigil of night and battlefield dim,
Vigil for boy of responding kisses, (never again on earth respond-
  ing,)
Vigil for comrade swiftly slain, vigil I never forget, how as day
  brighten'd,
I rose from the chill ground and folded my soldier well in his
  blanket,
And buried him where he fell.

Chapter Four

'By Broad Potomac's Shore'

(Washington scenes.)

Descriptions of life on many levels in the wartime capital: the hospitals, cavalry camps, soldiers, Congress, glimpses of the great, "pomp and circumstance." Arrival of the wounded from Chancellorsville; news of the victory at Gettysburg.

SPIRIT WHOSE WORK IS DONE

Spirit whose work is done—spirit of dreadful hours!
Ere departing fade from my eyes your forests of bayonets;
Spirit of gloomiest fears and doubts, (yet onward ever unfaltering
    pressing,)
Spirit of many a solemn day and many a savage scene—electric
    spirit,
That with muttering voice through the war now closed, like a tire-
    less phantom flitted,
Rousing the land with breath of flame, while you beat and beat the
    drum,
Now as the sound of the drum, hollow and harsh to the last, rever-
    berates round me,
As your ranks, your immortal ranks, return, return from the battles,
As the muskets of the young men yet lean over their shoulders,
As I look on the bayonets bristling over their shoulders,
As those slanted bayonets, whole forests of them appearing in the
    distance, approach and pass on, returning homeward,
Moving with steady motion, swaying to and fro to the right and
    left,
Evenly, lightly rising and falling while the steps keep time;
Spirit of hours I knew, all hectic red one day, but pale as death next
    day,
Touch my mouth ere you depart, press my lips close,
Leave me your pulses of rage—bequeath them to me—fill me with
    currents convulsive,
Let them scorch and blister out of my chants when you are gone,
Let them identify you to the future in these songs.

'By Broad Potomac's Shore'

Office Major Hapgood, Corner 15th and F Streets, Washington, February 1863.

. . . I have seen Preston King this morning for the second time.

(It is very amusing to hunt for an office—so the thing seems to me just now—even if one doesn't get it.) I have seen Charles Sumner three times; he says everything moves here as part of a great machine, and that I must consign myself to the fate of the rest. Still, in an interview I had with him yesterday, he talked and acted as though he had life in him and would exert himself to any reasonable extent for me to get something.

Meantime I make about enough to pay my expenses by hacking on the press here and copying in the paymasters' offices a couple of hours a day. One thing is favorable here, namely, pay for whatever one does is at a high rate. I have not yet presented my letters either to Seward or Chase; I thought I would get my forces all in a body and make one concentrated dash, if possible, with the personal introduction and presence of some big bug.

I like fat old Preston King very much—he is fat as a hogshead, with great hanging chops. The first thing he said to me the other day in the parlor chambers of the Senate, when I sent in for him and he came out, was: "Why, how can I do this thing or anything for you? How do I know but you are a Secessionist? You look for all the world like an old Southern planter—a regular Carolina or Virginia planter."

I treated him with just as much hauteur as he did me with bluntness (this was the first time). It afterward proved that Charles Sumner had not prepared the way for me, as I supposed—or rather not so strongly as I supposed—and Mr. King had even forgotten it; so I was an entire stranger. But the same day C. S. talked further with Mr. King in the Senate, and the second interview I had with the latter (this forenoon), he has given me a sort of general letter, endorsing me from New York; one envelope is addressed to Secretary Chase and another to General Meigs, head quartermaster's department.

Meantime, I am getting better and better acquainted with office-hunting wisdom and Washington peculiarities generally. I spent several hours in the Capitol the other day. The incredible gorgeousness of some of the rooms (interior decorations, etc.), rooms used perhaps but for merely three or four committee meetings in the course of the whole year, is beyond one's flightiest dreams.

Costly frescoes of the style of Taylor's saloon on Broadway, only really the best and choicest of their sort, done by imported French and Italian artists, are the prevailing sorts. (Imagine the work you see on the fine china vases in Tiffany's, the paintings of cupids and goddesses, etc. spread recklessly over the arched ceiling and broad panels of a big room—the whole floor underneath paved with tessellated pavement, which is a sort of a cross between marble and china, with little figures—drab, blue, cream color, etc.)

These things, with elaborately wrought balustrades, columns, and steps—all of the most beautiful marbles I ever saw, some white as milk, others of all colors—green, spotted, lined, or of our old chocolate color—all these marbles used as freely as if they were common blue flags, with rich doorframes and window casings of bronze and gold, heavy chandeliers and mantles and clocks in every room, and indeed by far the richest and the gayest and most unAmerican and inappropriate ornamenting and finest interior workmanship I ever conceived possible—spread in profusion through scores, hundreds (and almost thousands) of rooms—such are what I find, or rather, would find, to interest me if I would devote time to it. But a few of the rooms are enough for me—the style is without grandeur or simplicity.

These days, the state our country is in, and, especially, filled as I am from top to toe of late with scenes and thoughts of the hospitals (America seems to me now—though only in her youth but brought already here—feeble, bandaged, and bloody in hospital), these days, I say, . . . all the poppy-show goddesses and all the pretty blue and gold in which the interior Capitol is got up seem to me out of place beyond anything I could tell, and I get away from it as quick as I can when that kind of thought comes over me. . . .

Washington, February 11, 1863, Wednesday.

. . . Went with Mrs. O'Connor a while in the Senate gallery; then we went into the Supreme Court room (old Senate chamber); saw Chief Justice Taney and all the other black-gowned Supreme Judges—their faces old, wrinkled, heavy—a lot of old mummies. Went also into the Congressional Library—a splendid view from the high colonnade in front of it. Then went off into the rich chamber for the meeting of the agricultural committee of the Representatives—a magic, painted, marble, rich-hued palace room. Also in the House of Representatives session, the interior work of the new Capitol impresses me more and more with its beauty and perfect manipulation. . . .

63

Washington, February 16 [*1863*].

. . . This is the last day of the 37th Congress, the body during whose existence (1861, '62, '63) the most important, confusing and abnormal events in American history (shall I not say in the history of the world?) have happened. The 37th Congress, as I have watched their debates (wrangles, propositions, personal presences, physiognomies) in their magnificent skylighted halls; [have] gone night and day, sat, seen, listened—sometimes literally doubting for a moment my own eyes and ears.

I have learned many new things. These then are the men who do as they do—in the midst of the greatest historic chaos and gigantic tussle of the greatest of ages. Look at the little mannikins, shrewd, gabby, dressed in black, hopping about, making motions, amendments. It is very curious. Last night I have gone to the gallery to look at them down there, flooded with light stronger than sunshine, in the most magnificent and best proportioned rooms in the world.

What events are about them and all of us! Whither are we drifting? Who knows? It seems as if these electric and terrible days were enough to put life in a paving stone—as if these must needs form our representative men that have to do with them; [give them] faces of grandeur, actions of awe, vestments of majesty.

. . . I work somewhere among them [the wounded] every day or in the evening. It is not so exhausting as one might think—the endurance and spirit are supplied. My health, thank God, was never better—I feel strong and elastic—an obstinate cold and deafness of some weeks seems to be broken up at last. Yesterday I spent nearly all day at Armory-Square Hospital. This forenoon I take an intermission and go again at dusk.

You there North must not be so disheartened about Hooker's return to this side of the Rappahannock and supposed failure. The blow struck at Lee's and the Rebel Army in Virginia, and generally at Richmond and Jeff Davis, by this short but tremendous little campaign of 2nd, 3rd, 4th and 5th instants is, in my judgment, the heaviest and most staggering they have yet got from us, and has not only hit them nearer where they live than all McClellan ever did, but all that has been levelled at Richmond during the war. I mean this deliberately. We have paid for it with thousands of dear, noble lives—America's choicest blood. Yet the late battles are not without something decisive to show for them. Hooker will resume operations forthwith—maybe has returned there.

Do not be discouraged—I am not—even here amid all this huge mess of traitors, loafers, hospitals, axe-grinders, incompetencies and officials that goes by the name of Washington. I myself yet believe in Hooker, yet say he is a good man. . . .

The Wounded from Chancellorsville, May 1863.

As I write this, wounded have begun to arrive from Hooker's command from bloody Chancellorsville. I was down among the first arrivals. The men in charge told me the bad cases were yet to come. If that is so, I pity them—for these are bad enough. You ought to see the scene of the wounded arriving at the landing here at the foot of Sixth Street at night. Two boatloads came about half-past seven last night. A little after eight, it rained a long and violent shower. The pale, helpless soldiers had been debarked, and lay around on the wharf and neighborhood anywhere. The rain was probably grateful to them; at any rate, they were exposed to it. The few torches light up the spectacle.

All around—on the wharf, on the ground, out on side places—the men are lying on blankets, old quilts, etc., with

bloody rags bound 'round heads, arms, and legs. The attend-
ants are few, and at night few outsiders also; only a few
hard-worked transportation men and drivers. (The
wounded are getting to be common, and people grow
callous.)

The men, whatever their condition, lie there and patiently
wait till their turn comes to be taken up. Nearby, the am-
bulances are now arriving in clusters, and one after another
is called to back up and take its load. Extreme cases are
sent off on stretchers. The men generally make little or no
ado, whatever their sufferings. A few groans that cannot
be suppressed and occasionally a scream of pain, as they
lift a man into the ambulance. Today, as I write, hundreds
more are expected, and tomorrow and the next day more,
and so on for many days. Quite often they arrive at the rate
of one thousand a day.

Ambulance Processions, June 25, Sundown.

As I sit writing this paragraph, I see a train of about thirty
huge four-horse wagons, used as ambulances, filled with
wounded, passing up Fourteenth Street, on their way,
probably, to Columbian, Carver, and Mount Pleasant hos-
pitals. This is the way the men come in now—seldom in
small numbers, but almost always in these long, sad proces-
sions. Through the past winter, while our army lay opposite
Fredericksburg, the like strings of ambulances were of fre-
quent occurrence along Seventh Street, passing slowly up
from the steamboat wharf with loads from Aquia Creek.

Bad Wounds—the Young.

The soldiers are nearly all young men and far more Ameri-
can than is generally supposed; I should say nine tenths are
native-born. Among the arrivals from Chancellorsville, I
find a large proportion of Ohio, Indiana, and Illinois men.
As usual, there are all sorts of wounds. Some of the men

[are] fearfully burnt from the explosions of artillery cais-
sons. One ward has a long row of officers, some with ugly
hurts. Yesterday was perhaps worse than usual. Amputa-
tions are going on; the attendants are dressing wounds. As
you pass by, you must be on your guard where you look.
I saw the other day a gentlemen, a visitor, apparently from
curiosity, in one of the wards, stop and turn a moment to
look at an awful wound they were probing. He turned
pale, and in a moment more he had fainted away and fallen
on the floor.

The Most Inspiriting of All War's Shows. June 29, 1863.
Just before sundown this evening a very large cavalry
force went by—a fine sight. The men evidently had seen
service. First came a mounted band of sixteen bugles,
drums, and cymbals playing wild, martial tunes—made my
heart jump. Then the principal officers; then company af-
ter company, with their officers at their heads making of
course the main part of the cavalcade; then a long train of
men with led horses; lots of mounted Negroes with special
horses; and a long string of baggage wagons, each drawn by
four horses; and then a motley rear guard.

It was a pronouncedly warlike and gay show; the sabres
clanked; the men looked young and healthy and strong;
the electric trumping of so many horses on the hard road
and the gallant bearing, fine seat, and bright-faced appear-
ance of a thousand and more handsome young American
men were so good to see. An hour later another troop went
by, smaller in numbers—perhaps three hundred men. They,
too, looked like serviceable men, campaigners used to field
and fight.

July 3.
This forenoon, for more than an hour, again long strings of
cavalry, several regiments—very fine men and horses—

four or five abreast. I saw them in Fourteenth Street coming in town from north. Several hundred extra horses, some of them mares with colts, trotting along. (Appeared to be a number of prisoners, too.) How inspiriting always the cavalry regiments! Our men are generally well mounted, feel good, are young, gay on the saddle, their blankets in a roll behind them, their sabres clanking at their sides.

This noise and movement and the tramp of many horses' hoofs has a curious effect upon one. The bugles play; presently you hear them afar off, deadened, mixed with other noises. Then, just as they had all passed, a string of ambulances commenced from the other way, moving up Fourteen Street north, slowly wending along, bearing a large lot of wounded to the hospitals.

Boys in the Army.

As I walked home about sunset, I saw in Fourteenth Street a very young soldier, thinly clad, standing near the house I was about to enter. I stopped a moment in front of the door and called him to me. I knew that an old Tennessee regiment and also an Indiana regiment were temporarily stopping in new barracks near Fourteenth Street. This boy I found belonged to the Tennessee regiment. But I could hardly believe he carried a musket. He was but fifteen years old, yet had been twelve months a soldier and had borne his part in several battles, even historic ones. I asked him if he did not suffer from the cold. [He] had no overcoat, but could draw one whenever he wishes. His father was dead and his mother living in some part of East Tennessee; all the men were from that part of the country.

The next forenoon I saw the Tennessee and Indiana regiments marching down the Avenue. My boy was with the former, stepping along with the rest. There were many other boys no older. I stood and watched them as they tramped along with slow, strong, heavy, regular steps.

There did not appear to be a man over thirty years of age, and a large proportion were from fifteen to perhaps twenty-two or twenty-three. They had all the look of veterans—worn, stained, impassive, and a certain unbent, lounging gait—carrying in addition to their regular arms and knapsacks frequently a frying pan, broom, etc. They were all of pleasant physiognomy; no refinement, nor blanched with intellect, but as my eye picked them moving along, rank by rank, there did not seem to be a single repulsive, brutal, or markedly stupid face among them.

Paying the Bounties.

One of the things to note here now is the arrival of the paymaster with his strong box and the payment of bounties to veterans re-enlisting. Major H. is here today with a small mountain of greenbacks, rejoicing the hearts of the 2nd Division of the 1st Corps. In the midst of a ricketty shanty, behind a little table, sit the major and clerk Eldridge with the rolls before them and much moneys.

A re-enlisted man gets in cash about two hundred dollars down (and heavy installments following as the paydays arrive, one after another). The show of the men crowding around is quite exhilarating; I like to stand and look. They feel elated, their pockets full, and the ensuing furlough, the visit home. It is a scene of sparkling eyes and flushed cheeks. The soldier has many gloomy and harsh experiences, and this makes up for some of them.

Major H. is ordered to pay first all the re-enlisted men of the 1st Corps their bounties and back pay, and then the rest. You hear the peculiar sound of the rustling of new and crisp greenbacks by the hour, through the nimble fingers of the major and my friend, clerk Eldridge.

Battle of Gettysburg, July 4, 1863.

The weather today upon the whole is very fine, warm, but, from a smart rain last night, fresh enough, and no dust, which is a great relief for this city. I saw the parade about noon, Pennsylvania Avenue from Fifteenth Street down toward the Capitol. There were three regiments of infantry (I suppose the ones doing patrol duty here), two or three Societies of Odd Fellows, a lot of children in barouches, and a squad of policemen. (A useless imposition upon the soldiers—they have work enough on their backs without piling the like of this.)

As I went down the avenue, saw a big, flaring placard on the bulletin board of a newspaper office, announcing "Glorious Victory for the Union Army!" Meade had fought Lee at Gettysburg, Pennsylvania, yesterday and day before, and repulsed him most signally; taken three thousand prisoners, etc. (I afterwards saw Meade's dispatch, very modest, and a sort of order of the day from the President himself, quite religious, giving thanks to the Supreme, and calling on the people to do the same.)

I walked on to Armory Hospital; took along with me several bottles of blackberry and cherry syrup—good and strong, but innocent; went through several of the wards; announced to the soldiers the news from Meade; and gave them all a good drink of the syrups with ice water—quite refreshing; prepared it all myself and served it around.

Meanwhile, the Washington bells are ringing their sundown peals for Fourth of July, and the usual fusillades of boys' pistols, crackers, and guns.

Dispatch to the New York Times, December 11, 1864.
Back again in Washington.

They are breaking up the camp hospitals in Meade's Army, preparing for a move. As I write this, in March,

70

there are all the signs. Yesterday and last night the sick were arriving here in long trains, all day and night. I was among the newcomers most of the night. One train of a thousand came into the depot and others followed. The ambulances were going all night, distributing them to the various hospitals here. When they come in, some literally in a dying condition, you may well imagine it is a lamentable sight. I hardly know which is worse—to see the wounded after a battle or these wasted wrecks.

I remain in capital health and strength and go every day, as before, among the men in my own way, enjoying my life and occupation more than I can tell. . . .

A wanderer like me about Washington pauses on some high land which commands the sweep of the city (one never tires of the noble and ample views presented here, in the generally fine, soft, peculiar air and light), and has his eyes attracted by these white clusters of barracks in almost every direction. They make a great show in the landscape, and I often use them as landmarks. Some of these clusters are very full of inmates. Counting the whole, with the convalescent camps (whose inmates are often worse off than the sick in the hospitals), they have numbered in this quarter and just down the Potomac as high as fifty thousand invalid, disabled, or sick and dying men. . . .

April 10, 1864.

Unusual agitation all around concentrated here. Exciting times in Congress. The Copperheads are getting furious. "This is a pretty time to talk of recognizing such ———," said a Pennsylvania officer in hospital to me today, "after what has transpired in the last three years."

After First Fredericksburg, I felt discouraged myself and doubted whether our rulers could carry on the war. But that has passed away. The war *must* be carried on. I would

71

willingly go in the ranks myself if I thought it would profit more than as at present; and I don't know sometimes but I shall, as it is. Then there is certainly a strange, deep, fervid feeling formed or aroused in the land—hard to describe or name; it is not a majority feeling, but it will make itself felt. . . .

. . . You don't know what a nature a fellow gets, not only after being a soldier a while, but after living in the signs and influences of the camps, the wounded, etc.—a nature he never experienced before. The Stars and Stripes, the tune of Yankee Doodle, and similar things produce such an effect on a fellow as never before. I have seen them bring tears on some men's cheeks, and others turn pale with emotion.

I have a little flag (it belonged to one of our cavalry regiments), presented to me by one of the wounded. It was taken by the Secesh in a fight and rescued by our men in a bloody skirmish following. It cost three men's lives to get back that four-by-three flag—to tear it from the breast of a dead rebel for the name of getting their little "rag" back again.

The man that secured it was very badly wounded, and they let him keep it. I was with him a good deal; he wanted to give me some keepsake, he said—he didn't expect to live —so he gave me that flag. The best of it all is . . . there isn't a regiment, cavalry, or infantry that wouldn't do the like on the like occasion.

April 12, 1864. I will finish my letter this morning; it is a beautiful day. I was up in Congress very late last night. The house had a very excited night session about expelling the men that proposed recognizing the Southern Confederacy. You ought to hear (as I do) the soldiers talk; they are excited to madness. We shall probably have hot times here—not in the military fields alone. The body of the army is true and firm as the North Star.

Washington, 1864.

The happening to our America, abroad as well as at home these years, is indeed most strange. The democratic republic has paid her today the terrible and resplendent compliment of the united wish of all the nations of the world that her union should be broken, her future cut off, and that she should be compelled to descend to the level of kingdoms and empires ordinarily great.

There is certainly not one government in Europe but is watching the war in this country with the ardent prayer that the United States may be effectually split, crippled, and dismembered by it. There is not one but would help toward that dismemberment, if it dared. I say such is the ardent wish today of England and of France, as governments, and of all the nations of Europe, as governments.

I think indeed it is today the real, heartfelt wish of all the nations of the world, with the single exception of Mexico —Mexico, the only one to whom we have ever really done wrong, and now the only one who prays for us and for our triumph with genuine prayer. Is it not indeed strange? America, made up of all, cheerfully from the beginning opening her arms to all, the result and justifier of all—of Britain, Germany, France and Spain—all here; the accepter, the friend, hope, last resource, and general house of all; she who has harmed none but been bounteous to so many, to millions; the mother of strangers and exiles, all nations— should now, I say, be paid this dread compliment of general governmental fear and hatred?

Are we indignant? alarmed? Do we feel jeopardized? No; helped, braced, concentrated, rather. We are all too prone to wander from ourselves, to affect Europe, and watch her frowns and smiles. We need this hot lesson of general hatred and henceforth must never forget it. Never

73

again will we trust the moral sense nor abstract friendliness of a single *government* of the old world.

Heated Term.

There has been much suffering here from heat; we have had it upon us now eleven days. I go around with an umbrella and a fan. I saw two cases of sunstroke yesterday, one in Pennsylvania Avenue and another in Seventh Street. The city railroad company loses some horses every day. Yet, Washington is having a livelier August and is probably putting in a more energetic and satisfactory summer than ever before during its existence.

There is probably more human electricity, more population to make it, more business, more light-heartedness than ever before. The armies that swiftly circumambiated from Fredericksburg; marched, struggled, fought; had out their mighty clinch and hurl at Gettysburg; wheeled, circumambiated again, returned to their ways; touching us not either at their coming or going. And Washington feels that she has passed the worst; perhaps feels that she is henceforth mistress. So here she sits with her surrounding hills spotted with guns, and is conscious of a character and identity different from what it was five or six short weeks ago —and very considerably pleasanter and prouder.

Soldiers and Talks.

Soldiers, soldiers, soldiers, you meet everywhere about the city, often superb-looking men, though invalids dressed in worn uniforms and carrying canes or crutches. I often have talks with them, occasionally quite long and interesting. One, for instance, will have been all through the Peninsula under McClellan; narrates to me the fights, the marches, the strange, quick changes of the eventful campaign, and gives glimpses of many things untold in any official reports or books or journals. These, indeed, are the things that are genuine and precious: the man was there, has been out two years, has been through a dozen fights, the superfluous flesh of talking is long worked off him, and he gives me little but the hard meat and sinew.

I find it refreshing—these hardy, bright, intuitive American young men (experienced soldiers, with all their youth). The vocal play and significance moves one more than books. Then there hangs something majestic about a man who has borne his part in battles, especially if he is very quiet regarding it when you desire him to unbosom.

I am continually lost at the absence of blowing and blowers among these old-young American militaires. I have found some man or other who has been in every battle since the war began and have talked with them about each one, in every part of the United States, and many of the engagements on the rivers and harbors, too. I find men here from every state in the Union, without exception. (There are more Southerners, especially border state men, in the Union Army than is generally supposed.) I now doubt whether one can get a fair idea of what this war practically is, or what genuine America is and her character, without some such experience as this I am having.

A Silent Night Ramble, October 20, 1864.

Tonight, after leaving the hospital at ten o'clock (I had been on self-imposed duty some five hours, pretty closely confined), I wandered a long time around Washington. The night was sweet, very clear, sufficiently cool; a voluptuous half-moon, slightly golden, the space near it of a transparent blue-gray tinge.

I walked up Pennsylvania Avenue and then to Seventh Street, and for a long while around the Patent Office. Somehow it looked rebukefully strong, majestic, there in the delicate moonlight. The sky, the planets, the constellations

75

—all so bright, so calm, so expressively silent, so soothing after those hospital scenes. I wandered to and fro till the moist moon set, long after midnight.

Spiritual Characters Among the Soldiers.

Every now and then, in hospital or camp, there are beings I meet—specimens of unworldliness, disinterestedness, and animal purity and heroism—perhaps some unconscious Indianan or from Ohio or Tennessee, on whose birth the calmness of heaven seems to have descended and whose gradual growing up, whatever the circumstances of work-life or change or hardship or small or no education that attended it, the power of a strange spiritual sweetness, fibre, and inward health have also attended. Something veiled and abstracted is often a part of the manners of these beings.

I have met them, I say, not seldom in the army, in camp, and in the hospitals. The Western regiments contain many of them.

They are often young men obeying the events and occasions about them—marching, soldiering, fighting, foraging, cooking, working on farms or at some trade before the war, unaware of their own nature (as to that, who is aware of his own nature?), their companions only understanding that they are different from the rest, more silent, "something odd about them," and apt to go off and meditate and muse in solitude.

Cattle Droves About Washington.

Among other sights are immense droves of cattle with their drivers passing through the streets of the city. Some of the men have a way of leading the cattle by a peculiar call—a wild, pensive hoot, quite musical, prolonged, indescribable, sounding something between the cooing of a pigeon and the hoot of an owl. I like to stand and look at the sight of one of these immense droves—a little way off—as the dust is great. There are always men on horseback, cracking their whips and shouting; the cattle low; some obstinate ox or steer attempts to escape; then a lively scene—the mounted men, always excellent riders and on good horses; a dash after the recusant, and wheel and turn; a dozen mounted drovers, their great, slouched, broad-brimmed hats very picturesque; another dozen on foot; everybody covered with dust; long goads in their hands—an immense drove of perhaps one thousand cattle—the shouting, hooting, movement, etc.

. . . I have lately been down to the front on a short tour through the army; part of the time being in camp among the men. (I know a good many soldiers in the ranks and visit the division hospitals.) The hospitals in the field are at present thin—the main cases are here. The condition of the army the past winter has been surpassingly good; the talk here is that Grant is going to make things hop in this region presently.

The idea is that the means of railway transportation between here and the Southwest are to be increased to the extremest practical degree, so that he can swing large bodies to and fro with unprecedented dispatch, and have the use of the army in either quarter at a few days' notice. We hear he thinks it indispensable that we should smash Lee and the Richmond junta this summer, though more for our prestige than for any practical need of Richmond as a locality.

I can assure you from personal knowledge that the Army of the Potomac is in splendid condition; physically and in soul it has now the fibre of the most veteran troops—one of the historic armies. It is very youthful. I think well of Meade. He is very cautious and conscientious, yet very alert (would be perfect if he fused those qualities with the lightning of audacity and venturing all when it was worth

77

it, but he has not that dangerous but necessary crowning merit—Napoleon's).

I make no calculations on the course and result of the ensuing summer campaign, except that I believe it will be vehement. Meantime we are liable at any moment to have an incipient caving in of the South—parts of it like North Carolina; but the shrewd ones here still reckon on a desperate fight of the Richmond junta—ferocious, carrying things with as high a hand as ever the ensuing year.

I see the President often. I think better of him than many do. He has conscience and homely shrewdness; conceals an enormous tenacity under his mild, gawky Western manner. The difficulties of his situation have been unprecedented in the history of statesmanship. That he has conserved the government so far is a miracle. The difficulties have not been the South alone. The North has been, and is yet, honeycombed with semi-Secesh sympathizers every ready to undermine; and I am half disposed to predict that after the war closes, we shall see bevies of star-straps, two or three of our own major generals, shot for treachery, and fully deserve their fate.

I write this in hospital, having leisure here. I am sitting by the side of a soldier of the 6th Maine; he had his leg amputated lately. The sick are coming in pretty freely here—poor wrecks and phantoms, a sign of action, as they are breaking up the field hospitals. One's heart bleeds for them. Every day I am among them as usual. I desire you, if you have any friends able to send me aid and that feel to do so, that you would show them this letter, as I would like more means. It shall be sacred.

Brooklyn, April 7, 1865.

. . . The grand culminations of last week impress me profoundly, of course; I feel more than ever how America has been entirely restated by them, . . . and they will shape the destinies of the future of the whole of mankind. . . .

The Armies Returning. May 7, 1865, Sunday.

Today, as I was walking a mile or two south of Alexandria, I fell in with several large squads of the returning Western Army (Sherman's men, as they called themselves), about a thousand in all, the largest portion of them half sick, some convalescents, on their way to a hospital camp. These fragmentary excerpts, with the unmistakable Western physiognomy and idioms, crawling along slowly after a great campaign; blown this way, as it were, out of their latitude, I marked with curiosity and talked with off and on for over an hour.

Here and there was one very sick; but all were able to walk, except some of the last, who had given out and were seated on the ground, faint and despondent. These I tried to cheer; told them the camp they were to reach was only a little way further over the hill; and so got them up and started, accompanying some of the worst a little way and helping them or putting them under the support of stronger comrades.

May 21. Saw General Sheridan and his cavalry today; a strong, attractive sight. The men were mostly young (a few middle-aged), superb-looking fellows, brown, spare, keen, with well-worn clothing, many with pieces of waterproof cloth around their shoulders hanging down. They dashed along pretty fast, in wide, close ranks, all spattered with mud; no holiday soldiers; brigade after brigade. I could have watched for a week. Sheridan stood on a balcony under a big tree, coolly smoking a cigar. His looks and manner impressed me favorably.

May 22. Have been taking a walk along Pennsylvania Avenue and Seventh Street North. The city is full of soldiers, running around loose. Officers everywhere, of all

79

grades; all have the weatherbeaten look of practical serv-
ice. . . . All armies are now here (or portions of them)
for tomorrow's review. You see them swarming like bees
everywhere.

The Grand Review.

For two days now the broad spaces of Pennsylvania Ave-
nue along to Treasury Hill and so, by detour, around to
the President's house, and so up to Georgetown and across
the Aqueduct Bridge, have been alive with a magnificent
sight—the returning armies. In their wide ranks stretching
clear across the Avenue, I watch them march or ride along
at a brisk pace through two whole days—infantry, cavalry,
artillery—some two hundred thousand men. Some days
afterwards, one or two other corps; and then, still after-
wards, a good part of Sherman's immense army, brought
up from Charleston, Savannah, etc.

Washington, May 25, 1865.

. . . Well, the Review is over, and it was very grand. It
was too much and too impressive to be described, but you
will see a good bit about it in the papers.

If you can imagine a great, wide avenue like Flatbush
Avenue, quite flat and stretching as far as you can see, with
a great white building half as big as Fort Green on a hill at
the commencement of the avenue; and then, through this
avenue, marching, solid ranks of soldiers, twenty or
twenty-five abreast—just marching steady all day long,
for two days without intermission, one regiment after an-
other; real war-worn soldiers that have been marching and
fighting for years; sometimes for an hour nothing but cav-
alry, just solid ranks on good horses with sabres glistening
and carbines hanging by their saddles and their clothes
showing hard service, but they mostly all good-looking
young men; then great masses of guns, batteries of cannon

four or six abreast, each drawn by six horses, with the gunners seated on the ammunition wagons, and these perhaps a long while in passing—nothing but batteries (it seemed as if all the cannon in the world were here).

Then great battalions of blacks, with axes and shovels and pickaxes (real Southern darkies, black as tar); then again, hour after hour, the old infantry regiments, the men all sunburnt, nearly everyone with some old tatter all in shreds (that *had been* a costly and beautiful flag); the great drum corps of sixty or eighty drummers massed at the heads of the brigades, playing away; now and then a fine brass band, but oftener nothing but the drums and whistling fifes (but they sounded very lively); perhaps a band of sixty drums and fifteen or twenty fifes playing "Lannigan's Ball."

The different corps banners, the generals with their staffs, etc.; the Western Army, led by General Sherman ("old Bill," the soldiers all call him); . . . that, in a brief sketch, gives you some idea of the great panorama of the armies that have been passing through here the last few days.

. . . I saw the President [Johnson] several times, stood close by him and took a good look at him, and like his expression much. He is very plain but substantial; it seemed wonderful that just that plain, middling-sized, ordinary man, dressed in black without the least badge or ornament, should be the master of all these myriads of soldiers—the best that ever trod the earth—with forty or fifty major-generals around him or riding by with their broad yellow satin belts around their waists—and of all the artillery and cavalry, to say nothing of all the forts and ships, etc., etc.

I saw General Grant, too, several times—he is the noblest Roman of them all—none of the pictures do justice to him. About sundown I saw him again riding on a large, fine horse, with his hat off in answer to the hurrahs; he rode by where I stood and I saw him well as he rode by on a slow canter, with nothing but a single orderly after him. He looks like a good man (and I believe there is much in looks). I saw General Meade, General Thomas, Secretary Stanton, and lots of other celebrated officers and generals— but the *rank and file* was the greatest sight of all.

YEAR THAT TREMBLED AND REEL'D BENEATH ME

Year that trembled and reel'd beneath me!
Your summer wind was warm enough, yet the air I breathed froze me,
A thick gloom fell through the sunshine and darken'd me,
Must I change my triumphant songs? said I to myself,
Must I indeed learn to chant the cold dirges of the baffled?
And sullen hymns of defeat?

Chapter Five

'The Great Army of the Wounded'

A selection of pieces published in New York newspapers 1862–65, describing hospitals and soldiers; studies in individual heroism.

As I sit in twilight late alone by the flickering oak-flame,
Musing on long-pass'd war-scenes—of the countless buried un-
    known soldiers,
Of the vacant names, as unidentified air's and sea's—the unreturn'd,
The brief truce after battle, with grim burial-squads, and the deep-
    fill'd trenches
Of gather'd dead from all America, North, South, East, West,
    whence they came up,
From wooded Maine, New-England's farms, from fertile Penn-
    sylvania, Illinois, Ohio,
From the measureless West, Virginia, the South, the Carolinas,
    Texas,
(Even here in my room-shadows and half-lights in the noiseless
    flickering flames,
Again I see the stalwart ranks on-filing, rising—I hear the rhythmic
    tramp of the armies;)
You million unwrit names all, all—you dark bequest from all the
    war,
A special verse for you—a flash of duty long neglected—your mys-
    tic roll strangely gather'd here,
Each name recall'd by me from out the darkness and death's ashes,
Henceforth to be, deep, deep within my heart recording, for many
    a future year,
Your mystic roll entire of unknown names, or North or South,
Embalm'd with love in this twilight song.

'The Great Army of the Wounded'

Dispatch to the New York Times, February 26, 1863.
The military hospitals, convalescent camps, etc. in Washington and its neighborhood sometimes contain over fifty thousand sick and wounded men. Every form of wound (the mere sight of some of them having been known to make a tolerably hardy visitor faint away), every kind of malady—like a long procession, with typhoid, and diarrhoea at the head as leaders—are here in steady motion. The soldiers' hospital! How many sleepless nights, how many women's tears, how many long and waking hours and days of suspense from every one of the Middle, Eastern, and Western states have concentrated here! Our own New York, in the form of hundreds and thousands of her young men, may consider herself here; Pennsylvania, Ohio, Indiana, and all the West and Northwest the same, and all the New England States the same!

Upon a few of these hospitals I have been almost daily calling on a mission, on my own account, for the sustenance and consolation of some of the most needy cases of sick and dying men for the last two months. One has much to learn to do good in these places. Great tact is required. These are not like other hospitals. By far the greatest proportion (I should say five sixths) of the patients are American young men, intelligent, of independent spirit, tender feelings, used to a hardy and healthy life; largely the

85

farmers are represented by their sons—largely the mechanics and workingmen of the cities. Then they are soldiers. All these points must be borne in mind.

People through our Northern cities have little or no idea of the great and prominent feature which these military hospitals and convalescent camps make in and around Washington. There are not merely two or three or a dozen, but some fifty of them of different degrees of capacity. Some have a thousand and more patients. The newspapers here find it necessary to print every day a directory of the hospitals—a long list something like what a directory of the churches would be in New York, Philadelphia, or Boston.

The government (which really tries, I think, to do the best and quickest it can for these sad necessities) is gradually settling down to adopt the plan of placing the hospitals in clusters of one-story wooden barracks, with their accompanying tents and sheds for cooking and all needed purposes. Taking all things into consideration, no doubt these are best adapted to the purpose, better than using churches and large public buildings like the Patent Office. These sheds now adopted are long, one-story edifices, sometimes ranged along in a row with their heads to the street, and numbered either alphabetically—Wards A or B, C, D, and so on; or Wards 1, 2, 3, etc. The middle one will be marked by a flagstaff, and is the office of the establishment, with rooms for the ward surgeons, etc. One of these sheds or wards will contain sixty cots; sometimes, on an emergency, they move them close together and crowd in more. Some of the barracks are larger, with, of course, more inmates. Frequently there are tents—more comfortable here than one might think—whatever they may be down in the army.

Each ward has a ward-master and generally a nurse for every ten or twelve men. A ward surgeon has, generally, two wards—although this varies. Some of the wards have a woman nurse; the Armory-Square wards have some very good ones. The one in Ward E is one of the best.

A few weeks ago the vast area of the second story of that noblest of Washington buildings—the Patent Office— was crowded close with rows of the sick, badly wounded, and dying soldiers. They were placed in three very large apartments. I went there several times. It was a strange, solemn, and—with all its features of suffering and death— a sort of fascinating sight. I went sometimes at night to soothe and relieve particular cases; some, I found, needed a little cheering up and friendly consolation at that time, for they went to sleep better afterwards.

Two of the immense apartments are filled with high and ponderous glass cases crowded with models in miniature of every kind of utensil, machine, or invention it ever entered into the mind of man to conceive, and with curiosities and foreign presents. Between these cases were lateral openings perhaps eight feet wide and quite deep, and in these were placed many of the sick; besides, a great long double row of them up and down through the middle of the hall. Many of them were very bad cases, wounds, and amputations. Then there was a gallery running above the hall, in which there were beds also.

It was indeed a curious scene at night when lit up. The glass cases, the beds, the sick, the gallery above, and the marble pavement under foot; the suffering and the forti- tude to bear it in the various degrees; occasionally from some the groan that could not be repressed; sometimes a poor fellow dying, with emaciated face and glassy eyes, the nurse by his side, the doctor also there, but no friend, no relative—such were the sights but lately in the Patent Office. The wounded have since been removed from there, and it is now vacant again.

Of course, there are among these thousands of prostrated soldiers in hospital here all sorts of individual cases. On recurring to my notebook, I am puzzled which cases to select to illustrate the average of these young men and their experiences. I may say here, too, in general terms, that I could not wish for more candor and manliness among all their sufferings than I find among them.

Take this case in Ward 6, Campbell Hospital, a young man from Plymouth County, Massachusetts; a farmer's son, aged about twenty or twenty-one—a soldierly, American young fellow, but with sensitive and tender feelings. Most of December and January last he lay very low, and for quite a while I never expected he would recover. He had become prostrated with an obstinate diarrhoea; his stomach would hardly keep the least thing down; he was vomiting half the time. But that was hardly the worst of it. Let me tell you his story—it is but one of thousands.

He had been some time sick with his regiment in the field, in front, but did his duty as long as he could; was in the battle of Fredericksburg; soon after was put in the regimental hospital. He kept getting worse—could not eat anything they had there; the doctor told him nothing could be done for him there. The poor fellow had fever also; received (perhaps it could not be helped) little or no attention; lay on the ground getting worse. Toward the latter part of December, very much enfeebled, he was sent up from the front, from Falmouth Station, in an open platform car (such as hogs are transported upon North), and dumped with a crowd of others on the boat at Aquia Creek, falling down like a rag where they deposited him, too weak and sick to sit up or help himself at all. No one spoke to him or assisted him; he had nothing to eat or drink; was used (amid the great crowds of sick) with perfect indifference, or, as in two or three instances, with heartless brutality.

On the boat, when night came and when the air grew chilly, he tried a long time to undo the blankets he had in his knapsack, but was too feeble. He asked one of the employees who was moving around deck for a moment's assistance to get the blankets. The man asked him back if he could not get them himself. He answered, no, he had been trying for more than half an hour and found himself too weak. The man rejoined he might then go without them, and walked off. So H. lay chilled and damp on deck all night, without anything under or over him, while two good blankets were within reach. It caused him a great injury, nearly cost him his life.

Arrived at Washington, he was brought ashore and again left on the wharf or above it, amid the great crowds, as before, without any nourishment, not a drink for his parched mouth; no kind hand had offered to cover his face from the forenoon sun. Conveyed at last some two miles by the ambulance to the hospital and assigned a bed (Bed 49, Campbell Hospital, January and February, 1863), he fell down exhausted upon the bed. But the ward-master (he has since been changed) came to him with a growling order to get up; the rules, he said, permitted no man to lie down in that way with his own clothes on; he must sit up— must first go to the bathroom, be washed, and have his clothes properly changed. (A very good rule, properly applied.) He was taken to the bathroom and scrubbed well with cold water. The attendants, callous for a while, were soon alarmed, for suddenly the half-frozen and lifeless body fell limpsy in their hands, and they hurried it back to the cot, plainly insensible, perhaps dying.

Poor boy! The long train of exhaustion, deprivation, rudeness, no food, no friendly word or deed, but all kinds of upstart airs and impudent, unfeeling speeches and deeds from all kinds of small officials (and some big ones), cutting like razors into that sensitive heart, had at last done the job. He now lay, at times out of his head but quite silent, asking nothing of anyone for some days, with death getting a closer and a surer grip upon him; he cared not, or rather, he welcomed death. His heart was broken. He felt the struggle to keep up any longer to be useless. God, the world, humanity—all had abandoned him. It would feel so good to shut eyes forever on the cruel things around him and toward him.

As luck would have it, at this time I found him. I was passing down Ward No. 6 one day about dusk (4th January, I think), and noticed his glassy eyes, with a look of despair and hopelessness, sunk low in his thin, pallid-brown young face. One learns to divine quickly in the hospital, and as I stopped by him and spoke some commonplace remark (to which he made no reply), I saw as I looked that it was a case for ministering to the affection first and other nourishment and medicines afterward.

I sat down by him without any fuss; talked a little; soon saw that it did him good; led him to talk a little himself; got him somewhat interested; wrote a letter for him to his folks in Massachusetts (to L. H. Campbell, Plymouth County); soothed him down, as I saw he was getting a little too much agitated and tears in his eyes; gave him some small gifts and told him I should come again soon. (He has told me since that this little visit, at that hour, just saved him; a day more and it would have been perhaps too late.)

Of course I did not forget him, for he was a young fellow to interest anyone. He remained very sick—vomiting much every day, frequent diarrhoea, and also something like bronchitis, the doctor said. For a while, I visited him almost every day, cheered him up, took him some little gifts, and gave him small sums of money (he relished a drink of new milk when it was brought through the ward for sale). For a couple of weeks his condition was uncertain; sometimes I thought there was no chance for him at all, but of late he is doing better—is up and dressed and goes around more and more (February 21) every day. He will not die but will recover.

The other evening, passing through the ward, he called

me—he wanted to say a few words, particular. I sat down by his side on the cot in the dimness of the long ward, with the wounded soldiers there in their beds, ranging up and down. H. told me I had saved his life. He was in the deepest earnest about it. It was one of those things that repay a soldiers' hospital missionary a thousandfold—one of the hours he never forgets.

A benevolent person, with the right qualities and tact, cannot, perhaps, make a better investment of himself at present anywhere upon the varied surface of the whole of this big world than in these military hospitals, among such thousands of most interesting young men. The army is very young—and so much more American than I supposed.

Reader! How can I describe to you the mute appealing look that rolls and moves from many a manly eye, from many a sick cot, following you as you walk slowly down one of these wards? To see these and to be incapable of responding to them, except in a few cases (so very few compared to the whole of the suffering men), is enough to make one's heart crack. I go through in some cases, cheering up the men, distributing now and then little sums of money—and, regularly, letter-paper and envelopes, oranges, tobacco, jellies, etc., etc.

Many things invite comment, and some of them sharp criticism, in these hospitals. The Government, as I said, is anxious and liberal in its practice toward its sick; but the work has to be left, in its personal application to the men, to hundreds of officials of one grade or another about the hospitals, who are sometimes entirely lacking in the right qualities. There are tyrants and shysters in all positions and especially those dressed in subordinate authority. Some of the ward doctors are careless, rude, capricious, needlessly strict. One I found who prohibited the men from all enlivening amusements; I found him sending men to the guardhouse for the most trifling offence. In general, perhaps, the officials—especially the new ones with their straps or badges—put on too many airs. Of all places in the world, the hospitals of American young men and soldiers, wounded in the volunteer service of their country, ought to be exempt from mere conventional military airs and etiquette of shoulder-straps. But they are not exempt.

Dispatch to Brooklyn Eagle, March 19, 1863.

A military hospital here in Washington is a little city in itself and contains a larger population than most of the well-known country towns down in the Queens and Suffolk County portions of Long Island. I say one of the government hospitals here is a little city in itself, and there are some fifty of these hospitals in the District of Columbia alone. In them are collected the tens of thousands of sick and wounded soldiers, the legacies of many a bloody battle and of the exposure of two years of camp life. I find these places full of significance. They have taken up my principal time and labour for some months past.

Imagine a long, one-story wooden shed, like a short, wide ropewalk, well whitewashed; then cluster ten or a dozen of these together, with several smaller sheds and tents, and you have the soldiers' hospital as generally adopted here. It will contain perhaps six or seven hundred men, or perhaps a thousand—and occasionally more still. There is a regular staff and a substaff of big and little officials. Military etiquette is observed, and it is getting to become very stiff. I shall take occasion before long to show up some of this ill-fitting nonsense. The harvest is large, the gleaners few.

Beginning at first with casual visits to these establishments to see some of the Brooklyn men wounded or sick here, I became by degrees more and more drawn in, until I have now been for many weeks quite a devotee to the business—a regular self-appointed missionary to these thousands and tens of thousands of wounded and sick young men here, left upon government hands, many of them languishing, many of them dying. I am not connected with any society, but go on my own individual account, and to the work that appears to be called for.

Almost every day and frequently in the evenings, I visit, in this informal way, one after another of the wards of a hospital and always find cases enough where I can be of service. Cases enough, do I say? Alas! there is, perhaps, not one ward or tent—out of the seven or eight hundred now hereabout filled with sick—in which I am sure I might not profitably devote every hour of my life to the abstract work of consolation and sustenance for its suffering inmates. And indeed, beyond that, a person feels that in some one of these crowded wards he would like to pick out two or three cases and devote himself wholly to them.

Meanwhile, however, to do the best that is permitted, I go around distributing myself and the contents of my pockets and haversack in infinitesimal quantities, with faith that nearly all of it will, somehow or other, fall on good ground. In many cases, where I find a soldier "dead broke" and pretty sick, I give half a tumbler of good jelly. I carry a good-sized jar to a ward, have it opened, get a spoon and, taking the head nurse in tow, I go around and distribute it to the most appropriate cases. To others I give an orange or an apple, to others some spiced fruits, to others a small quantity of pickles. Many want tobacco; I do not encourage any of the boys in its use, but where I find they crave it, I supply them. I always carry some cut up in small plugs in my pocket. Then I have commissions: some New York or Connecticut or other soldier will be going home on sick leave or perhaps discharged, and I must fit him out with good new undershirt, drawers, stockings, etc.

But perhaps the greatest welcome is for writing paper, envelopes, etc. I find these always a rare reliance. When I go into a new ward, I always carry two or three quires of

93

paper and a good lot of envelopes and walk up and down and circulate them around to those who desire them. Then some will want pens, pencils, etc. In some hospitals there is quite a plenty of reading matter; but others, where it is needed, I supply.

By these and like means, one comes to be better acquainted with individual cases and so learns every day peculiar and interesting characters and gets on intimate and soon affectionate terms with noble American young men; and now is where the real good begins to be done, after all. Here, I will egotistically confess, I like to flourish. Even in a medical point of view it is one of the greatest things and in a surgical point of view the same. I can testify that friendship has literally cured a fever, and the medicine of daily affection, a bad wound. In these sayings are the final secret of carrying out well the role of a hospital missionary for our soldiers—which I tell for those who will understand them.

As I write, I have lying before me a little discarded notebook, filled with memoranda of things wanted by the sick—special cases. I use one of these little books in a week. See from this sample, for instance, after walking through a ward or two: Bed 53 wants some licorice; Bed 6 (erysipelas), bring some raspberry vinegar to make a cooling drink with water; Bed 18 wants a good book—a romance; Bed 25 (a manly, friendly young fellow, H.D.B. of the Twenty-Seventh, Connecticut, an independent young soul) refuses money and eatables, so I will bring him a pipe and tobacco, for I see he much enjoys a smoke; Bed 45 (sore throat and cough), wants horehound candy; Bed 11, when I come again, don't forget to write a letter for him; etc.

The wants are a long and varied list; some need to be humored and forgotten; others need to be especially remembered and obeyed. One poor German, dying—in the last stage of consumption—wished me to find him in Washington a German Lutheran clergyman and send him to him; I did so. One patient will want nothing but a toothpick, another a comb, and so on. All whims are represented and all the states. There are many New York State soldiers here; also Pennsylvanians. I find, of course, many from Massachusetts, Connecticut, and all the New England States, and from the Western and Northwestern States. Five sixths of the soldiers are young men.

Among other cases of young men from our own city of Brooklyn I have encountered and have had much to do with in hospital here, is John Lowery, wounded and arm amputated, at Fredericksburg. I saw this young fellow down there last December, immediately after the battle, lying on a blanket on the ground, the stump of his arm bandaged— but he was not a bit disheartened. He was soon afterward sent up from the front by way of Aquia Creek, and has for the past three months been in the Campbell Hospital here, in Ward 6, on the gain slowly but steadily.

He thinks a great deal of his physician here, Dr. Frank Hinkle, and as some other soldiers in the ward do the same, and bear testimony to their hearty gratitude and medical and surgical improvement to the quality of Dr. H., I think he deserves honorable mention in this letter to the people of our city—especially as another Brooklyn soldier in Ward 6, Amos H. Vliet, expresses the same feeling of obligation to the doctor for his faithfulness and kindness.

Vliet and Lowery both belong to that old war regiment whose flag has flaunted through more than a score of hot-contested battles—the 51st New York, Colonel Potter; and it is to be remembered that no small portion of the fame of this old veteran regiment may be claimed near home, for many of her officers and men are from Brooklyn. The friends of these two young soldiers will have a chance to talk to them soon in Brooklyn. I have seen a good deal of Jack Lowery, and I find him, and heard of him on the field, as a brave, soldierly fellow. Amos Vliet, too, made a first-rate soldier. He has had frozen feet pretty bad, but now better.

Occasionally I meet some of the Brooklyn 14th. In Ward E, of Armory Hospital I found a member of Company C of that regiment, Isaac Snyder; he is now acting as nurse there, and makes a very good one. Charles Dean, of Company H of the same regiment, is in Ward A of Armory, acting as ward-master. I also got very well acquainted with a young man of the Brooklyn 14th who lay sick some time in Ward F; he lately got his discharge and has gone home. I have met with others in the H-Street and Patent Office hospitals. Colonel Fowler of the 14th is in charge, I believe, of the convalescent camp at Alexandria. Lieutenant Colonel Debevoise is in Brooklyn, in poor health, I am sorry to say. Thus, the Brooklyn invalids are scattered around.

Off in the mud, a mile east of the Capitol, I found the other day in Emory Hospital there, in Ward C, three Brooklyn soldiers—Allen V. King, Michael Lally, and Patrick Hennessy—none of them, however, are very sick.

At a rough guess, I should say I have met from one hundred and fifty to two hundred young and middle-aged men whom I specifically found to be Brooklyn persons. Many of them I recognized as having seen their faces before, and very many of them knew me. Some said they had known me from boyhood. Some would call to me as I passed down a ward and tell me they had seen me in Brooklyn. I have had this happen at night, and have been entreated to stop and sit down and take the hand of a sick and restless boy and talk to him and comfort him awhile, for old Brooklyn's sake.

Some pompous and every way improper persons, of course, get in power in hospitals, and have full swing over the helpless soldiers. There is great state kept at Judiciary-Square Hospital, for instance. An individual, who probably has been a waiter somewhere for years past, has got into the high and mighty position of sergeant-at-arms at this hospital; he is called "Red Stripe" (from his artillery trimmings) by the patients, of whom he is at the same time the tyrant and the laughingstock. Going in to call on some sick New York soldiers here the other afternoon, I was stopped and treated to a specimen of the airs of this powerful officer. Surely the Government would do better to send such able-bodied loafers down into service in front, where they would earn their rations, than keep them here in the idle, shallow sinecures of military guard over a collection of sick soldiers, to give insolence to their visitors and friends. I found a shallow old person also here named Dr. Hall, who told me he had been eighteen years in the service.

I must give this Judiciary establishment the credit, from my visits to it, of saying that while in all the other hospitals I met with general cordiality and deference among the doctors, ward officers, nurses, etc., I have found more impudence and more dandy doctorism and more needless airs at this Judiciary than in all the twoscore other establishments in and around Washington. But the corps of management at the Judiciary has a bad name anyhow, and I only specify it here to put on record the general opinion and in hopes it may help in calling the attention of the Government to a remedy. For this hospital is half filled with New York soldiers, many noble fellows, and many sad and interesting cases. Of course, there are exceptions of good officials here, and some of the women nurses are excellent, but the Empire State has no reason to be oversatisfied with this hospital.

But I should say, in conclusion, that the earnest and continued desire of the Government and much devoted labor are given to make the military hospitals here as good as they can be, considering all things. I find no expense spared and great anxiety manifested in the highest quarters to do well by the national sick. I meet with first-class surgeons in charge of many of the hospitals and often the ward surgeons, medical cadets, and head nurses are fully faithful and competent. Dr. Bliss, head of Armory-Square, and Dr. Baxter, head of Campbell, seem to me to try to do their best and to be excellent in their posts. Dr. Bowen, one of the ward surgeons of Armory, I have known to fight as hard for many a poor fellow's life under his charge as a lioness would fight for her young. I mention such cases because I think they deserve it, on public grounds.

I thought I would include in my letter a few cases of soldiers, especially interesting, out of my notebook, but I find that my story has already been spun out to sufficient length. I shall continue here in Washington for the present and maybe for the summer to work as a missionary, after my own style, among these hospitals, for I find it in some respects curiously fascinating—with all its sadness. Nor do I find it ended by my doing some good to the sick and dying soldiers. They do me good in return, more than I do them.

Washington, February, 1864.

The hospitals here in and around Washington are still pretty full and contain in some respects the most needy cases of all the suffering (though there are plenty such everywhere). For the past few weeks I have been on a tour down to the front, through the division hospitals, especially those around Culpepper and Brandy Station, mostly of the 1st, 2nd, and 3rd Corps, to see how the sick were situated there. A year ago I spent December and part of January (after First Fredericksburg) among the wounded in front from Aquia Creek to Falmouth, and saw perhaps the saddest scenes of the war then.

But there is nothing like it now. I have made up my mind that the camp hospitals are pretty well cleaned out; the worst cases are here in Washington, and so I have returned here for good. In the field hospitals I find diarrhoea getting more and more prevalent and chronic. It is the great disease of the army. The doctors, as always, give too much medicine and hold on to the poor young men in camp too long; then when the [malady] is deeply rooted, send them up here. How many such wrecks of young men have I seen, from boat and railroad, from front, come crawling pale and faint along here, many to linger awhile and die, during the past year, sent up in this way after being kept too long!

I suppose you will be interested in knowing that our troops in the field in Virginia are this Winter remarkably well in health, however, as a general thing, and in the cheeriest temper. They have better houses than ever before, no shelter tents now but huts of logs and mud with fireplaces. In the tour I allude to I was much in contact with the rank and file, lived among them in their camps, among the common soldiers and teamsters, etc.

I never go among the army in this way but what, after making all allowances, I feel that our general stock of young men shows all other races meager and pale and puny in comparison. The more I see of them in the army, the higher and broader my estimate of them. (I mean the Americans, I don't make account of any other—Americans both west and east and from all the agricultural regions of the great states.) And then to be among them also, as I have been for the past fifteen months—among them, seeing them in hospitals—thousands, so young and manly, with such fearful suffering, wounds, amputations, and weary sickness. O how one gets to love them—indeed it brings people very, very close, such circumstances!

As to the temper of the army in Virginia, I should say it was never so resolute, so full of the right spirit for endurance and work as it is today. The filled-up regiments gathering around the nucleus of the old veterans make better regiments than any. I was with several such and found them excellent. These re-enlisted regiments returning from their furloughs, thus filled up, are streaming down to front fast already. The opinion of Meade is full of respect for him—he is thought an earnest, alert, conscientious, cautious commander.

I write these, doctor, thinking they may interest you, coming from late direct contact with the army on the ground. So, doctor, I still remain here in Washington, occupying my time nearly altogether among the wounded and sick, as when I last wrote you. I act as an independent visitor and helper among the men, fixing as before on the cases that most need. I never miss a single day or night, weekday or Sunday, visiting some poor young soul in bodily and mental tribulation. It is a great privilege to me, more to me than to them, I think.

Dispatch to New York Times, December 11, 1864.

As this tremendous war goes on, the public interest becomes more general and gathers more and more closely about the wounded, the sick, and the government hospitals, the surgeons, and all appertaining to the medical department of the army. Up to the date of this writing (December 9, 1864) there have been, as I estimate, near four hundred thousand cases under treatment, and there are today, probably, taking the whole service of the United States, two hundred thousand, or an approximation to that number, on the doctors' list. Half of these are comparatively slight ailments or hurts. Every family has directly or indirectly some representative among this vast army of the wounded and sick. . . .

December 22–31, 1862.

Am among the regimental brigade and division hospitals somewhat. Few at home realize that these are merely tents

—and sometimes very poor ones—the wounded lying on the ground, lucky if their blanket is spread on a layer of pine or hemlock twigs or some leaves. No cots, seldom even a mattress on the ground. It is pretty cold. I go around from one case to another. I do not see that I can do any good, but I cannot leave them. Once in a while some youngster holds on to me convulsively, and I do what I can for him; at any rate stop with him and sit near him for hours, if he wishes it.

Besides the hospitals, I also go occasionally on long tours through the camps, talking with the men, etc.; sometimes at night among the groups around the fires, in their shebang enclosures of bushes. I soon get acquainted anywhere in camp with officers or men, and am always well used. Sometimes I go down on picket with the regiments I know best.

As to rations, the army here at present seems to be tolerably well supplied, and the men have enough, such as it is. Most of the regiments lodge in the flimsy little shelter tents. A few have built themselves huts of logs and mud with fireplaces.

I might give a long list of special cases, interesting items of the wounded men here, but have not space. . . .

. . . This afternoon, July 22, 1863, I spent a long time with a young man I have been with considerably, named Oscar F. Wilber, Company G, 154th, New York, low with chronic diarrhoea and a bad wound also. He asked me to read him a chapter in the New Testament. I complied and asked him what I should read. He said: "Make your own choice." I opened at the close of one of the first books of the Evangelists and read the chapters describing the latter hours of Christ and the scenes at the Crucifixion.

The poor wasted young man asked me to read the following chapter also, how Christ rose again. I read very slowly, for Oscar was feeble. It pleased him very much, yet the tears were in his eyes. He asked me if I enjoyed religion.

I said: "Perhaps not, my dear, in the way you mean, and yet maybe it is the same thing." He said: "It is my chief reliance." He talked of death and said he did not fear it. I said: "Why, Oscar, don't you think you will get well?" He said: "I may, but it is not probable."

He spoke calmly of his condition. The wound was very bad; it discharged much. Then the diarrhoea had prostrated him, and I felt that he was even then the same as dying. He behaved very manly and affectionate. The kiss I gave him as I was about leaving, he returned fourfold. He gave me his mother's address, Mrs. Sally D. Wilber, Alleghany Post Office, Cattaraugus County, N.Y. I had several such interviews with him. He died a few days after the one just described.

August, September, October, [1863] etc.

I continue among the hospitals in the same manner, getting still more experience, and daily and nightly meeting with most interesting cases. Through the winter of 1863–64, the same. The work of the army hospital visitor is indeed a trade, an art requiring both experience and natural gifts, and the greatest judgment. A large number of the visitors to the hospitals do no good at all, while many do harm. The surgeons have great trouble from them. Some visitors go from curiosity—as to a show of animals. Others give the men improper things. Then there are always some poor fellows, in the crises of sickness or wounds, that imperatively need perfect quiet—not to be talked to by strangers. Few realize that it is not the mere giving of gifts that does good; it is the proper adaption. Nothing is of any avail among the soldiers except conscientious personal investigation of cases, each for itself; with sharp, critical faculties, but in the fullest spirit of human sympathy and boundless love. The men feel such love more than anything else. I have met very few persons who realize the importance of humoring the yearnings for love and friendship of these American young men, prostrated by sickness and wounds. . . .

. . . My sketch has already filled up so much room that I shall have to omit any detailed account of the wounded of May and June, 1864, from the battles of the Wilderness, Spottsylvania, etc. They would be a long history in itself. The arrivals, the numbers, and the severity of the wounds outviewed anything that we have seen before. For days and weeks a melancholy tide set in upon us. The weather was very hot. The wounded had been delayed in coming and much neglected. Very many of the wounds had worms in them. An unusual proportion mortified. It was among these that, for the first time in my life, I began to be prostrated with real sickness, and was, before the close of the summer, imperatively ordered North by the physician to recuperate and have an entire change of air.

What I know of first Fredericksburg, Chancellorsville, Wilderness, etc. makes clear to me that there has been, and is yet, a total lack of science in elastic adaptation to the needs of the wounded after a battle. The hospitals are long afterward filled with proofs of this.

I have seen many battles, their results, but never one where there was not, during the first few days, an unaccountable and almost total deficiency of everything for the wounded—appropriate sustenance, nursing, cleaning, medicines, stores, etc. (I do not say surgical attendance, because the surgeons cannot do more than human endurance permits.) Whatever pleasant accounts there may be in the papers of the North, this is the actual fact.

No thorough previous preparation, no system, no foresight, no genius. Always plenty of stores, no doubt, but always miles away; never where they are needed, and never the proper application. Of all harrowing experiences, none is greater than that of the days following a heavy battle. Scores, hundreds, of the noblest young men on earth, uncomplaining, lie helpless, mangled, faint, alone, and so bleed to death or die from exhaustion, either actually untouched at all, or with merely the laying of them down and leaving them, when there ought to be means provided to save them. . . .

. . . He who goes among the soldiers with gifts, etc. must beware how he proceeds. It is much more of an art than one would imagine. They are not charity patients but American young men of pride and independence. The spirit in which you treat them and bestow your donations is just as important as the gifts themselves; sometimes more so. Then there is continual discrimination necessary. Each case requires some peculiar adaptation to itself. It is very important to slight nobody—not a single case. Some hospital visitors, especially the women, pick out the handsomest-looking soldiers, or have a few for their pets. Of course, some will attract you more than others, and some will need more attention than others; but be careful not to ignore any patient. A word, a friendly turn of the eye or touch of the hand in passing, if nothing more. . . .

Washington, October 11, 1863.

. . . Above all, the poor boys (in Armory-Square Hospital) welcome a magnetic personality (some are so fervent, so hungry for this); poor fellows, too young they are, lying there with their pale faces and that mute look in the eyes. O how one gets to love them, often particular cases, so suffering, so manly and affectionate!

. . . You would all smile to see me among them—some of them like children; ceremony is mostly discarded; they suffer and get exhausted and so weary; lots of them have grown to expect as I leave at night that we should kiss each other—sometimes quite a number. I have to go around; poor boys—there is little petting in a soldier's life in the field, but . . . I know what is in their hearts—always waiting—though they may be unconscious of it themselves.

. . . I could not describe to you what mutual attachments and how passing deep and tender these boys. Some have died, but the love for them lives as long as I draw breath; these soldiers know how to love, too, when once they have the right person and the right love offered them. It is wonderful. You see how I am running off into the clouds—but this is my element. . . .

. . . Through Fourteenth Street to the river, and then over the long bridge and some three miles beyond, is the huge collection called the convalescent camp. It is a respectable-sized army in itself, for these hospitals, tents, sheds, etc. at times contain from five to ten thousand men. Of course there are continual changes. Large squads are sent off to their regiments or elsewhere and new men received. Sometimes I found large numbers of paroled returned prisoners here.

. . . I have lately been (November 25) in the Central Park Hospital, near One Hundred and Fourth Street; it seems to be a well-managed institution. During September, and previously, went many times to the Brooklyn City Hospital, in Raymond Street, where I found (taken in by contract) a number of wounded and sick from the army. Most of the men were badly off and without a cent of money, many wanting tobacco. I supplied them and a few special cases with delicacies; also repeatedly with letter paper, stamps, envelopes, etc., writing the addresses myself plainly (a pleased crowd gathering around me as I directed for each one in turn).

This Brooklyn Hospital is a bad place for soldiers, or anybody else. Cleanliness, proper nursing, watching, etc. are more deficient than in any hospital I know. For dinner

on Sundays I invariably found nothing but rice and mo-
lasses. The men all speak well of Drs. Yale and Kissam for
kindness, patience, etc., and I think, from what I saw, there
are also [good] young medical men. In its management
otherwise this is the poorest hospital I have been in, out of
many hundreds.

Among places, apart from soldiers', visited lately (Decem-
ber 7), I must specially mention the great Brooklyn Gen-
eral Hospital and other public institutions at Flatbush, in-
cluding the extensive lunatic asylum under charge of Drs.
Chapin and Reynolds. Of the latter (and I presume I might
include these county establishments generally), I have de-
liberately to put on record about the profoundest satisfac-
tion with professional capacity, completeness of house ar-
rangements to ends required, and the right vital spirit ani-
mating all, that I have yet found in any public curative
institution among civilians.

In Washington, in camp, and everywhere, I was in the
habit of reading to the men. They were very fond of it, and
liked declamatory, poetical pieces. Mike O'Reilly's pieces
were also great favorites. I have had many happy evenings
with the men. We would gather in a large group by our-
selves after supper and spend the time in such readings, or
in talking, and occasionally by an amusing game called the
game of "Twenty Questions."

For nurses, middle-aged women and mothers of families
are best. I am compelled to say young ladies, however re-
fined, educated, and benevolent, do not succeed as army
nurses, though their motives are noble; neither do the Cath-
olic nuns, among these home-born American young men.
Mothers full of motherly feeling, and however illiterate
but bringing reminiscences of home and with the magnetic
touch of hands, are the true women nurses. Many of the
wounded are between fifteen and twenty years of age.

I should say that the Government, from my observation,

is always full of anxiety and liberality toward the sick and wounded. The system in operation in the permanent hospitals is good, and the money flows without stint. But the details have to be left to hundreds and thousands of subordinates and officials. Among these, laziness, heartlessness, gouging, and incompetency are more or less prevalent. Still, I consider the permanent hospitals generally well conducted.

. . . I must bear most emphatic testimony to the zeal, manliness, and professional spirit and capacity generally prevailing among the surgeons, many of them young men, in the hospitals and the army. I will not say much about the exceptions, for they are few (but I have met some of those few, and how very foolish and airish they were). I never ceased to find the best young men, and the hardest and most disinterested workers, among these surgeons in the hospitals. They are full of genius, too, and this is my testimony. . . .

AS I WALK THESE BROAD MAJESTIC DAYS

As I walk these broad majestic days of peace,
(For the war, the struggle of blood finish'd, wherein, O terrific
  Ideal,
Against vast odds erewhile having gloriously won,
Now thou stridest on, yet perhaps in time toward denser wars,
Perhaps to engage in time in still more dreadful contests, dangers,
Longer campaigns and crises, labors beyond all others,)
Around me I hear that eclat of the world, politics, produce,
The announcements of recognized things, science,
The approved growth of cities and the spread of inventions.

I see the ships, (they will last a few years,)
The vast factories with their foremen and workmen,
And hear the indorsement of all, and do not object to it.

But I too announce solid things,
Science, ships, politics, factories, are not nothing,

Like a grand procession to music of distant bugles pouring, tri-
umphantly moving, and grander heaving in sight,
They stand for realities—all is as it should be.

Then my realities;
What else is so real as mine?
Libertad and the divine average, freedom to every slave on the face
of the earth,
The rapt promises and luminè of seers, the spiritual world, these
centuries-lasting songs,
And our visions, the visions of poets, the most solid announcements
of any.

Chapter Six

'*Dear Love of Comrades*'

More descriptions of soldiers, hospital scenes, and war impressions, in memo form, often from notes made on the spot.

Over the carnage rose prophetic a voice,
Be not dishearten'd, affection shall solve the problems of freedom yet,
Those who love each other shall become invincible,
They shall yet make Columbia victorious.

Sons of the Mother of All, you shall yet be victorious,
You shall yet laugh to scorn the attacks of all the remainder of the earth.

No danger shall balk Columbia's lovers,
If need be a thousand shall sternly immolate themselves for one.

One from Massachusetts shall be a Missourian's comrade,
From Maine and from hot Carolina, and another an Oregonese, shall be friends triune,
More precious to each other than all the riches of the earth.

To Michigan, Florida perfumes shall tenderly come,
Not the perfumes of flowers, but sweeter, and wafted beyond death.

It shall be customary in the houses and streets to see manly affection,
The most dauntless and rude shall touch face to face lightly,
The dependence of Liberty shall be lovers,
The continuance of Equality shall be comrades.

These shall tie you and band you stronger than hoops of iron,
I, ecstatic, O partners! O lands! with the love of lovers tie you.

(Were you looking to be held together by lawyers?
Or by an agreement on a paper? or by arms?
Nay, nor the world, nor any living thing, will so cohere.)

'Dear Love of Comrades'

"He went out with the tide and the sunset," was a phrase I heard from a surgeon describing an old sailor's death under peculiarly gentle conditions.

During the Secession War, 1863 and '64, visiting the army hospitals around Washington, I formed the habit and continued it to the end, whenever the ebb or flood tide began the latter part of day, of punctually visiting those at that time populous wards of suffering men. Somehow (or I thought so) the effect of the hour was palpable. The badly wounded would get some ease and would like to talk a little or be talked to. Intellectual and emotional natures would be at their best; deaths were always easier; medicines seemed to have better effect when given then; and a lulling atmosphere would pervade the wards.

Similar influences, similar circumstances and hours, day-close, after great battles, even with all their horrors. I had more than once the same experiences on the fields covered with fallen or dead.

June 18, 1863.

In one of the hospitals I find Thomas Haley, Company M, 4th New York Cavalry—a regular Irish boy, a fine specimen of youthful physical manliness—shot through the lungs, inevitably dying. Came over to this country from

Ireland to enlist; has not a single friend or acquaintance here; is sleeping soundly at this moment (but it is the sleep of death); has a bullethole through the lungs. I saw Tom when first brought here, three days since, and didn't suppose he could live twelve hours (yet he looks well enough in the face to a casual observer).

He lies there with his frame exposed above the waist, all naked for coolness, a fine-built man, the tan not yet bleached from his cheeks and neck. It is useless to talk to him, as with his sad hurt and the stimulants they give him and the utter strangeness of every object, face, furniture, etc., the poor fellow, even when awake, is like some frightened, shy animal. Much of the time he sleeps or half sleeps. (Sometimes I thought he knew more than he showed.)

I often come and sit by him in perfect silence; he will breathe for ten minutes as softly and evenly as a young babe asleep. Poor youth—so handsome, athletic, with profuse, beautiful, shining hair. One time, as I sat looking at him while he lay asleep, he suddenly—without the least start—awakened, opened his eyes, gave one clear, silent look, a slight sigh, then turned back and went into his doze again. Little he knew, poor death-stricken boy, the heart of the stranger that hovered near. . . .

Thomas Lindly, 1st Pennsylvania Cavalry, shot very badly through the foot—poor young man, he suffers horridly, has to be constantly dosed with morphine—his face ashy and glazed, his bright young eyes. . . . I gave him a large, handsome apple; [hold] it in sight; tell him to have it roasted in the morning, as he generally feels easier then and can eat a little breakfast. I write two letters for him.

Opposite, an old Quaker lady sits by the side of her son, Amer Moore, 2nd U.S. Artillery—shot in the head two weeks since, very low, quite rational—from hips down paralyzed—he will surely die. I speak a very few words to

him every day and evening; he answers pleasantly, wants nothing (he told me soon after he came about his home affairs. His mother had been an invalid, and he feared to let her know his condition). He died soon after she came.

I adapt myself to each case and to temperaments—some need to be humored; some are rather out of their head; some merely want me to sit with them and hold them by the hand. One will want a letter written to mother or father (yesterday I wrote over a dozen letters); some like to have me feed them (wounded perhaps in shoulder or wrist); perhaps a few of my peaches; some want a cooling drink (I have some very nice syrup from raspberries); others want writing paper, envelopes, a stamp, etc.

I could fill a sheet with one day's items—I often go just at dark; sometimes stay nearly all night. I like to go just before supper, carrying a pot or jar of something good, and go around with a spoon distributing a little here and there; yet, after all this succoring of the stomach (which is, of course, most well and indispensable), I should say that I believe my profoundest help to these sick and dying men is probably the soothing invigoration I steadily bear in mind to infuse in them through affection, cheering love, and the like between them and me. It has saved more than one life. There is a strange influence here. I have formed attachments here in hospital that I shall keep to my dying day, and they will the same, without doubt.

Home-Made Music, August 8th.

Tonight, as I was trying to keep cool, sitting by a wounded soldier in Armory-Square, I was attracted by some pleasant singing in an adjoining ward. As my soldier was asleep, I left him, and entering the ward where the music was, I walked halfway down and took a seat by the cot of a young Brooklyn friend, S.R., badly wounded in the hand at Chancellorsville—who has suffered much, but at that moment in the evening was wide-awake and comparatively easy. He had turned over on his left side to get a better view of the singers, but the mosquito curtains of the adjoining cots obstructed the sight. I stepped round and looped them all up, so that he had a clear show, and then sat down again by him and looked and listened.

The principal singer was a young lady-nurse of one of the wards, accompanied on a melodeon and joined by the lady-nurses of other wards. They sat there making a charming group, with their handsome, healthy faces; and standing up a little behind them were some ten or fifteen of the convalescent soldiers, young men, nurses, etc., with books in their hands, singing. Of course, it was not such a performance as the great soloists at the New York Opera House take in, yet I am not sure but I received as much pleasure under the circumstances, sitting there, as I have had from the best Italian compositions, expressed by world-famous performers.

The men lying up and down the hospitals in their cots (some badly wounded—some never to rise thence); the cots themselves with their drapery of white curtains, and the shadows down the lower and upper parts of the ward; then the silence of the men, and the attitudes they took—the whole was a sight to look around upon again and again. And there sweetly rose those voices up to the high, whitewashed wooden roof, and pleasantly the roof sent it all back again. They sang very well, mostly quaint old songs and declamatory hymns, to fitting tunes. Here, for instance:

My days are swiftly gliding by, and I a pilgrim stranger,
Would not detain them as they fly, those hours of toil and danger;
For O we stand on Jordan's strand, our friends are passing over,
And just before, the shining shore we may almost discover.
We'll gird our loins, my brethren dear, our distant home discerning,

Our absent Lord has left us word, let every lamp be burning;
For O we stand on Jordan's strand, our friends are passing over,
And just before, the shining shore we may almost discover.

8th September, 1863.

Here now is a specimen army hospital case: Lorenzo Strong,
Co. A., 9th U.S. Cavalry, shot by a shell last Sunday; right
leg amputated on the field. Sent up here Monday night,
14th. Seemed to be doing pretty well till Wednesday noon,
16th, when he took a turn for the worse, and a strangely
rapid and fatal termination ensued. Though I had much to
do, I stayed and saw all.

It was a death picture characteristic of these soldiers'
hospitals—the perfect specimen of physique, one of the most
magnificent I ever saw, the convulsive spasms and working
of muscles, mouth, and throat. There are two good women
nurses, one on each side. The doctor comes in and gives
him a little chloroform. One of the nurses constantly fans
him, for it is fearfully hot. He asks to be raised up, and they
put him in a half-sitting posture. He called for "Mark" re-
peatedly, half-deliriously, all day.

Life ebbs, runs now with the speed of a mill race; his
splendid neck, as it lays all open, works still slightly; his
eyes turn back. A religious person coming in offers a prayer
in subdued tones, bent at the foot of the bed; and in the
space of the aisle a crowd including two or three doctors,
several students, and many soldiers has silently gathered.
It is very still and warm, as the struggle goes on, and dwin-
dles—a little more and a little more—and then welcome
oblivion, painlessness, death. A pause, the crowd drops
away, a white bandage is bound around and under the jaw,
the propping pillows are removed, the limpsy head falls
down, the arms are softly placed by the side, all composed,
all still—and the broad white sheet is thrown over every-
thing.

Burial of a Lady Nurse.

Here is an incident just occurred in one of the hospitals. A lady named Miss or Mrs. Billings—who has long been a practical friend of soldiers and nurse in the army, and had become attached to it in a way that no one can realize but him or her who has had experience—was taken sick early this winter, lingered some time, and finally died in the hospital. It was her request that she should be buried among the soldiers and after the military method. This request was fully carried out. Her coffin was carried to the grave by soldiers with the usual escort, buried, and a salute fired over the grave. This was at Annapolis a few days since.

Female Nurses for Soldiers.

There are many women in one position or another among the hospitals—mostly as nurses here in Washington and among the military stations, quite a number of them young ladies acting as volunteers. They are a help in certain ways and deserve to be mentioned with respect. Then it remains to be distinctly said that few or no young ladies, under the irresistible conventions of society, answer the practical requirements of nurses for soldiers. Middle-aged or healthy and good conditioned elderly women, mothers of children, are always best.

Many of the wounded must be handled. A hundred things which cannot be gainsayed must occur and must be done. The presence of a good middle-aged or elderly woman, the magnetic touch of hands, the expressive features of the mother, the silent soothing of her presence, her words, her knowledge and privileges, arrived at only through having had children, are precious and final qualification. It is a natural faculty that is required; it is not merely having a genteel young woman at a table in a ward. One of the finest nurses I met was a red-faced, illiterate old Irish woman; I have seen her take the poor, wasted, naked boys so tenderly up in her arms. There are plenty of excellent, clean old black women that would make tiptop nurses.

An Army Hospital Ward.

Let me specialize a visit I made to the collection of barrack-like one-story buildings, Campbell Hospital, out on the flats at the end of the then horse railway route on Seventh Street.

There is a long building appropriated to each ward. Let us go into Ward 6. It contains today, I should judge, eighty or a hundred patients, half sick, half wounded. The edifice is nothing but boards, well whitewashed inside, and the usual slender-framed iron bedsteads, narrow and plain. You walk down the central passage, with a row on either side, their feet towards you and their heads to the wall. There are fires in large stoves, and the prevailing white of the walls is relieved by some ornaments, stars, circles, etc. made of evergreens.

The view of the whole edifice and occupants can be taken at once, for there is no partition. You may hear groans or other sounds of unendurable suffering from two or three of the cots, but in the main there is quiet—almost a painful absence of demonstration. But the pallid face, the dulled eye, and the moisture on the lip are demonstration enough.

Most of these sick or hurt are evidently young fellows from the country, farmers' sons and such like. Look at the fine, large frames, the bright and broad countenances, and the many yet-lingering proofs of strong constitution and physique. Look at the patient and mute manner of our American wounded as they lie in such a sad collection; representatives from all New England and from New York and New Jersey and Pennsylvania—indeed from all the states and all the cities—largely from the West. Most of them are entirely without friends or acquaintances here—

no familiar face and hardly a word of judicious sympathy or cheer through their sometimes long and tedious sickness or the pangs of aggravated wounds. . . .

. . . How much I know of diarrhoea in the hospitals—the army—diarrhoea was of all troubles the most prevalent . . . a bad form, it meant death, death. I nursed many and many a man down with diarrhoea . . . There was a young man . . . a miserable scamp and scalawag he was, too— yet with elements in his nature that I liked. He liked me, too, I think; came there, down with diarrhoea—oh! it was very bad. We nursed him; I was there once, twice, often three times a day; posted the nurses, the doctors. Finally the man came around, was better. The doctor came to me one evening, said to me: "We're going to get your boy about again"; next day he got a big mess of pork and beans. His mother, sister, smuggled them in—surreptitiously brought them in. The fellow was ravenously hungry; he swallowed the whole mess with gusto; was taken with a relapse, then died . . . That finished him.

I can see him now—it is one of those days long ago—the devilishly obstinate, illiterate boy he was; no one could do anything with him—doctors, nurses—no one but me. For me he would do anything. Yet I was a perfect tyrant with him. Yes, yes: I can see him now—the close-cropped hair, the beautiful, full, eloquent eye, the bullet head, the strong mouth. Then, as he lay there, pale, sick, thin . . . I had seen many such cases, seemingly insignificant in themselves, yet part of the real history of that time. . . .

. . . One Sunday night, in a ward in the South Building, I spent one of the most agreeable evenings of my life amid such a group of convalescent young soldiers of a Maine regiment. We drew around together on our chairs in the dimly lighted room, and after interchanging the few magnetic remarks that show people it is well for them to be together, they told me stories of country life and adventures, etc., away up there in the Northeast. They were to leave the next day in a vessel for the Gulf where their regiment was, and they felt so happy at the prospect. I shook hands with them all around at parting, and I know we all felt as if it were the separation of old friends.

. . . In one case, the wife sat by the side of her husband, his sickness typhoid fever, pretty bad. In another, by the side of her son, a mother—she told me she had seven children and this was the youngest. (A fine, kind, healthy, gentle mother, good-looking, not very old, with a cap on her head and dressed like home—what a charm it gave to the whole ward!)

I liked the woman nurse in Ward E—I noticed how she sat a long time by a poor fellow who just had that morning, in addition to his other sickness, bad hemmorhage. She gently assisted him, relieved him of the blood, holding a cloth to his mouth as he coughed it up—he was so weak he could only just turn his head over on the pillow.

Death of a Wisconsin Officer.

Another characteristic scene of that dark and bloody 1863, from notes of my visit to Armory-Square Hospital one hot but pleasant summer day. In Ward H we approach the cot of a young lieutenant of one of the Wisconsin regiments. Tread the bare board floor lightly here—for the pain and panting of death are in this cot.

I saw the lieutenant when he was first brought here from Chancellorsville, and have been with him occasionally from day to day and night to night. He had been getting along pretty well till night before last, when a sudden hemorrhage that could not be stopped came upon him, and today it still

119

continues at intervals. Notice that water-pail by the side of the bed, with a quantity of blood and bloody pieces of muslin, nearly full—that tells the story.

The poor young man is struggling painfully for breath, his great dark eyes with a glaze already upon them and the choking faint but audible in his throat. An attendant sits by him, and will not leave him till the last—yet little or nothing can be done. He will die in an hour or two, without the presence of kith or kin. Meantime the ordinary chat and business of the ward a little way off goes on indifferently. Some of the inmates are laughing and joking; others are playing checkers or cards; others are reading, etc.

I have noticed through most of the hospitals that as long as there is any chance for a man, no matter how bad he may be, the surgeon and nurses work hard, sometimes with curious tenacity for his life—doing everything and keeping somebody by him to execute the doctor's orders, and minister to him every night and day. See that screen there. As you advance through the dusk of early candlelight, a nurse will step forth on tiptoe and silently but imperiously forbid you to make any noise or perhaps to come near at all. Some soldier's life is flickering there, suspended between recovery and death. Perhaps at this moment the exhausted frame has just fallen into a light sleep that a step might shake. You must retire. The neighboring patients must move in their stocking feet.

I have several times been struck with such marked efforts—everything bent to save a life from the very grip of the destroyer. But when that grip is once firmly fixed, leaving no hope or chance at all, the surgeon abandons the patient. If it is a case where stimulus is any relief, the nurse gives milk-punch or brandy or whatever is wanted, ad libitum. There is no fuss made. Not a bit of sentimentalism or whining have I seen about a single deathbed in hospital or on the field, but generally impassive indifference. All is over, as far as any efforts can avail; it is useless to expend emotions or labors. While there is a prospect, they strive hard—at least most surgeons do; but death certain and evident, they yield the field. . . .

Hospital Perplexity.

To add to other troubles amid the confusion of this great army of sick, it is almost impossible for a stranger to find any friend or relative unless he has the patient's specific address to start upon. Besides the directory printed in the newspapers here, there are one or two general directories of the hospitals kept at provost's headquarters, but they are nothing like complete. They are never up to date and, as things are, with the daily streams of coming and going and changing, cannot be. I have known cases for instance, such as a farmer coming here from Northern New York to find a wounded brother, faithfully hunting around for a week, and then compelled to leave and go home without getting any trace of him. When he got home he found a letter from the brother giving the right address.

Sept. 23, 1863.

Talked with Ben in Ward A about the tyrannisings and unnecessary exposure of the soldiers. —So many officers there are who dare not go into engagements nor even out on picket with their men for fear of their lives from their own men.

Yesterday I spent a good part of the afternoon with a young soldier of seventeen, Charles Cutter, of Lawrence City, Mass., 1st Massachusetts Heavy Artillery, Battery M. He was brought to one of the hospitals mortally wounded in abdomen. Well, I thought to myself, as I sat looking at him, it ought to be a relief to his folks if they could see how little he really suffered. He lay very placid, in a half-lethargy, with his eyes closed. As it was extremely hot, and I sat a good while silently fanning him and wiping the sweat, at length he opened his eyes quite wide and clear and looked inquiringly around. I said: "What is it, my boy? Do you want anything?" He answered quietly, with a good-natured smile: "Oh, nothing; I was only looking around to see who was with me." His mind was somewhat wandering, yet he lay in an evident peacefulness that sanity and health might have envied. I had to leave for other engagements. He died, I heard afterward, without any special agitation, in the course of the night.

Summer of 1864.

I am back again in Washington, on my regular daily and nightly rounds. Of course, there are many specialties. Dotting a ward here and there are always cases of poor fellows long-suffering under obstinate wounds, or weak and disheartened from typhoid fever or the like; marked cases needing special and sympathetic treatment. These I sit down and either talk to, or silently cheer them up. They always like this hugely (and so do I).

Each case has its peculiarities and needs some new adaptation. I have learnt to thus conform—learnt a good deal of hospital wisdom. Some of the poor young chaps, away from home for the first time in their lives, hunger and thirst for affection; this is sometimes the only thing that will reach their condition. The men like to have a pencil and something to write in. I have given them cheap pocket diaries and almanacs for 1864, interleaved with blank paper. For reading I generally have some old pictorial magazines or story papers—they are always acceptable. Also the morning or evening papers of the day. The best books I do not give but lend to read through the wards, and then take them to others, and so on; they are very punctual about returning the books.

In these wards, or on the field, as I thus continue to go round, I have come to adapt myself to each emergency, after its kind or call—however, trivial, however solemn, every one justified and made real under its circumstances—not only visits and cheering talk and little gifts, not only washing and dressing wounds (I have some cases where the patient is unwilling anyone should do this but me), but passages from the Bible, expounding them, prayer at the bedside, explanations of doctrine, etc. (I think I see my friends smiling at this confession, but I was never more in earnest in my life.)

In camp and everywhere I was in the habit of reading or giving recitations to the men. They were very fond of it, and liked declamatory poetic pieces. We would gather in a large group by ourselves after supper, and spend the time in such readings or in talking, and occasionally by an amusing game called the game of "Twenty Questions."

Gifts—Money—Discrimination.

As a very large proportion of the wounded came up from the front without a cent of money in their pockets, I soon discovered that it was about the best thing I could do to raise their spirits, and show them that somebody cared for them and practically felt a fatherly or brotherly interest in them, to give them small sums in such cases, using tact and discretion about it. I am regularly supplied with funds for this purpose by good women and men in Boston, Salem, Providence, Brooklyn, and New York. I provide myself with a quantity of bright new ten-cent and five-cent bills, and when I think it incumbent, I give twenty-five or thirty cents or perhaps fifty cents, and occasionally a still larger sum to some particular case.

As I have started this subject, I take opportunity to ventilate the financial question. My supplies, altogether voluntary, mostly confidential, often seeming quite providential, were numerous and varied. For instance, there were two distant and wealthy ladies, sisters, who sent regularly for two years quite heavy sums, enjoining that their names should be kept secret. The same delicacy was indeed a frequent condition. From several I had carte blanche. Many were entire strangers. From these sources, during from two to three years, in the manner described, in the hospitals I bestowed as almoner for others many, many thousands of dollars. I learned one thing conclusively—that beneath all the ostensible greed and heartlessness of our times there is no end to the generous benevolence of men and women in the United States, when once sure of their object. Another thing became clear to me—while *cash* is not amiss to bring up the rear, tact and magnetic sympathy and unction are, and ever will be, sovereign still.

Christmas Night.

The men had a theatrical performance, *Rob Roy*, second floor, "front seats reserved for the cripples." Where they were all in one building, the men had the run of the whole building.

An Incident.

In one of the fights before Atlanta, a rebel soldier of large size, evidently a young man, was mortally wounded top of the head, so that the brains partially exuded. He lived three days, lying on his back on the spot where he first dropped. He dug with his heel in the ground during that time a hole big enough to put in a couple of ordinary knapsacks. He just lay there in the open air and with little intermission kept his heel going night and day. Some of our soldiers then moved him to a house, but he died in a few minutes.

Another.

After the battles at Columbia, Tennessee, where we repulsed about a score of vehement rebel charges, they left a great many wounded on the ground, mostly within our range. Whenever any of these wounded attempted to move away by any means, generally by crawling off, our men, without exception, brought them down by a bullet. They let none crawl away, no matter what his condition.

Two Brothers, One North, One South. May 28–9.

I stayed tonight a long time by the bedside of a new patient, a young Baltimorean aged about nineteen years. W.S.P. (2nd Maryland, Southern), very feeble, right leg amputated, can't sleep hardly at all; has taken a great deal of morphine, which, as usual, is costing more than it comes to. Evidently very intelligent and well bred, very affectionate, held on to my hand and put it by his face, not willing to let me leave.

As I was lingering, soothing him in his pain, he says to me suddenly: "I hardly think you know who I am; I don't wish to impose on you—I am a Rebel soldier." I said I did not know that, but it made no difference. Visited him daily for about two weeks after that, while he lived (death had marked him and he was quite alone). I loved him much, always kissed him, and he did me.

In an adjoining ward I found his brother, an officer of rank, a Union soldier, a brave and religious man, Colonel Clifton K. Prentiss, 6th Maryland Infantry, 6th Corps, wounded in one of the engagements at Petersburg, April 2; lingered, suffered much, died in Brooklyn August 20, '65. It was in the same battle both were hit. One was a strong Unionist, the other Secesh; both fought on their respective sides, both badly wounded, and both brought together here after a separation of four years. Each died for his cause.

June 9–10.

I have been sitting late tonight by the bedside of a wounded captain, a special friend of mine, lying with a painful fracture of left leg in one of the hospitals, in a large ward partially vacant. The lights were put out, all but a little candle far from where I sat. The full moon shone in through the windows, making long, slanting, silvery patches on the floor. All was still, my friend too was silent, but could not sleep; so I sat there by him, slowly wafting the fan, and occupied with the musings that arose out of the scene—the long, shadowy ward; the beautiful, ghostly moonlight on the floor; the white beds, here and there an occupant with huddled form, the bedclothes thrown off. The hospitals have a number of cases of sunstroke and exhaustion by heat from the late reviews. There are many such from the 6th Corps, from the hot parade of day before yesterday. (Some of these shows cost the lives of scores of men.)

. . . I wonder if I could ever convey to another—to you, for instance, reader dear—the tender and terrible realities of such cases (many, many happened) as the one I am now going to mention. Stewart C. Glover, Company E, 5th Wisconsin—was wounded May 5th, in one of those fierce tussles of the Wilderness—died May 21, aged about twenty. He was a small and beardless young man—a splendid soldier—in fact almost an ideal American of his age. He had served nearly three years, and would have been entitled to his discharge in a few days. He was in Hancock's Corps.

The fighting had about ceased for the day, and the general commanding the brigade rode by and called for volunteers to bring in the wounded. Glover responded among the first—went out gaily—but while in the act of bearing in a wounded sergeant to our lines, was shot in the knee by a rebel sharpshooter; consequence—amputation and death. He had resided with his father, John Glover, an aged and feeble man, in Batavia, Genesee County, New York, but was at school in Wisconsin after the war broke out and there enlisted—soon took to soldier life, liked it, was very manly, was beloved by officers and comrades. He kept a little diary, like so many of the soldiers. On the day of his death, he wrote the following in it: "Today the doctor says I must die—all is over with me—ah, so young to die." On another blank leaf he pencilled to his brother: "Dear brother Thomas, I have been brave but wicked—pray for me."

. . . As I read over even my own story, it all vividly comes back to me—I see all that over again. I often read the Bible, read anything. My point was to please the boys—to do for them just what they most wished done. If I had any rule at all that I observed, it was just this: satisfy the boys themselves at whatever sacrifice; always, except in rare cases, humor them. . . .

There were cases in which good reasons obliged me to run counter to them; I hated to do it; I did it with some pain. The doctors would most times leave the boys absolutely in my hands; sometimes, however, their mandates, especially concerning diet, were imperative. Many Bibles —oh, many of them; fruit, tobacco—heaven only knows what not. I read to them! From the Bible if they wished it; from anything else if they preferred—always seriously, always happily . . . I can't recall a single case in which I gave away *Leaves of Grass*. Now and then some individuals would ask for something from my pen—something wholly mine—then I would hunt up a magazine or newspaper article somewhere—some slip—give them that.

THE WOUND-DRESSER

I

An old man bending I come among new faces,
Years looking backward resuming in answer to children,
Come tell us old man, as from young men and maidens that love me,
(Arous'd and angry, I'd thought to beat the alarum, and urge relentless war,

But soon my fingers fail'd me, my face droop'd and I resign'd my-
self,
To sit by the wounded and soothe them, or silently watch the
dead;)
Years hence of these scenes, of these furious passions, these chances,
Of unsurpass'd heroes, (was one side so brave? the other was equally
brave;)
Now be witness again, paint the mightiest armies of earth,
Of those armies so rapid so wondrous what saw you to tell us?
What stays with you latest and deepest? of curious panics,
Of hard-fought engagements or sieges tremendous what deepest
remains?

2

O maidens and young men I love and that love me,
What you ask of my days those the strangest and sudden your talk-
ing recalls,
Soldier alert I arrive after a long march cover'd with sweat and
dust,
In the nick of time I come, plunge in the fight, loudly shout in the
rush of successful charge,
Enter the captur'd works—yet lo, like a swift-running river they
fade,
Pass and are gone they fade—I dwell not on soldiers' perils or sol-
diers' joys,
(Both I remember well—many of the hardships, few the joys, yet I
was content.)

But in silence, in dreams' projections,
While the world of gain and appearance and mirth goes on,
So soon what is over forgotten, and waves wash the imprints off
the sand,
With hinged knees returning I enter the doors, (while for you up
there,
Whoever you are, follow without noise and be of strong heart.)

Bearing the bandages, water and sponge,
Straight and swift to my wounded I go,
Where they lie on the ground after the battle brought in,

Where their priceless blood reddens the grass the ground,
Or to the rows of the hospital tent, or under the roof'd hospital,
To the long rows of cots up and down each side I return,
To each and all one after another I draw near, not one do I miss,
An attendant follows holding a tray, he carries a refuse pail,
Soon to be fill'd with clotted rags and blood, emptied, and fill'd
    again.

I onward go, I stop,
With hinged knees and steady hand to dress wounds,
I am firm with each, the pangs are sharp yet unavoidable,
One turns to me his appealing eyes—poor boy! I never knew you,
Yet I think I could not refuse this moment to die for you, if that
    would save you.

3

On, on I go, (open doors of time! open hospital doors!)
The crush'd head I dress, (poor crazed hand tear not the bandage
    away,)
The neck of the cavalry-man with the bullet through and through
    I examine,
Hard the breathing rattles, quite glazed already the eye, yet life
    struggles hard,
(Come sweet death! be persuaded O beautiful death!
In mercy come quickly.)
From the stump of the arm, the amputated hand,
I undo the clotted lint, remove the slough, wash off the matter and
    blood,
Back on his pillow the soldier bends with curv'd neck and side fall-
    ing head,
His eyes are closed, his face is pale, he dares not look on the bloody
    stump,
And has not yet look'd on it.

I dress a wound in the side, deep, deep,
But a day or two more, for see the frame all wasted and sinking,
And the yellow-blue countenance see.
I dress the perforated shoulder, the foot with the bullet-wound,
Cleanse the one with a gnawing and putrid gangrene, so sickening,
    so offensive,

129

While the attendant stands behind aside me holding the tray and
pail.

I am faithful, I do not give out,
The fractur'd thigh, the knee, the wound in the abdomen,
These and more I dress with impassive hand, (yet deep in my breast
a fire, a burning flame.)

4

Thus in silence in dreams' projections,
Returning, resuming, I thread my way through the hospitals,
The hurt and wounded I pacify with soothing hand,
I sit by the restless all the dark night, some are so young,
Some suffer so much, I recall the experience sweet and sad,
(Many a soldier's loving arms about this neck have cross'd and
rested,
Many a soldier's kiss dwells on these bearded lips.)

Chapter Seven

'Dearest Mother'

A selection of Whitman's wartime letters to his mother, published posthumously. The letters, sometimes written most colloquially, give intimate details of Whitman's important impressions during the war period.

DELICATE CLUSTER

Delicate cluster! flag of teeming life!
Covering all my lands—all my seashores lining!
Flag of death! (how I watch'd you through the smoke of battle
   pressing!
How I heard you flap and rustle, cloth defiant!)
Flag cerulean—sunny flag, with the orbs of night dappled!
Ah my silvery beauty—ah my woolly white and crimson!
Ah to sing the song of you, my matron mighty!
My sacred one, my mother!

*   *   *

AS AT THY PORTALS ALSO DEATH

As at thy portals also death,
Entering thy sovereign, dim, illimitable grounds,
To memories of my mother, to the divine blending, maternity,
To her, buried and gone, yet buried not, gone not from me,
(I see again the calm benignant face fresh and beautiful still,
I sit by the form in the coffin,
I kiss and kiss convulsively again the sweet old lips, the cheeks, the
   closed eyes in the coffin;)
To her, the ideal woman, practical, spiritual, of all of earth, life,
   love, to me the best,
I grave a monumental line, before I go, amid these songs,
And set a tombstone here.

'Dearest Mother'

. . . I wrote my mother voluminously from the war; ah! those letters—my dear, dear mother. She in Brooklyn, alone—I wrote every day or so—sometimes in a general way—frequently all sorts of personal quips, bits, oddities, interspersed—family jottings—no letter in the whole lot absolutely clear of them. . . .

. . . The letters to my mother are all here—I have them —I got them after she died—a hundred or more—all scrupulously kept together—still about somewhere with my manuscripts. The reality, the simplicity, the transparency of my dear, dear mother's life was responsible for the main things in the letters, as in *Leaves of Grass* itself. How much I owe her! It could not be put in a scale—weighed—it could not be measured—be even put in the best words; it can only be apprehended through the intuitions. *Leaves of Grass* is the flower of her temperament active in me. My mother was illiterate in the formal sense, but strangely knowing; she excelled in narrative—had great mimetic power; she could tell stories, impersonate; she was very eloquent in the utterance of noble moral axioms—was very original in her manner, her style. . . .

Washington, Wednesday forenoon, April 15, 1863.
Dearest Mother: I believe I weigh about two hundred, and as to my face (so scarlet) and my beard and neck, they are

133

terrible to behold. I fancy the reason I am able to do some good in the hospitals among the poor languishing and wounded boys is that I am so large and well—indeed like a great wild buffalo, with much hair. Many of the soldiers are from the West and far North, and they take to a man that has not the bleached, shiny, and shaved cut of the cities and the East. . . .

Washington, April 28, 1863.

. . . Tell Jeff I am going to write to Mr. Lane either today or tomorrow. Jeff asks me if I go to hospitals as much as ever. If my letters home don't show it, you don't get 'em. I feel sorry sometimes after I have sent them, I have said so much about hospitals and so mournful. O mother, the young man in Armory Square, Dennis Barrett in the 169th N.Y. I mentioned before, is probably going to get up after all; he is like one saved from the grave. Saturday last I saw him and talked with him and gave him something to eat, and he was much better—it is the most unexpected recovery I have yet seen. . . .

. . . How contemptible all the usual little worldly prides and vanities and striving after appearances seems in the midst of such scenes as these—such tragedies of soul and body. To see such things and not be able to help them is awful—I feel amost ashamed of being so well and whole. . . .

. . . Our wounded from Hooker's battles are worse wounded and more of them than any battle of the war, and indeed any, I may say, of modern times—besides, the weather has been very hot here, very bad for new wounds. Yet, as Jeff writes so downhearted, I must tell him the Rebellion has lost worse and more than we have. The more I find out about it, the more I think they, the Confederates, have received an irreparable harm and loss in Virginia—I should not be surprised to see them (either voluntarily or by force) leaving Virginia before many weeks; I don't see how on earth they can stay there. I think Hooker is already reaching them again. . . .

Washington, Tuesday morning, June 9, 1863.

. . . Well, mother, the war still goes on, and everything as much in a fog as ever—and the battles as bloody, and the wounded and sick getting worse and plentier all the time. I see a letter in the *Tribune* from Lexington, Ky., June 5th, headed "The 9th Army Corps departing for Vicksburg"— but I cannot exactly make it out on reading the letter carefully—I don't see anything in the letter about the 9th Corps moving from Vicksburg; at any rate I think the 2nd Division is more likely to be needed in Kentucky (or, as I said, in Eastern Tennessee) as the Secesh are expected to make trouble there. But one can hardly tell—the only thing is to resign one's self to events as they occur; it is a sad and dreary time for so many thousands of parents and relatives, not knowing what will occur next. . . .

. . . Mother, I think something of commencing a series of lectures and reading, etc., through different cities of the North, to supply myself with funds for my hospital and soldiers' visits, as I do not like to be beholden to the medium of others. I need a pretty large supply of money, etc., to do the good I would like to, and the work grows upon me and fascinates me—it is the most affecting thing you ever see, the lots of poor, sick, and wounded young men that depend so much, in one word or another, upon my petting or soothing or feeding, sitting by them and feeding them their dinner or supper—some are quite helpless, some wounded in both arms—or giving some trifle (for a novelty or a change, it isn't for the value of it), or stopping a little while with them. Nobody will do but me—so, mother, I feel I would like to inaugurate a plan by which I could

135

raise means on my own hook, and perhaps quite plenty too. Best love to you, dearest mother, and to sister Mat and Jeff.

Washington, Monday morning, June 22, 1863.

. . . Well, mother, we are generally anticipating a lively time here, or in the neighborhood, as it is probable Lee is feeling about to strike a blow on Washington, or perhaps right into it—and, as Lee is no fool, it is perhaps possible he may give us a good shake. He is not very far off—yesterday was a fight to the southwest of here all day; we heard the cannons nearly all the day. The wounded are arriving in small squads every day, mostly cavalry, a great many Ohio men; they send off today from the Washington hospitals a great many to New York, Philadelphia, etc., all who are able, to make room—which looks ominous—indeed, it is pretty certain that there is to be some severe fighting, maybe a great battle again, the pending week. I am getting so callous that it hardly arouses me at all. I fancy I should take it very quietly if I found myself in the midst of a desperate conflict here in Washington. . . .

. . . I have quite made up my mind about the lecturing, etc., project—I have no doubt it will succeed well enough the way I shall put it in operation. You know, mother, it is to raise funds to enable me to continue my hospital ministrations on a more freehanded scale. As to the Sanitary Commissions and the like, I am sick of them all, and would not accept any of their berths. You ought to see the way the men, as they lay helpless in bed, turn away their faces from the sight of those agents, chaplains, etc. (hirelings, as Elias Hicks would call them—they seem to me always a set of foxes and wolves). They get well paid, and are always incompetent and disagreeable; as I told you before, the only good fellows I have met are the Christian Commissioners— they go everywhere and receive no pay.

We here think Vicksburg is ours. The probability is that it has capitulated—and there has been no general assault—can't tell yet whether the 51st went there.

Washington, June 30, 1863.

. . . I am told that I hover too much over the beds of the hospitals, with fever and putrid wounds, etc. One soldier brought here about fifteen days ago, very low with typhoid fever, Livingston Brooks, Company B., 17th Pennsylvania Cavalry, I have particularly stuck to, as I found him to be in what appeared to be a dying condition, from negligence and a horrible journey of about forty miles, bad roads and fast driving; and then after he got here, as he is a simple country boy, very shy and silent, and made no complaint, they neglected him.

I found him something like I found John Holmes last winter. I called the doctor's attention to him, shook up the nurses, had him bathed in spirits, gave him lumps of ice and ice to his head; he had a fearful bursting pain in his head, and his body was like fire. He was very quiet, a very sensible boy, old-fashioned; he did not want to die, and I had to lie to him without stint, for he thought I knew everything, and I always put in, of course, that what I told him was exactly the truth, and that if he got really dangerous I would tell him and not conceal it.

The rule is to remove bad fever patients out from the main wards to a tent by themselves, and the doctor told me he would have to be removed. I broke it gently to him, but the poor boy got it immediately that he was marked with death and was to be removed on that account. It had a great effect upon him, and although I told the truth, this time it did not have as good a result as my former fibs. I persuaded the doctor to let him remain. For three days he lay just about an even chance, go or stay, with a little leaning toward the first.

But . . . to make a long story short, he is now out of any immediate danger. He has been perfectly rational throughout—begins to taste a little food (for a week he ate nothing; I had to compel him to take a quarter of an orange now and then), and I will say, whether anyone calls it pride or not, that if he *does* get up and around again, it's me that saved his life.

Mother, as I have said in former letters, you can have no idea how these sick and dying youngsters cling to a fellow, and how fascinating it is, with all its hospital surroundings of sadness and scenes of repulsion and death. . . .

. . . It seems to me, as I go through these rows of cots, as if it was too bad to accept these *children*, to subject them to such premature experiences. I devote myself much to Armory-Square Hospital because it contains by far the worst cases, most repulsive wounds, has the most suffering and most need of consolation. I go every day without fail and often at night—sometimes stay very late. No one interferes with me, guards, nurses, doctors, nor anyone. I am let to take my own course.

Well, mother, I suppose you folks think we are in a somewhat dubious position here in Washington, with Lee in strong force almost between us and you Northerners. Well, it does look ticklish; if the Rebs cut the connection, then there will be fun. The Reb cavalry come quite near us, dash in, and steal wagon trains, etc.; it would be funny if they should come some night to the President's country house (Soldiers' Home) where he goes out to sleep every night; it is in the same direction as their saucy raid last Sunday. . . .

About an hour [ago] we had a large cavalry regiment pass, with blankets, arms, etc., on the war march over the same track. The regiment was very full, over a thousand—indeed thirteen or fourteen hundred. It was an old regiment, veterans, *old fighters*, young as they were. They were preceded by a fine mounted band of sixteen (about ten bugles, the rest cymbals and drums).

I tell you, mother, it made everything ring—made my heart leap. They played with a will. Then the accompaniment; the sabers rattled on a thousand men's sides—they had pistols, their heels were spurred—handsome American young men (I made no account of any other); rude uniforms, well worn, but good cattle, prancing—all good riders, full of the devil; nobody shaved, very sunburnt. The regimental officers (splendidly mounted but just as roughly dressed as the men) came immediately after the band; then company after company, with each its officers at its head; the tramps of so many horses (there is a good hard turnpike); then a long train of men with led horses; mounted Negroes; and a long, long string of baggage wagons, each with four horses; and then a strong rear guard.

I tell you it had the look of *real war*—noble-looking fellows; a man feels so proud on a good horse and armed. They are off toward the region of Lee's (supposed) rendezvous, toward Susquehannah, for the great anticipated battle. Alas! how many of these healthy, handsome, rollicking young men will lie cold in death before the apples ripen in the orchard.

Mother, it is curious and stirring here in some respects. Smaller or larger bodies of troops are moving continually —many just-well men are turned out of the hospitals. I am where I see a good deal of them. There are getting to be *many black troops*. There is one very good regiment here, black as tar; they go around, have the regular uniform— they submit to no nonsense. Others are constantly forming. It is getting to be a common sight.

Washington, Wednesday forenoon, July 15, 1863.

. . . So the mob has risen at last in New York—I have been expecting it, but as the day for the draft had arrived, and everything was so quiet, I supposed all might go on smoothly; but it seems the passions of the people were only sleeping, and have burst forth with terribly fury, and they have destroyed life and property, the enrollment buildings, etc., as we hear.

The feeling here is savage and hot as fire against New York (the mob—"Copperhead mob" the papers here call it), and I hear nothing in all directions but threats of ordering up the gunboats, cannonading the city, shooting down the mob, hanging them in a body, etc., etc. Meantime I remain silent, partly amused, partly scornful, or occasionally put a dry remark, which only adds fuel to the flame. I do not feel it in my heart to abuse the poor people, or call for a rope or bullets for them, but that is all the talk here, even in the hospitals. The accounts from New York this morning are that the Government has ordered the draft to be suspended there—I hope it is true, for I find that the deeper they go in with the draft, the more trouble it is likely to make. I have changed my opinion and feelings on the subject—we are in the midst of strange and terrible times—one is pulled a dozen different ways in his mind, and hardly knows what to think or do. . . .

. . . My hospital life still continues the same—I was in Armory all day yesterday—and day and night before. They have the men wounded in the railroad accident at Laurel Station (between here and Baltimore), about thirty soldiers, some of them horribly injured at 3 o'clock a.m. last Saturday by collision—poor, poor, poor men. I go again this afternoon and night—I see so much of butcher sights, so much sickness and suffering, I must get away a while, I believe, for self-preservation.

Washington, August 18, 1863.
. . . I had a letter in the *New York Times* of last Sunday —did you see it? I wonder if George can't get a furlough

and come home for a while; that furlough he had was only a fleabite? If he could, it would be no more than right, for no man in the country has done his duty more faithful, and without complaining of anything or asking for anything, than George. I suppose they will fill up the 51st with conscripts, as that seems to be the order of the day—a good many are arriving here from the North and passing through to join Meade's army. We are expecting to hear of more rows in New York about the draft; it commences there right away, I see—this time it will be no such doings as a month or five weeks ago; the Government here is forwarding a large force of regulars to New York to be ready for anything that may happen—there will be no blank cartridges this time.

Well, I thought when I first heard of the riot in New York, I had some feeling for them, but soon as I found what it really was, I felt it was the devil's own work all through. I guess the strong arm will be exhibited this time up to the shoulder. . . .

Washington, August 25, 1863.

. . . The letter from George and your lines, and a few from Jeff, came yesterday, and I was glad indeed to be certain George had got back to Kentucky safe and well—while so many fall that we know, or, what is about as bad, get sick or hurt in the fight and lie in hospital—it seems almost a miracle that George should have gone through so much, South and North and East and West, and yet have stood it so, and be yet alive and in good health and spirits.

O mother, what would we [have] done if it had been otherwise—if he had met the fate of so many we know—if he had been killed or badly hurt in some of those battles? I get thinking about it sometimes, and it works upon me so I have to stop and turn my mind on something else. . . .

I have seen so much horrors that befall men (so bad and such suffering and mutilations, etc., that the poor men can defy their fate to do anything more or any harder misfortune or worse a-going) that I sometimes think I have grown callous—but no, I don't think it is that, but nothing of ordinary misfortune seems as it used to, and death itself has lost all its terrors—I have seen so many cases in which it was so welcome and such a relief.

Mother, you must just resign yourself to things that occur —but I hardly think it is necessary to give you any charge about it, for I think you have done so for many years, and stood it all with good courage. . . .

Washington, September 1, 1863.

. . . I have been thinking today and all yesterday about the draft in Brooklyn, and whether Jeff would be drafted; you must some of you write me just as soon as you get this— I want to know; I feel anxious enough I can tell you—and besides, it seems a good while since I have received any letters from home. Of course it is impossible for Jeff to go, in case it should turn out he was drafted—the way our family is all situated now, it would be madness. If the Common Council raise the money to exempt men with families dependent on them, I think Jeff ought to have no scruples in taking advantage of it, as I think he is in duty bound—but we will see what course to take when we know the result, etc., write about it right away. . . .

Dear mother, how are you nowadays? I do hope you feel well and in good spirits—I think about you every day of my life out here. Sometimes I see women in the hospitals, mothers come to see their sons, and occasionally one that makes me think of my dear mother—one did very much, a lady about 60, from Pennsylvania, come to see her son, a captain, very badly wounded and his wound gangrened, and they after a while removed him to a tent by himself.

Another son of hers, a young man, came with her to see his brother. She was a pretty full-size lady, with spectacles; she dressed in black—looked real Velsory.[1] I got very well acquainted with her; she had a real Long Island old-fashioned way—but I had to avoid the poor captain, as it was that time that my hand was cut in the artery, and I was liable to gangrene myself—but she and the two sons have gone home now, but I doubt whether the wounded one is alive, as he was very low. . . . You have no idea how many soldiers there are who have lost their voices and have to speak in whispers—there are a great many, I meet some almost every day.

Washington, September 8, 1863.

. . . O, I was so pleased that Jeff was not drawn, and I know how Mat must have felt too; I have no idea the Government will try to draft again, whatever happens—they have carried their point, but have not made much out of it. O how the conscripts and substitutes are deserting down in front and on their way there—you don't hear anything about it, but it is incredible—they don't allow it to get in the papers. . . .

. . . I was gratified to hear you went up among the soldiers—they are rude in appearance, but they know what is decent, and it pleases them much to have folks, even old women, take an interest and come among them. Mother, you must go again, and take Mat . . . I am first-rate in health, so much better than a month and two months ago—my hand has entirely healed. I go to hospital every day or night—I believe no men ever loved each other as I and some of these poor wounded, sick and dying men love each other. Good bye, dearest mother, for present.

[1] Mrs. Whitman's maiden name was Louisa Van Velsor.

WHEN I PERUSE THE CONQUER'D FAME

When I peruse the conquer'd fame of heroes and the victories of
    mighty generals, I do not envy the generals,
Nor the President in his Presidency, nor the rich in his great house,
But when I hear of the brotherhood of lovers, how it was with them,
How together through life, through dangers, odium, unchanging,
    long and long,
Through youth and through middle and old age, how unfaltering,
    how affectionate and faithful they were,
Then I am pensive—I hastily walk away fill'd with the bitterest
    envy.

Tuesday afternoon.

. . . It seems to be certain that Meade has gained the day,
and that the battles there in Pennsylvania have been about
as terrible as any in the war—I think the killed and wounded
there on both sides were as many as eighteen or twenty
thousand—in one place, four or five acres, there were a
thousand dead at daybreak on Saturday morning.

Mother, one's heart grows sick of war, after all, when
you see what it really is; every once in a while I feel so
horrified and disgusted—it seems to me like a great slaugh-
terhouse and the men mutually butchering each other—
then I feel how impossible it appears, again, to retire from
this contest until we have carried our points (it is cruel to
be so tossed from pillar to post in one's judgment).

. . . Washington is a pleasant place in some respects—it
has the finest trees and plenty of them everywhere, on the
streets and grounds. The Capitol grounds, though small,
have the finest cultivated trees I ever see—there is a great
variety, and not one but is in perfect condition.

As I finish this letter, I am going out there for an hour's
recreation. The great sights of Washington are the public
buildings, the wide streets, the public grounds, the trees,
the Smithsonian Institute and grounds. I go to the latter oc-

casionally—the Institute is an old-fogy concern, but the grounds are fine. Sometimes I go up to Georgetown, about two-and-a-half miles up the Potomac, an old town—just opposite it in the river is an island, where the [Negroes] have their first Washington regiment encamped. They make a good show; are often seen in the streets of Washington in squads. Since they have begun to carry arms, the Secesh here and in Georgetown (about three fifths) are not insulting to them as formerly.

One of the things here always on the go is long trains of army wagons—sometimes they will stream along all day; it seems as if there was nothing else but army wagons and ambulances. They have great camps here in every direction, of army wagons, teamsters, ambulance camps, etc.; some of them are permanent, and have small hospitals. I go to them (as no one else goes; ladies would not venture). I sometimes have the luck to give some of the drivers a great deal of comfort and help.

Indeed, . . . , there are camps here of everything—I went once or twice to the contraband camp, to the hospital, etc., but I could not bring myself to go again; when I meet black men or boys among my own hospitals, I use them kindly, give them something, etc. I believe I told you that I do the same to the wounded Rebels, too—but as there is a limit to one's sinews and endurance and sympathies etc., I have got in the way, after going lightly, as it were, all though the wards of a hospital and trying to give a word of cheer, if nothing else, to everyone, then confining my special attentions to the few where the investment seems to tell best, and who want it most.

Mother, I have real pride in telling you that I have the consciousness of saving quite a number of lives by saving them from giving up—and being a good deal with them; the men say it is so, and the doctors say it is so—and I will candidly confess I can see it is true, though I say it of myself. I know you will like to hear it, mother, so I tell you.

I am finishing this in Major Hapgood's office, about 1 o'clock—it is pretty warm, but has not cleared off yet. The trees look so well from where I am, and the Potomac—it is a noble river; I see it several miles, and the Arlington Heights. Mother, I see some of the 47th Brooklyn every day or two; the regiment is on the heights back of Arlington House, a fine camp ground. . . .

Washington, Sept. 15, 1863.

. . . Have you heard anything whether the 51st went on with Burnside, or did they remain as a reserve in Kentucky? Burnside has managed splendidly so far, his taking Knoxville and all together—it is a first-class success. I have known Tennessee Union men here in hospital, and I understand it, therefore—the region where Knoxville [is] is mainly Union, but the Southerners could not exist without it, as it is in their midst, so they determined to pound and kill and crush out the Unionists—all the savage and monstrous things printed in the papers about their treatment are true, at least that kind of thing is, as bad as the Irish in the mob treated the poor [Negroes] in New York. . . .

Washington, September 29, 1863.

. . . Well, here I sit this forenoon in a corner by the window in Major Hapgood's office, all the Potomac and Maryland and Virginia hills in sight, writing my Tuesday letter to you . . . Major has gone home to Boston on sick leave, and only the clerk and me occupy the office, and he not much of the time. At the present moment there are two wounded officers come in to get their pay—one has crutches; the other is dressed in the light-blue uniform of the invalid corps. Way up here on the fifth floor it is pretty hard scratching for cripples and very weak men to journey up here—often they come up here very weary and faint, and then find out they can't get their money, some red-tape hitch, and the poor soldiers look so disappointed—it always makes me feel bad. . . .

Mother, I don't think the 51st has been in any of the fighting we know of down there yet—what is to come of course nobody can tell. As to Burnside, I suppose you know he is among his *friends,* and I think this quite important, for such the main body of East Tennesseans are, and are far truer Americans anyhow than the Copperheads of the North. The Tennesseans will fight for us too.

. . . You have no idea how the soldiers, sick, etc. (I mean the American ones, to a man) all feel about the Copperheads; they never speak of them without a curse; and I heard them say, with an air that shows they mean it, they would shoot them sooner than they would a Rebel. . . . The troops from Meade's army are passing through here night and day, going west and so down to reinforce Rosecrans, I suppose—the papers are not permitted to mention it, but it is so. Two army corps, I should think, have mostly passed—they go through night and day—I hear the whistle of the locomotive screaming away any time at night when I wake up, and the rumbling of the trains. . . .

. . . I am in the hospitals as usual—I stand it better the last three weeks than ever before—I go among the worst fevers and wounds with impunity. I go among the small pox, etc., just the same—I feel to go without apprehension, and so I go. Nobody else goes; and as the darkey said there at Charleston when the boat run on a flat and the Reb sharpshooters were peppering them: "Somebody must jump in de water and shove de boat off."

Washington, October 6, 1863.

. . . I think Rosecrans and Burnside will be too much for the Rebels down there yet. I myself make a great account of Burnside being in the midst of *friends,* and such friends, too—they will fight and fight up to the handle, and kill somebody (it seems as if it was coming to that pass where we will either have to destroy or be destroyed). . . .

Mother, it is lucky I like Washington in many respects, and that things are upon the whole pleasant personally, for every day of my life I see enough to make one's heart ache with sympathy and anguish here in the hospital, and I do not know as I could stand it if it was not counterbalanced outside. It is curious, when I am present at the most appalling things—deaths, operations, sickening wounds (perhaps full of maggots)—I do not fail, although my sympathies are very much excited, but keep singularly cool; but often hours afterward, perhaps when I am home or out walking alone, I feel sick and actually tremble when I recall the thing and have it in my mind again before me. . . . Did you see my letter in the *New York Times* of Sunday, October 4? . . . .

Washington, October 13, 1863.

Nothing particular new with me. I am well and hearty—think a good deal about home. . . . There is a new lot of wounded now again. They have been arriving sick and wounded for three days—first long strings of ambulances with the sick, but yesterday many with bad and bloody wounds, poor fellows. Our troops got the worst of it, but fought like devils. Our men engaged were Kilpatrick's Cavalry. They were in the rear as part of Meade's retreat, and the Reb cavalry cut in between and cut them off and attacked them and shelled them terribly. But Kilpatrick brought them out mostly—this was last Sunday. . . .

Washington, October 27, 1863.

. . . Mother, if any of my soldier boys should ever call upon you (as they are often anxious to have my address in Brooklyn) you just use them as you know how to, without ceremony, and if you happen to have pot luck and feel to ask them to take a bite, don't be afraid to do so.

Well, dear mother, how the time passes away—to think it will soon be a year I have been away. It has passed away very swiftly, somehow, to me. O what things I have witnessed during that time—I shall never forget them! And the war is not settled yet, and one does not see anything at all certain about the settlement yet; but I have finally got for good, I think, into the feeling that our triumph is assured, whether it be sooner, or whether it be later, or whatever roundabout way we are led there, and I find I don't change that conviction from any reverses we meet, or any delays or government blunders. There are blunders enough, heaven knows, but I am thankful things have gone as well for us as they have—thankful the ship rides safe and sound at all. Then I have finally made up my mind that Mr. Lincoln has done as good as a human man could do. I still think him a pretty big president. I realize here in Washington that it has been a big thing to have just kept the United States from being thrown down and having its throat cut; and now I have no doubt it will throw down Secession and cut its throat—and I have not had any doubt since Gettysburg. . . .

Washington, Friday Afternoon, January 29, 1864.

. . . The young man that I took care of, Lewis Brown, is pretty well, but very restless—he is doing well now, but there is a long road before him yet; it is torture for him to be tied to his cot this weather; he is a very noble young man and has suffered very much. . . . But I find so many noble men in the ranks I have ceased to wonder at it. I think the soldiers from the New England States and the Western States are splendid, and the country parts of New York and Pennsylvania, too. I think less of the great cities than I used to. I know there are black sheep enough even in the

ranks, but the general rule is the soldiers are noble, very.
. . . Congress is in session; I see Odell, Kalbfleisch, etc. often. I have got acquainted with Mr. Garfield, an M. C. from Ohio, and like him very much indeed (he has been a soldier West, and I believe a good brave one—was a major general). I don't go much to the debates this session yet. Congress will probably keep in session till well into the summer. As to what course things will take, political or military, there's no telling. I think, though, the Secesh military power is getting more and more shaky. How they can make any headway against our new, large, and fresh armies next season passes my wit to see.

. . . I was talking with a pretty high officer here, who is behind the scenes—I was mentioning that I had a great desire to be present at a first-class battle; he told me if I would only stay around here three or four weeks longer, my wish would probably be gratified. I asked him what he meant, what he alluded to specifically, but he would not say anything further—so I remain as much in the dark as before —only there seemed to be some meaning in his remark, and it was made me only as there was no one else in hearing at the moment (he is quite an admirer of my poetry).

The re-enlistment of the veterans is the greatest thing yet; it pleases everybody but the Rebels—and surprises everybody too. . . .

Washington, March 2, 1864.

. . . Well, dear mother, I am just the same here—nothing new. I am well and hearty, and constantly moving around among the wounded, the sick. There are a great many of the latter coming up—the hospitals here are quite full—lately they have [been] picking out in the hospitals all that had pretty well recovered and sending them back to their regiments. They seem to be determined to strengthen the army this spring to the utmost. They are sending down many to their regiments that are not fit to go in my opinion—then there are squads and companies, and regiments, too, passing through here in one steady stream, going down to the front, returning from furlough home; but then there are quite a number leaving the army on furlough, re-enlisting, and going North for a while. They pass through here quite largely.

. . . Lewis Brown is getting quite well; he will soon be able to have a wooden leg put on. He is very restless and active and wants to go round all the time. . . .

If I can get a chance, I think I shall come home for a while. I want to try to bring out a book of poems, a new one, to be called *Drum-Taps*, and I want to come to New York for that purpose, too.

. . . I haven't given up the project of lecturing either, but whatever I do, I shall for the main thing devote myself for years to come to these wounded and sick, what little I can. . . .

Washington, March 22, 1864.

I am writing this in Major Hapgood's old office, corner 15th and F Streets, where I have my old table and window. It is dusty and chilly today, anything but agreeable. General Grant is expected every moment now in the Army of the Potomac to take active command. I have just this moment heard from the front—there is nothing yet of a movement, but each side is continually on the alert, expecting something to happen.

O mother, to think that we are to have here soon what I have seen so many times, the awful loads and trains and boatloads of poor, bloody, and pale and wounded young men again—for that is what we certainly will, and before very long. I see all the little signs, getting ready in the hospitals, etc.; it is dreadful when one thinks about it. I sometimes think over the sights I have myself seen: the arrival of the wounded after a battle, and the scenes on the field, too, and I can hardly believe my own recollections. What an awful thing war is! Mother, it seems not men but a lot of devils and butchers butchering each other. . . .

Washington, March 29, 1864.

. . . Mother, it was a dreadful night (last Friday night)—pretty dark, the wind gusty, and the rain fell in torrents. One poor boy—this is a sample of one case out of the six hundred—he seemed to be quite young, he was quite small (I looked at his body afterwards), he groaned some as the stretcher bearers were carrying him along, and again as they carried him through the hospital gate. They set down the stretcher and examined him, and the poor boy was dead. They took him into the ward, and the doctor came immediately, but it was all of no use.

The worst of it is, too, that he is entirely unknown—there was nothing on his clothes, or anyone with him to identify him, and he is altogether unknown. Mother, it is enough to rack one's heart—such things. Very likely his folks will never know in the world what was become of him. Poor, poor child, for he appeared as though he could be but eighteen.

I feel lately as though I must have some intermission. I feel well and hearty enough, and was never better, but my feelings are kept in a painful condition a great part of the time. Things get worse and worse as to the amount and sufferings of the sick, and, as I have said before, those who have to do with them are getting more and more callous and indifferent. Mother, when I see the common soldiers, what they go through, and how everybody seems to try to pick upon them, and what humbug there is over them every how, even the dying soldier's money stolen from his body by some scoundrel attendant, or from [the] sick one, even from under his head—which is a common thing—and then the agony I see every day, I get almost frightened at the world. . . . I will try to write more cheerfully next time —but I see so much. Well, goodbye for present, dear mother.

Washington, Tuesday noon, April 19, 1864.

. . . I went down to the Capitol the nights of the debate on the expulsion of Mr. Long last week. They had night sessions, very late. I like to go to the House of Representatives at night; it is the most magnificent hall, so rich and large, and lighter at night than it is days, and still not a light visible—it comes through the glass roof—but the speaking and the ability of the members is nearly always on a low scale.

It is very curious and melancholy to see such a rate of talent there, such tremendous times as these—I should say about the same range of genius as our old friend, Dr. Swaim, just about. You may think I am joking, but I am not, mother—I am speaking in perfect earnest. The Capitol grows upon one in time, especially as they have got the great figure on top of it now, and you can see it very well. It is a great bronze figure, the Genius of Liberty, I suppose. It looks wonderful towards sundown. I love to go and look at it. The sun when it is nearly down shines on the headpiece and it dazzles and glistens like a big star; it looks quite curious. . . .

. . . We have commenced on another summer, and what it will bring forth who can tell? The campaign of this summer is expected here to be more active and severe than any yet. As I told you in a former letter, Grant is determined to bend everything to take Richmond and break up the banditti of scoundrels that have stuck themselves up there as a "government." He is in earnest about it; his whole soul and all his thoughts night and day are upon it. He is probably the most in earnest of any man in command or in the Government either—that's something, ain't it, mother?—and they are bending everything to fight for their last chance—calling in their forces from Southwest, etc. . . .

Washington, April 26, 1864.

. . . Burnside's army passed through here yesterday. I saw George and walked with him in the regiment for some distance and had quite a talk. He is very well; he is very much tanned and looks hardy. I told him all the latest news from home. George stands it very well, and looks and behaves the same noble and good fellow he always was and always will be. It was on Fourteenth Street. I watched three hours before the 51st came along. I joined him just before they came to where the President and General Burnside were standing with others on a balcony, and the interest of seeing me, etc., made George forget to notice the President and salute him. He was a little annoyed at forgetting it. I called his attention to it, but we had passed a little too far on, and George wouldn't turn round even ever so little.

However, there was a great many more than half the army passed without noticing Mr. Lincoln and the others, for there was a great crowd all through the streets, especially here, and the place where the President stood was not conspicuous from the rest.

The 9th Corps made a very fine show indeed. There were, I should think, five very full regiments of new black troops, under General Ferrero. They looked and marched very well. It looked funny to see the President standing with his hat off to them just the same as the rest as they passed by. Then there [were the] Michigan regiments; one of them was a regiment of sharpshooters, partly composed of Indians. Then there was a pretty strong force of artillery and a middling force of cavalry—many New York, Pennsylvania, Massachusetts, Rhode Island, regiments. All except the blacks were veterans [that had] seen plenty of fighting.

. . . It is very different to see a real army of fighting men, from one of those shows in Brooklyn, or New York, or on Fort Green. . . . It was a curious sight to see these ranks after rank of our own dearest blood of men, mostly young, march by, worn and sunburnt and sweaty, with well-worn clothes and thin bundles, and knapsacks, tin cups, and some with frying pans strapt over their backs, all dirty and sweaty, nothing real neat about them except their muskets, but they were all as clean and bright as silver.

They were four or five hours passing along, marching with wide ranks pretty quickly, too. It is a great sight to see an army twenty-five or thirty thousand on the march. They are all so gay, too. Poor fellows, nothing dampens their spirits. They all got soaked with rain the night before. I saw Fred McReady and Captain Sims and Colonel Le-Gendre, etc.

I don't know exactly where Burnside's army is going. Among other rumors it is said they [are] to go [with] the Army of the Potomac to act as a reserve force, etc. Another is that they are to make a flank march, to go round and get Lee on the side, etc.

I haven't been out this morning and don't know what news—we know nothing, only that there is without doubt to be a terrible campaign here in Virginia this summer, and that all who know deepest about it are very serious about it. Mother, it is serious times. I do not feel to fret or whimper, but in my heart and soul about our country, the forthcoming campaign with all its vicissitudes and the wounded and slain—I daresay . . . I feel the reality more than some because I am in the midst of its saddest results so much. Others may say what they like: I believe in Grant and in Lincoln, too. I think Grant deserves to be trusted. He is working continually. No one knows his plans; we will only know them when he puts them in operation. Our army is very large here in Virginia this spring, and they are still pouring in from east and west. You don't see about it in the papers, but we have a very large army here. . . .

I have given a Michigan soldier his breakfast with me. He relished it, too; he has just gone. Mother, I have just heard again that Burnside's troops are to be a reserve to protect Washington, so there may be something in it. . . .

Washington, April 28, 1864.

. . . I thought I would write you just a line, though I have nothing of importance—only the talk of the street here seems more and more to assert that Burnside's army is to remain near here to protect Washington and act as a reserve, so that Grant can move the Army of the Potomac upon Richmond, without being compelled to turn and be anxious about the Capital; also that Burnside can attend to Lee if the latter should send any force up west of here (what they call the Valley of the Shenandoah), or invade Pennsylvania again. I thought you would like to hear this; it looks plausible, but there are lots of rumors of all kinds. I cannot hear where Burnside's army is, as they don't allow the papers to print army movements, but I fancy they are very near Washington, the other side of Arlington Heights, this moment. . . .

2 o'clock, 28th April.

Just as I was going to mail this I received authentic information [that] Burnside's army is now about sixteen or eighteen miles south of here, at a place called Fairfax Court House. They had last night no orders to move at present, and I rather think they will remain there or near there. What I have written before as a rumor about their being to be held as a reserve, to act whenever occasion may need them, is now quite decided on. You may hear a rumor in

New York that they have been shipped in transports from Alexandria—there is no truth in it at all. Grant's Army of the Potomac is probably to do the heavy work. His army is strong and full of fight. Mother, I think it is today the noblest army of soldiers that ever marched—nobody can know the men as well as I do, I sometimes think. . . .

Washington, May 3, 1864.

. . . I have nothing different to write about the war or movements here. What I wrote last Thursday, about Burnside's Corps being probably used as a reserve, is still talked of here, and seems to be probable. A large force is necessary to guard the railroad between here and Culpepper, and also to keep from any emergency that might happen; and I shouldn't wonder if the 9th would be used for such purpose, at least for the present. I think the 51st must be down not very far from Fairfax Court House yet, but I haven't heard certain.

Mother, I have seen a person up from front this morning. There is no movement yet and no fighting started. The men are in their camps yet. General Grant is at Culpepper. You need not pay the slightest attention to such things as you mention in the *Eagle* about the 9th Corps—the writer of it, and very many of the writers on war matters in those papers, don't know one bit more on what they are writing about them Ed [1] does. . . .

Washington, May 6, 1864.

. . . I write you a few lines, as I know you feel anxious these times. The New York papers, I suppose, must have it in this morning that the Army of the Potomac has made a move and has crossed the Rapidan River. At any rate, that is the case.

As near as I can learn about Burnside's army that lies

[1] Whitman's brother.

157

in the rear of the Army of the Potomac (from Warrenton, Virginia, and so to Rappahannock River, and up toward Manassas), it still appears to be kept as a reserve and for emergencies, etc. I have not heard anything from the 51st. Mother, of course you got my letter of Tuesday, 3rd, with the letter from George dated Bristoe Station. I have writ to George since, and addressed the letter Warrenton, Va., or elsewhere, thinking he might get it.

. . . The idea is entertained quite largely here that the Rebel Army will retreat to Richmond, as it is well known that Grant is very strong (most folks say too strong for Lee). I suppose you know we menace them almost as much from up Fortress Monroe as we do from the Rapidan. Butler and W. F. Smith are down there with at least fifty or sixty thousand men, and will move up simultaneously with Grant. The occasion is very serious and anxious, but somehow I am full of hope, and feel that we shall take Richmond (I hope to go there yet before the hot weather is past). . . .

Monday, Washington, 2 o'clock, May 9, 1864.

. . . There is nothing from the army more than you know in the New York papers. The fighting has been hard enough, but the papers make lots of additional items, and a good deal that they just entirely make up. There are from six hundred to one thousand wounded coming up here— not six thousand to eight thousand as the papers have it. I cannot hear what part the 9th Corps took in the fight of Friday and afterwards, nor whether they really took any at all (they, the papers, are determined to make up just anything).

. . . So far as we get news here, we are gaining the day, so far *decidedly*. If the news we hear is true that Lee has been repulsed and driven back by Grant, and that we are masters of the field, and pursuing them—then I think Lee will retreat south and Richmond will be abandoned by the Rebs. But of course time only can develop what will happen.

Washington, May 10, '64 (half-past 2 p.m.).

. . . There is nothing perhaps more than you see in the New York papers. The fighting down in the field on the 6th I think ended in our favor, though with pretty severe losses to some of our divisions. The fighting is about seventy miles from here and fifty from Richmond—on the 7th and 8th, followed up by the Rebel Army hauling off, they say retreating, and Meade pursuing. It is quite mixed yet, but I guess we have the best of it. If we really have, Richmond is a goner, for they cannot do any better than they have done. The 9th Corps was in the fight, and where, I cannot tell yet, but from the wounded I have seen I don't think that corps was deeply in.

I have seen three hundred wounded. They came in last night. I asked for men of 9th Corps, but could not find any at all. These three hundred men were not badly wounded, mostly in arms, hands, trunk of body, etc. They could all walk, though some had an awful time of it. They had to fight their way with the worst in the middle out of the region of Fredericksburg, and so on, where they could get across the Rappahannock and get where they found transportation to Washington. The Government has decided (or rather General Meade has) to occupy Fredericksburg for depot and hospital (I think that is a first-rate decision), so the wounded men will receive quick attention and surgery, instead of being racked through the long journey up here. Still, many come in here. Mother, my impression is that we have no great reason for alarm or sadness about George so far. Of course, I *know* nothing. . . .

[Washington] May 12, half-past 5 p.m.

. . . George is all right, unhurt, up to Tuesday morning, 10th instant. The 51st was in a bad battle last Friday; lost twenty killed, between forty and fifty wounded. I have just seen some of the 51st wounded just arrived, one of them, Fred Saunders, Corporal Company K, George's company. He said when he left the 51st was in rear on guard duty. He left Tuesday morning last. The papers have it that Burnside's Corps was in a fight Tuesday, but I think it most probable the 51st was not in it.

Fred McReady is wounded badly, but not seriously. Sims is safe. You see, Le Gendre is wounded—he was shot through the bridge of the nose . . .

Washington, May 13, 1864, 2 o'clock p.m.

. . . The battle of Friday, 6th, was very severe. George's Company K lost one acting sergeant, Sturgis, killed; two men killed; four wounded. As I wrote yesterday, I have seen here Corporal Fred Saunders of Company K, who was wounded in side, nothing serious, in Friday's fight, and came up here. I also talked with Sergeant Brown, Company F, 51st, rather badly wounded in right shoulder. Saunders said when he left Tuesday morning he heard (or saw them there, I forget which) the 51st and its whole division were on guard duty toward the rear. The 9th Corps, however, has had hard fighting since, but whether the division or brigade the 51st is in was in the fights of Tuesday, 10th (a pretty severe one), or Wednesday, I cannot tell, and it is useless to make calculations—and the only way is to wait and hope for the best. As I wrote yesterday, there were some thirty of 51st Regiment killed and fifty wounded in Friday's battle, 6th inst. I have seen Colonel Le Gendre. He is here in Washington not far from where I am; 485 Twelfth Street is his address. Poor man, I feel sorry indeed for him. He is badly wounded and disfigured. He is shot through the bridge of the nose and left eye probably lost. I spent a little time with him this forenoon. He is suffering very much, spoke of George very kindly; said: "Your brother is well." His orderly told me he saw him, George, Sunday night last, well.

Fred McReady is wounded in hip, I believe bone fractured—bad enough, but not deeply serious. I cannot hear of his arrival here. If he comes I shall find him immediately and take care of him myself. He is probably yet at Fredericksburg, but will come up, I think. Yesterday and today the badly wounded are coming in. The long lists of *previous arrivals* (I suppose they are all reprinted at great length in New York papers) are of men, three fourths of them quite slightly wounded, and the rest hurt pretty bad.

. . . I see such awful things. I expect one of these days, if I live, I shall have awful thoughts and dreams—but it is such a great thing to be able to do some real good; assuage these horrible pains and wounds, and save life even—that's the only thing that keeps a fellow up. . . .

Washington, Monday forenoon, May 23, 1864.

. . . I suppose it is idle to say I think George's chances are very good for coming out of this campaign safe, yet at present it seems to me so—but it is indeed idle to say so, for no one can tell what a day will bring forth. Sometimes I think that should it come, when it *must* be, to fall in battle, one's anguish over a son or brother killed would be tempered with much to take the edge off. I can honestly say it has no terrors for me, if I had to be hit in battle, as far as I myself am concerned. It would be a noble and manly death, and in the best cause.

Then one finds, as I have the past year, that our feelings and imaginations make a thousand times too much of the whole matter. Of the many I have seen die, or known of, the past year, I have not seen or heard of *one* who met death with any terror. . . .

Washington, June 3, 1864.

. . . I think the news from the army is very good. You know, of course, that it is now very near Richmond indeed —from five to ten miles. . . . If this campaign was not in progress, I should not stop here, as it is now beginning to tell a little upon me—so many bad wounds, many putrefied and all kinds of dreadful ones I have been rather too much with—but as it is, I certainly remain here while the thing remains undecided. . . .

I saw Captain Baldwin of the 14th this morning; he has lost his left arm; is going home soon. Mr. Kalbfleisch and Anson Herrick (member of Congress from New York) came in one of the wards where I was sitting writing a letter this morning, in the midst of the wounded. Kalbfleisch was so much affected by the sight that he burst into tears. . . .

. . . Mother, I believe I am homesick—something new for me—then I have seen all the horrors of soldiers' life and not been kept up by its excitement. It is awful to see so much, and not be able to relieve it.

Washington, June 7, 1864.

. . . I cannot write you anything about the 51st, as I have not heard a word. I felt very much disturbed yesterday afternoon, as Major Hapgood came up from the paymaster general's office and said that news had arrived that Burnside was killed, and that the 9th Corps had had a terrible slaughter. He said it was believed at the paymaster general's office. Well, I went out to see what reliance there was on it. The rumor soon spread over town, and was believed by many —but, as near as I can make it out, it proves to be one of those unaccountable stories that get started these times.

Saturday night we heard that Grant was routed completely, etc. etc.—so that's the way stories fly. I suppose you hear the same big lies there in Brooklyn.

Well, the truth is sad enough, without adding anything to it—but Grant is not destroyed yet, but I think is going into Richmond yet, but the cost is terrible.

Mother, I have not felt at all well the last week. I had spells of deathly faintness and bad trouble in my head too, and sore throat (quite a little budget, ain't they?). My head was the worst, though, I don't know, the faint spells were not very pleasant—but I feel so much better this forenoon, I believe it has passed over.

There is a very horrible collection in Armory Building (in Armory-Square Hospital), about two hundred of the worst cases you ever see, and I had been probably too much with them. . . . Things are going pretty badly with the wounded. They are crowded here in Washington in immense numbers, and all those that come up from the Wilderness and that region arrived here so neglected and in such plight, it was awful (those that were at Fredericksburg and also from Ball Plain).

The papers are full of puffs, etc., but the truth is the largest proportion of worst cases get little or no attention. We receive them here with their wounds full of worms—some all swelled and inflamed. Many of the amputations have to be done over again. One new feature is that many of the poor afflicted young men are crazy. Every ward has some in it that are wandering. They have suffered too much, and it is perhaps a privilege that they are out of their senses. . . .

Washington, June 14, 1864.

. . . I am not feeling very well these days—the doctors have told me not to come inside the hospitals for the present. I send things and aid to some cases every day and hear from there also, but I do not go myself at present. It is probable that the hospital poison has affected my system, and I find it worse than I calculated. I have spells of faintness and very bad feeling in my head, fullness and pain—and besides sore throat. My boarding place, 502 Pennsylvania Avenue, is a miserable place—very bad air. But I shall feel better, I know—the doctors say it will pass over —they have long told me I was going in too strong. Some days I think it has all gone, and I feel well again, but in a few hours I have a spell again. . . . If I don't feel better before the end of this week or beginning of next, I may come home for a week or fortnight for a change . . . The rumor is very strong here that Grant is over the James River on south side—but it is not in the papers. . . .

Washington, June 17, 1864.

. . . I got your letter this morning. This place and the hospitals seem to have got the better of me. I do not feel so badly this forenoon—but I have bad nights and bad days too. Some of the spells are pretty bad—still I am up some and around every day. The doctors have told me for a fortnight that I must leave; that I need an entire change of air, etc. . . .

NOT YOUTH PERTAINS TO ME

Not youth pertains to me,
Nor delicatesse, I cannot beguile the time with talk,
Awkward in the parlor, neither a dancer nor elegant,
In the learn'd coterie sitting constrain'd and still, for learning inures
not to me,
Beauty, knowledge, inure not to me—yet there are two or three
things inure to me,
I have nourish'd the wounded and sooth'd many a dying soldier,
And at intervals waiting or in the midst of camp,
Composed these songs.

164

PENSIVE ON HER DEAD GAZING

Pensive on her dead gazing I heard the Mother of All,

Desperate on the torn bodies, on the forms covering the battle-
fields gazing,

(As the last gun ceased, but the scent of the powder-smoke
linger'd,)

As she call'd to her earth with mournful voice while she stalk'd,

Absorb them well O my earth, she cried, I charge you lose not my
sons, lose not an atom,

And you streams absorb them well, taking their dear blood,

And you local spots, and you airs that swim above lightly im-
palpable,

And all you essences of soil and growth, and you my rivers' depths,

And you mountain sides, and the woods where my dear children's
blood trickling redden'd,

And you trees down in your roots to bequeath to all future trees,

My dead absorb or South or North—my young men's bodies ab-
sorb, and their precious precious blood,

Which holding in trust for me faithfully back again give me many a
year hence,

In unseen essence and odor of surface and grass, centuries hence,

In blowing airs from the fields back again give me my darlings,
give my immortal heroes,

Exhale me them centuries hence, breathe me their breath, let not an
atom be lost,

O years and graves! O air and soil! O my dead, an aroma sweet!

Exhale them perennial sweet death, years, centuries hence.

'O My Soldiers, My Veterans'

Letters written, during the war for the most part, by Whitman to soldiers, or for soldiers to their families.

DIRGE FOR TWO VETERANS

The last sunbeam
Lightly falls from the finish'd Sabbath,
On the pavement here, and there beyond it is looking,
Down a new-made double grave.

Lo, the moon ascending,
Up from the east the silvery round moon,
Beautiful over the house-tops, ghastly, phantom moon,
Immense and silent moon.

I see a sad procession,
And I hear the sound of coming full-key'd bugles,
All the channels of the city streets they're flooding,
As with voices and with tears.

I hear the great drums pounding,
And the small drums steady whirring,
And every blow of the great convulsive drums,
Strikes me through and through.

For the son is brought with the father,
(In the foremost ranks of the fierce assault they fell,
Two veterans son and father dropt together,
And the double grave awaits them.)

Now nearer blow the bugles,
And the drums strike more convulsive,
And the daylight o'er the pavement quite has faded,
And the strong dead-march enwraps me.

In the eastern sky up-buoying,
The sorrowful vast phantom moves illumin'd,
('Tis some mother's large transparent face,
In heaven brighter growing.)

O strong dead-march you please me!
O moon immense with your silvery face you soothe me!
O my soldiers twain! O my veterans passing to burial!
What I have I also give you.

The moon gives you light,
And the bugles and the drums give you music,
And my heart, O my soldiers, my veterans,
My heart gives you love.

'O My Soldiers, My Veterans'

. . . I urged the men to write; and myself, when called upon, wrote all sorts of letters for them (including love letters, very tender ones). . . .

"*Fort Bennett, July 21, 1863. Adjutant General Thomas.*
General: I have the honor to forward this, my application for an officer's position in one of the Colored Regiments now forming in the District of Columbia. I have been in the military service of the government as a private since the beginning of the War—enlisted first in the 8th New York Militia 19th April, 1861, for three months—subsequently on the 25th August 1862, in the 2nd New York Artillery for three years—and am still in the regiment. I was born in the State of New York, am in sound health, and 26 years of age.
    Herewith please see testimonials from my officers.
    I have the honor General to remain, etc.
        Samuel S. Freyer,
        Co. E 2nd New York Vol. Artillery."

. . . I wrote hundreds of such similar letters for the boys —letters for their friends, for their folks—fathers, mothers, sweethearts. They were too sick to write, or not sure of themselves, or something. Why, I even said their prayers for them—some of them. What didn't I do? . . .

. . . Yes, it was from the midst of things to the midst of things. When I went to New York, I would write to the hospitals; when I was in the hospitals, I would write to New York. I could not forget the boys—they were too precious. . . .

Washington, March 19, 1863.

Dear Nat and Fred Gray: . . . Since I left New York I was down in the Army of the Potomac in front with my brother a good part of the winter, commencing time of the battle of Fredericksburg—have seen *war-life*, the real article—folded myself in a blanket, lying down in the mud with composure—relished salt pork and hard tack—have been on the battlefield among the wounded, the faint and the bleeding, to give them nourishment—have gone over with a flag of truce the next day to help direct the burial of the dead—have struck up a tremendous friendship with a young Mississippi captain (about 19) that we took prisoner, badly wounded at Fredericksburg—he has followed me here, is in the Emory Hospital here minus a leg—he wears his Confederate uniform, proud as the devil—I met him first at Falmouth, in the Lacy house middle of December last, his leg just cut off, and cheered him up—poor boy, he has suffered a great deal and still suffers—his eyes bright as a hawk, but face pale—our affection is an affair quite romantic—sometimes when I lean over to say I am going, he puts his arms around my neck, draws my face down, etc., quite a scene for the New Bowery.

I spent the Christmas holidays on the Rappahannock—during January came up hither, took a lodging room here.

Did the Thirty-seventh Congress, especially the night sessions the last three weeks; explored the Capitol, meandering the gorgeous painted interminable Senate corridors, getting lost in them (a new sensation, rich and strong, that endless painted interior at night)—got very much interested in some particular cases in hospitals here—go now steadily to more or less of said hospitals by day or night—find always the sick and dying soldiers forthwith begin to cling to me in a way that makes a fellow feel funny enough.

These hospitals, so different from all others—these thousands, and tens and twenties of thousands of American young men, badly wounded, all sorts of wounds, operated on, pallid with diarrhoea, languishing, dying with fever, pneumonia, etc., open a new world somehow to me, giving closer insights, new things, exploring deeper mines than any yet, showing our humanity. (I sometimes put myself in fancy in the cot, with typhoid, or under the knife) tried by terrible, fearfullest tests, probed deepest, the living soul's, the body's tragedies, bursting the petty bonds of art.

To these, what are your dramas and poems, even the oldest and the fearfullest? Not old Greek mighty ones where man contends with fate (and always yields)—not Virgil showing Dante on and on among the agonized and damned—approach what here I see and take part in. For here I see, not at intervals, but quite always, how certain man, our American man—how he holds himself cool and unquestioned, master above all pains and bloody mutilations. It is immense, the best thing of all—nourishes me, of all men. This then, what frightened us all so long? Why, it is put to flight with ignominy—a mere stuffed scarecrow of the fields. Oh death, where is thy sting? Oh grave, where is thy victory?

In the Patent Office, as I stood there one night, just off the cot-side of a dying soldier, in a large ward that had received the worst cases of Second Bull Run, Antietam and Fredericksburg, the surgeon, Dr. Stone (Horatio Stone, the sculptor) told me, of all who had died in that crowded ward the past six months, he had still to find the *first man* or *boy* who had met the approach of death with a single tremor of unmanly fear.

But let me change the subject—I have given you screed enough about death and the hospitals—and too much—since I got started. Only I have some curious yarns I promise you, my darlings and gossips, by word of mouth whene'er we meet.

Washington and its points, I find, bear a second and a third perusal, and doubtless many. My first impressions, architectural, etc., were not favorable; but upon the whole, the city, the spaces, buildings, etc. make no unfit emblem of our country—so far, so broadly planned, everything in plenty, money and materials staggering with plenty, but the fruit of the plans, the knit, the combination yet wanting —determined to express ourselves greatly in a Capitol but no fit Capital yet here (time, associations, wanting, I suppose) many a hiatus yet—many a thing to be taken down and done over again—perhaps an entire change of base— maybe a succession of bases.

Congress does not seize very hard upon me; I studied it and its members with curiosity, and long—much gab, much fear of public opinion, plenty of low business talent, but no masterful man in Congress (probably best so). I think well of the President. He has a face like a Hoosier Michelangelo—so awful ugly it becomes beautiful—with its strange mouth, its deep-cut, crisscross lines, and its doughnut complexion. My notion is, too, that underneath his outside smutched mannerism, and stories from third-class county barrooms (it is his humor), Mr. Lincoln keeps a fountain of first-class practical telling wisdom.

I do not dwell on the supposed failures of his government; he has shown, I sometimes think, an almost supernatural tact in keeping the ship afloat at all, with head steady—not only not going down—and now certain not to—but with

proud and resolute spirit, and flag flying in sight of the
world, menacing and high as ever. I say never yet captain,
never ruler, had such a perplexing, dangerous task as his
the past two years. I more and more rely upon his idiomatic
western genius, careless of court dress or court decorum.

I am living here without much definite aim (except going
to the hospitals)—yet I have quite a good time—I make
some money by scribbling for the papers, and as copyist.
I have had (and have) thoughts of trying to get a clerk-
ship or something, but I only try in a listless sort of a way,
and of course do not succeed. I have strong letters of intro-
duction from Mr. Emerson to Mr. Seward and Mr. Chase,
but I have not presented them. I have seen Mr. Summer
several times anent my office hunting—he promised fair
once—but he does not seem to be finally fascinated.

I hire a bright little third-story front room, with service,
etc., for seven dollars a month, dine in the same house (394
L Street, a private house)—and remain yet much of the old
vagabond that so gracefully becomes me. I miss you all,
my darlings and gossips, Fred Gray, and Bloom, and
Russell, and everybody. I wish you would all come here in
a body—that would be divine (we would drink ale, which
is here the best).

My health, strength, personal beauty, etc. are, I am
happy to inform you, without diminution, but on the con-
trary quite the reverse. I weigh full 220 pounds avoirdupois,
yet still retain my usual perfect shape—a regular model.
My beard, neck, etc., are woolier, fleecier, whiteyer than
ever. I wear army boots with magnificent black morocco
tops, the trousers put in, wherein, shod and legged, con-
front I Virginia's deepest mud with supercilious eyes.

The scenery around Washington is really fine, the Poto-
mac a lordly river, the hills, woods, etc. all attractive. I
poke about quite a good deal. Much of the weather here is
from heaven—of late, though, a stretch decidedly from

the other point. Tonight (for it is night, about 10) I sit alone writing this epistle (which will doubtless devour you all with envy and admiration) in a room adjoining my own particular. A gentleman and his wife who occupy the two other apartments on this floor have gone to see Heron in "Medea"—have put their little child in bed and left me in charge. The little one is sleeping soundly there in the back room, and I (plagued with a cold in the head) sit here in the front by a good fire, writing as aforesaid to my gossips and darlings. The evening is lonesome and still; I am entirely alone—"Oh, Solitude where are the charms, etc."

Now you write to me good long letters, my own boys. You, Bloom, give me your address particular, dear friend. Tell me Charles Russell's address, particular—also write me about Charles Chauncey. Tell me about everybody. For, dearest gossips, as the hart panteth, etc., so my soul after any and all sorts of items about you all. My darling, dearest boys, if I could be with you this hour, long enough to take only just three mild hot rums, before cool weather closes.

Friday morning, 20th. I finish my letter in the office of Major Hapgood, a paymaster, and a friend of mine. This is a large building filled with paymasters' offices, some thirty or forty or more. This room is up on the fifth floor (a most noble and broad view from my window), curious scenes around here—a continual stream of soldiers, officers, cripples, etc., some climbing wearily up the stairs. They seek their pay, and every hour, almost every minute, has its incident, its hitch, its romance, farce, or tragedy.

There are two paymasters in this room. A sentry at the street door, another halfway up the stairs, another at the chief clerk's door, all with muskets and bayonets—sometimes a great swarm, hundreds around the sidewalk in front waiting (everybody is waiting for something here). I take a pause, look up a couple of minutes from my pen and

paper—see spread, off there, the Potomac, very fine, nothing petty about it—the Washington monument, not half finished—the public grounds around it filled with ten thousand beeves on the hoof—to the left the Smithsonian with its brown turrets—to the right, far across, Arlington Heights, the forts, eight or ten of them—then the long bridge, and down a ways, but quite plain, the shipping of Alexandria. Opposite me, and in a stone throw, is the Treasury building, and below, the bustle and life of Pennsylvania Avenue. I shall hasten with my letter, and then go forth and take a stroll down "the avenue," as they call it here.

Now you boys, don't you think I have done the handsome thing by writing this astoundingly magnificent letter —certainly the longest I ever wrote in my life? Fred, I wish you to present my best respects to your father, Bloom and all; one of these days we will meet and make up for lost time, my dearest boys.

21 April 1863.

. . . I thought I would write you [Tom Sawyer] a few words, and take chances of its getting to you—though there is great excitement now about the Army of the Potomac, no passes allowed, mails held over, etc., etc.: still I thought I would write, and take chances.

There is nothing very special here about Washington; they seem to be shoving troops off from here now all the time in small or large bodies. The convalescents are doing guard duty, etc. in the hospitals—even the old regiments doing patrol and provost are sent off, so I suppose something is up.

Tom, I was at Armory last evening; saw Lewy Brown; sat with him a good while. He was very cheerful; told me how he laid out to do when he got well enough to go from the hospital (which he expects soon); says he intends to go to home to Maryland—go to school and learn to write better, and learn a little bookkeeping, etc., so that he can be fit for some light employment.

Lew is so good, so affectionate; when I came away he reached up his face; I put my arm around him, and we gave each other a long kiss, half a minute long. We talked about you while I was there. I saw Hiram, but did not speak to him. He lay pale and pretty sick, sound asleep. I could not help stopping before I came away and looking at him—it was pitiful to see him so pale, sound asleep. Poor Hiram— he is a good boy—he gets no better. Johnny Mahay does not get any better—in Ward E. He is going to have an operation performed on him by Dr. Bliss. Tom, I do not know who you was most intimate with in the hospital or I would write you about them.

As to me, there is nothing new with me or my affairs. I manage to pay my way here in Washington—what I make writing letters for the New York papers, etc. When I stopped here last January on my return from Falmouth, I thought I would stop only a few days, before returning to New York, and see if I could not get some berth, clerkship, or something; but I have not pushed strong enough; have not got anything; and I don't now as I could be satisfied with the life of a clerk in the departments anyhow. So I have hung along here ever since. I guess I enjoy a kind of vagabond life anyhow. I go around some nights, when the spirit moves me, sometimes to the gay places just to see the sights. Tom, I wish you was here—somehow I don't find the comrade that suits me to a dot—and I won't have any other—not for good.

Well, Tom, the war news is not lovely, is it? We feel disappointed here about Charleston—I felt as blue about it as anybody. I was so in hopes they would take the conceit out of that gassy city. It seems to me always as if Charleston has done the biggest business of blowing and mischief on a small capital of industry or manliness of any city the world ever knew.

But for all our bad success at Charleston, and even if we fail for a while elsewhere, I believe this Union will conquer in the end, as sure as there's a God in heaven. This country can't be broken up by Jeff Davis and all his damned crew. Tom, I sometimes feel as if I didn't want to live—life would have no charm for me, if this country should fail after all and be reduced to take a third-rate position—to be domineered over by England and France and the haughty nations of Europe, etc., and we unable to help ourselves. But I have no thought that this will ever be; this country—I hope—would spend her last drop of blood and last dollar rather than submit to such humiliation.

O, I hope Hooker will have good success in his plans, whatever they may be. We have been foiled so often in our plans—it seems as though it was too much. And our noble Army of the Potomac—so brave, so capable, so full of good men—I really believe they are this day the best in the world. God grant Hooker may have success, and his brave boys may at last achieve the victory they deserve. O how much I think about them though! (I suppose that does no good.)

Tom, you tell the boys of your company there is an old pirate up in Washington, with the white wool growing all down his neck—an old comrade who thinks about you and them every day, for all he don't know them and will probably never see them—but thinks about them as comrades and younger brothers of his—just the same. My old mother, in Brooklyn, New York, when she sees the troops marching away or returning, always begins to cry.

[*July, 1863*]

. . . You [Tom Sawyer] did not write any answer to my last two letters now quite a while ago; still, I will write again. I still remain here in Washington finding just about work enough to pay my expenses. Occasionally I go to Armory Hospital. I see Lewy Brown always; he has returned from his furlough. He told me a few days ago he had written to you, and had sent you my best respects. —I told him he must never send my respects to you but always my love. Lewy's leg has not healed; gives him trouble yet. He goes around with crutches, but not very far. He is the same good young man as ever, and always will be.

Well Tom, it looks as though Secesh was nearly played out—if they lose Charleston, as I believe they will soon, seems to me they may as well give it up. Some think that Lee will make another dash up this way, but I should think Gettysburg might last him a while yet.

Dear brother, how I should like to see you and would like to know how things have gone with you for three months past! I can't understand why you have ceased to correspond with me. Anyhow, I hope we shall meet again and have some good times. So, dearest comrade, good-bye for present and God bless you.

October 8, 1863.

Dear Hugo: I don't know why I have delayed so long as a month to write to you, for your affectionate and lively letter of September 5th gave me as much pleasure as I ever received from correspondence. I read it [every day?], and have taken the liberty to show it to one or two persons I knew would be interested.

Dear comrade, you must be assured that my heart is much with you in New York and with my other dear friends, your associates—and, my dear, I wish you to excuse me to Fred Gray and to Perk and Ben Knower for not yet writing to them—also to Charley Kingsley, should you see him. I am contemplating a tremendous letter to my dear comrade

Frederickus which will make up for deficiencies—my own comrade Fred—how I should like to see him and have a good heart's time with him and a mild orgy—just as a basis, you know, for talk and interchange of reminiscences and the play of the quiet lambent electricity of real friendship.

O Hugo, as my pen glides along writing these thoughts, I feel as if I could not delay coming right off to New York and seeing you all—you and Fred and Bloom and everybody—I want to see you, to be within hands' reach of you, and hear your voices, even if only for one evening for only three hours. I want to hear Perk's fiddle—I want to hear Perk himself (and I will humbly submit to drink to the Church of England); I want to be with Bloom (that wretched young man who I hear continually adorns himself outwardly, but I hear nothing of the interior); and I want to see Charley Russell, and if he is in New York [and] you see him, I wish you to say that I sent him my love, particular; and that he and Fred and Charles Chauncey remain a group of itself in the portrait-gallery of my heart and mind yet and forever—for so it happened for our dear times, when we first got acquainted (we recked not of them as they passed) were so good, so hearty, those friendship times—our talk, our knitting together—it may be a whim, but I think nothing could be better or quieter and more happy of the kind—and is there any better kind in life's experiences?

Dear comrade, I still live here as a hospital missionary after my own style and on my own hook—I go every day or night without fail to some of the great government hospitals. O the sad scenes I witness—scenes of death, anguish, the fevers, amputations, friendlessness, hungering and thirsting young hearts, for some loving presence—such noble young men as some of these wounded are—such endurance, such native decorum, such candor—I will confess to you, dear Hugo, that in some respects I find myself

181

in my element amid these scenes—shall I not say to you that I find I supply often to some of these dear suffering boys in my presence and magnetism that which nor doctors, nor medicines, nor skill, nor any routine assistance can give?

Dear Hugo, you must write to me often as you can and not delay it—your letters are very dear to me. Did you see my newspaper letter in *New York Times* of Sunday, October 4? About my dear comrade Bloom, is he still out in Pleasant Valley? Does he meet you often? Do you and the fellows meet at Gray's or anywhere?

O, Hugo, I wish I could hear with you the current opera—I saw "Devereux" in the New York papers of Monday announced for that night, and I knew in all probability you would be there—tell me how it goes and about the principal singers—only don't run away with that theme and occupy too much of your letter with it, but tell me mainly about all my dear friends and every little personal item and what you all do and say, etc.

I am excellent well. I have cut my beard short and hair ditto (all my acquaintances are in anger and despair and go about wringing their hands); my face is all tanned and red. If the weather is moist, or has been lately, or looks as if it thought of going to be, I perambulate this land in big army boots outside and up to my knees. Then around my majestic brow, around my well-brimmed felt hat—a black and gold cord with acorns. Altogether the effect is satisfactory. The guards as I enter or pass places often salute me. All of which I tell, as you will of course take pride in your friend's special and expanding glory.

Fritschy, I am writing this in Major Hapgood's office, fifth story, by a window that overlooks all down the city and over and down the beautiful Potomac, and far across the hills and shores for many a mile. We have had superb weather lately, yes, for a month. It has just rained, so the dust is provided for (that is the only thing I dread in Washington—the dust—I don't mind the mud). It is now between one and two o'clock Thursday afternoon. I am much alone in this pleasant far-up room, as Major is absent sick, and the clerk lays off a good deal. From three to five hours a day or night I go regularly among the sick, wounded, dying—our men. I am enabled to give them things, food. There are very few visitors; amateurs now. It has become an old story. The suffering ones cling to me, poor children, very close. I think of coming to New York quite soon to stay perhaps three weeks; then, sure return here.

Washington, August 1, 1863.

. . . Both your letters have been received, Lewy; the second one came this morning and was welcome—as anything from you will always be, and the sight of your face welcomer than all, my darling. I see you write in good spirits and appear to have first-rate times. Lew, you must not go around too much, nor eat and drink too promiscuous, but be careful and moderate and not let the kindness of friends carry you away, lest you break down again, dear son.

I was at the hospital yesterday four or five hours, was in Ward K. Taber has been down sick, so he had to lay abed, but he is better now and goes around as usual. Curly is the same as usual; most of the others are the same. There have been quite a good many deaths. The young man who lay in Bed 2 with a very bad leg is dead. I saw Johnny Mahay in Ward E—poor fellow, he is very poorly, he is very thin and his face is like wax.

Lew, I must tell you what a curious thing happened in the Chaplain's house night before last—there had been a man in Ward I, named Lane, with two fingers amputated— very bad with gangrene—so they removed him to a tent by himself. Last Thursday his wife came to see him. She seemed a nice woman, very poor. She stopped at the Chaplain's. About three o'clock in the morning she got up and went to the sink, and there she gave birth to a child, which fell down the sink into the sewer runs beneath. Fortunately the water was not turned on; the Chaplain got up, carried Mrs. Lane out, and then roused up a lot of men from the hospital. With spades, etc. they dug a trench outside and got into the sink and took out the poor little child. It lay there on its back in about two inches of water. —Well, strange as it may seem, the child was alive (it fell about five feet through the sink), and is now living and likely to live, is quite bright, has a head of thick black hair. The Chaplain took me in yesterday, showed me the child; and Mrs. Jackson, his wife, told me the whole story, with a good deal I haven't told you, and then she treated me to a good plate of ice cream—so I stayed there nearly an hour and had quite a pleasant visit. Mrs. Lane lay in an adjoining room.

Lew, as to me and my affairs, there is nothing very new or important—I have not succeeded in getting any employment here, except that I write a little (newspaper correspondence, etc.), barely enough to pay my expenses—but it is my fault, for I have not tried enough for anything. The last three weeks I have not felt very well—for two or three days I was down sick, for the first time in my life (as I have never before been sick). I feel pretty fair today; I go round most every day the same as usual. I have some idea of giving myself a furlough of three or four weeks and going home to Brooklyn, N.Y., but I should return again to Washington, probably.

Lew, it is pretty hot weather here and the sun affects me (I had a sort of sunstroke about five years ago). You speak of being here in Washington again about the last of August. O how glad I should be to see you, to have you with me. I have thought that if it could be so that you and one other person and myself could be where we could work and live together and have each other's society, we three, I should like it so much—but it is probably a dream.

Well, Lew, they had the great battle of Gettysburg, but it does not seem to have settled anything, except to have killed and wounded a great many thousand men. It seems as though the two armies were falling back again to near their old positions on the Rappahannock. It is hard to tell what will be the next move, yet, Lewy, I think we shall conquer yet. I don't believe it is destined that this glorious Union is to be broken up by all the Secesh South or Copheads either.

Well, my darling, I have scribbled you off something to show you where I am and that I have received your welcome letters—but my letter is not of much interest, for I don't feel very bright today. Dear son, you must write me whenever you can—take opportunity—when you have nothing to do and write me a good long letter. Your letters and your love for me are very precious to me, for I appreciate it all, Lew, and give you the like in return. It is now about 3 o'clock, and I will go out and mail this letter and then go and get my dinner—so goodbye, Lewy—goodbye, my dear son and comrade, and I hope it will prove God's will that you get well and sound yet, and have many good years yet. . . ."

Washington, August 7, 1863.

. . . Well, Hugo, I am still as much as ever, indeed more. in the great military hospitals here. Every day or night I spend four, five, or six hours among my sick, wounded, prostrate boys. It is fascinating, sad, and with varied fortune, of course. Some of my boys get well, some die. . . . I am welcomed by the surgeons as by the soldiers—very grateful to me. . . .

Let me see, Hugo. I will not write anything about the

185

topics of the horrible riots of last week, nor General Meade nor Vicksburg, nor Charleston—I have to leave them to the newspapers. Nor will I write you this time as much about hospitals as I did last. Tell Fred his letter was received. I appreciate it, received real pleasure from it— 'twas a true friend's letter, characteristic, full of vivacity, off-hand, and, below all, a thorough base of genuine remembrance and good will. Was not wanting in the sentimental either (so I take back all about the apostate, do you understand, Freddy, my dear?), and only write this for you till I reply to that said letter a good long and special measure to yourself.

. . . Tell Nat Bloom that if he expects to provoke me into a dignified not mentioning him nor writing anything about him, by his studious course of heartbreaking neglect (which has already reduced me to a skeleton of but little over two hundred pounds and a countenance of raging hectic, indicating an early grave), I was determined not to do anything of the sort, but shall speak of him every time, and send him love, just as if he were adorned with faithful troth instead of (as I understood) beautiful whiskers. Does he think that beautiful whiskers can fend off the pangs of remorse? In conclusion, I have to say, Nathaniel, you just keep on, if you think there's no hell.

Hugo, I suppose you were at Charles Channing's funeral —tell me all you hear about the particulars of his death . . . tell me of course about the boys—what you do, say, anything, everything.

Hugo, write oftener—you express your thoughts perfectly—do you know how much more agreeable to me is the conversation or writing that does not take hard paved tracks, the usual and stereotyped, but has little peculiarities and even kinks of its own, making its genuineness—its vitality? Dear friend, your letters are precious to me— none I have ever received from anyone are more so.

Ah, I see in your letter, Hugo, you speak of my being reformed—no, I am not so frightfully reformed either, only the hot weather here does not admit of drinking heavy drinks, and there is no good lager here—then besides I have no society—I expect to prove to you and all yet that I am no backslider. But here I go nowhere for mere amusement, only occasionally a walk.

And Charles Russell—how I should like to see him—how like to have one of our old times again! Ah Fred and you, dear Hugo, and you, repentant one with the dark shining whiskers—must there not be an hour, an evening, in the future when we four returning, concentrating New York-ward or elsewhere, shall meet, allowing no interloper, and have our drinks and things, and resume the chain, and consolidate and achieve a night better and mellower than ever—we four?

Hugo, I wish you to give my love to all the boys. I received a letter from Ben Knower, very good—I shall answer it soon. Give my love to Ben; if Charles Kingsley is in town, same to him—ditto Mullen—ditto Perk (I hope to hear that sweet fiddler one of these days, that strain, again). I wish to have Fred Gray say something for me, giving my love to his mother and father—I bear them both in mind— I count on having good interviews with them when I see New York. . . .

. . . My honest thanks to you, Hugo, for your letter posting me up not only about yourself but about my dear boys, Fred, Nat Bloom—always so welcome to me to hear personally or in any way and every item about them. Dear friend, the same evening I received your letter, I saw in the New York papers (which get here about five every evening) the announcement of Charles Chauncey's death. When I went up to my room that night towards eleven, I took a seat by the open window in the splendid soft moonlit night and, there alone by myself, I devoted (as is my custom sometimes under such circumstances) to the dead boy the silent cheerful tribute of an hour or so of floating thought about him, and whatever rose up from the thought of him—his looks, his handsome face, his hilarious fresh ways, his sunny smile, his voice, his blonde hair, his talk, his caprices—the way he and I first met—how we spoke together impromptu, no introduction; and then our easy falling into intimacy—he, with his affectionate heart, thought so well of me, and I loved him then and love him now.

I thought over our meetings together, our drinks and groups so friendly, our suppers with Fred and Charley Russell etc., off by ourselves at some table, at Pfaff's, off the other end. O how charming those early times, adjusting our friendship, I to the three others, although it needed little adjustment—for I believe we all loved each other more than we supposed! Chauncey was frequently the life and the soul of these gatherings—was full of sparkle, and so good, really witty—then, for an exception, he would have a mood come upon him, and right after the outset of our party, he would grow still and cloudy and up and unaccountably depart—but these were seldom. Then I got to occasionally quite a long walk with him, only us two, and then he would talk well and freely about himself, his experiences, feelings, quite confidential, etc. All these I resumed, sitting by myself. Hugo, that's the way I sat there Wednesday night till after midnight (the pleasant Virginia breeze coming up the Potomac) and, certainly without what they call mourning, thought of the boy. That's often my little way of celebrating the death of my friends.

Dear Hugo, you speak of your all remembering me and wishing to see me. It would be happiness for me to be with you all at one of your friendly meetings, especially at Fred's room, so pleasant, with its effect, I remember, of pictures, fine color, etc., to have the delight of my dear boys' company and their gayety and electricity, their precious friendship, the talk and laughter, the drinks, me surrounded by you all (so I will for a moment fancy myself), tumbled upon by you all with all sorts of kindness, smothered with you all in your hasty, thoughtless, magnificent way, overwhelmed with questions. Walt this, Walt that, and Walt everything.

Ah, if one could float off to New York this afternoon! It is Sunday afternoon now, and perhaps you are at this moment gathered at Fred's or at your house, and having a good time. I suppose you were at Charles Chauncey's funeral—tell me about it and all particulars about his death. When you write, tell.

Washington, August 10, 1863. Mr. and Mrs. Haskell.
Dear Friends: I thought it would be soothing to you to have a few lines about the last days of your son Erastus Haskell, of Company K 141st New York Volunteers—I write in haste, but I have no doubt anything about Erastus will be welcome.

From the time he came into Armory-Square, until he died, there was hardly a day but I was with him a portion of the time—if not in the day, then at night (I am merely a friend visiting the wounded and sick soldiers). From almost the first I felt somehow that Erastus was in danger, or at least was much worse than they supposed in the hospital. As he made no complaint, they thought him nothing so bad. I told the doctor of the ward over and over again he was a very sick boy, but he took it lightly, and said he would certainly recover; he said: "I know more about these fever cases than you do—he looks very sick to you, but I shall bring him out all right."

Probably the doctor did his best; at any rate, about a

week before Erastus died, he got really alarmed, and after that he and all the doctors tried to help him, but it was too late. Very possibly it would not have made any difference. I think he was broken down before he came to hospital here.

I believe he came here about July 11th; I took to him. He was a quiet young man, behaved always so correct and decent, said little. I used to sit on the side of his bed. I said once, jokingly, "You don't talk much, Erastus, you leave me to do all the talking." He only answered quietly, "I was never much of a talker."

The doctor wanted every one to cheer him up very lively; I was always pleasant and cheerful with him, but never tried to be lively. Only I tried once to tell him amusing narratives, etc., but after I had talked a few minutes, I saw that the effect was not good, and after that I never tried it again. I used to sit by the side of his bed, generally silent. He was oppressed for breath and with the heat, and I would fan him. Occasionally he would want a drink; some days he dozed a good deal; sometimes when I would come in, he woke up, and I would lean down and kiss him. He would reach out his hand and pat my hair and beard as I sat on the bed and leaned over him—it was painful to see the working in his throat to breathe.

They tried to keep him up by giving him stimulants, wine, etc. These affected him, and he wandered a good deal of the time—I would say, "Erastus, don't you remember me? don't you remember my name, dear son?" Once he looked at me quite a while when I asked him; he mentioned over a name or two (one sounded like Mr. Satchell), and then he said sadly, quite slow, as if to himself: "I don't remember—I don't remember—I don't remember." It was quite pitiful.

One thing was that he could not talk very comfortably at any time—his throat and chest were bad. I have no doubt he had some complaint beside the typhoid. In my limited talks with him, he told me about his brothers and sisters and his parents; wished me to write to them and send them all his love. I think he told me about his brothers being away, living in New York City or elsewhere.

From what he told me, I take it that he had been poorly for several months before he came. The first week in July, I think, he told me he was at the regimental hospital, at a place called Baltimore Corners, down not very many miles from White House, on the Peninsula. For quite a long time previous, although he kept around, he was not well; didn't do much; was in the band as fifer. While he lay sick here he had the fife on the little stand by his cot. He once told me that if he got well, he would play me a tune on it, "but," he says, "I am not much of a player yet."

I was very anxious he should be saved, and so were they all; he was well used by attendants; he was tanned and looked well in the face when he came; was in pretty good flesh; never complained; behaved manly and proper. I assure you I was attracted to him very much. —Some nights I sat by his cot till far into the night. The lights would be put out and I sat there silently hour after hour. He seemed to like to have me sit there, but he never cared much to talk.

I shall never forget those nights, in the dark hospital. It was a curious and solemn scene, the sick and wounded lying all around, and this dear young man close by me, lying on what proved to be his deathbed. I do not know his past life, but what I saw and know of, he behaved like a noble boy. I feel if I could have seen him under right circumstances of health, etc., I should have got much attached to him. He made no display or talk; he met his fate like a man. I think you have reason to be proud of such a son and all his relatives have cause to treasure his memory.

He is one of the thousands of our unknown American young men in the ranks about whom there is no record or fame, no fuss made about their dying unknown, but who are the real precious and royal ones of this land, giving up—aye even their young and precious lives—in the country's cause. Poor dear son, though you were not my son, I felt to love you as a son what short time I saw you, sick and dying there.

But it is well as it is—perhaps better. Who knows whether he is not far better off, that patient and sweet young soul, to go, than we are to stay? Farewell, deary boy, it was my opportunity to be with you in your last days. I had no chance to do much for you; nothing could be done—only you did not lay there among strangers without having one near who loved you dearly, and to whom you gave your dying kiss.

Mr. and Mrs. Haskell, I have thus written rapidly whatever came up about Erastus, and must now close. Though we are strangers and shall probably never see each other, I send you and all Erastus' brothers and sisters my love. I live when at home in Brooklyn, New York, in Portland Avenue, fourth floor, north of Myrtle.

. . . As I write I sit in a large, pretty well-filled ward by the cot of a lad of eighteen belonging to Company M, 2nd New York Cavalry, wounded three weeks ago at Culpepper—hit by fragment of a shell in the leg below the knee—a large part of the calf of the leg is torn away. (It killed his horse). Still, no bones broken, but a pretty large ugly wound. I have been writing to his mother at Comac, Suffolk Co., N.Y. She must have a letter just as if from him about every three days. It pleases the boy very much; he has four married sisters—them also I have to write to occasionally.

Although so young, he has been in many fights and tells me shrewdly about them, but only when I ask him. He is a cheerful, good-natured child—has to lie in bed constantly, his leg in a box. I bring him things; he says little or nothing in the way of thanks; is a country boy; always smiles and brightens much when I appear; looks straight in my face and never at what I may have in my hand for him.

. . . Poor young men, how many have I seen and known; how pitiful it is to see them! One must be calm and cheerful; not let on how their case really is; must stop much with them; find out their idiosyncrasies—do anything for them —nourish them, judiciously give them right things to drink —bringing in the affections; soothe them, brace them up, kiss them, discard all ceremony, and fight for them, as it were, with all weapons. I need not tell your womanly soul that such work blesses him that works as much as the object of it. I have never been happier than in some of these hospital ministering hours.

It is now between eight and nine evening—the atmosphere is rather solemn here tonight. There are some very sick men here; the scene is a curious one. The ward is perhaps 120 or 130 feet long; the cots each have their white mosquito curtains—all is quiet. Still an occasional sigh or groan. Up in the middle of the ward the lady nurse sits at a little table with a shaded lamp, reading—the walls, roof, etc. are all whitewashed; the light up and down the ward from a few gas burners about half turned down. . . .

Brooklyn, Nov. 8, 1863.

Dear son and comrade and all my dear comrades in the hospital: I sit down this pleasant Sunday forenoon intending to write you all a good stout letter to try to amuse you, as I am not able at present to visit you like I did. Yet what

I shall write about I hardly know until I get started—but, my dear comrades, I wish to help you pass away the time, for a few minutes anyhow. . . .

Lew, I wish you was here with me, and I wish my dear comrade Elijah Fox in Ward G was here with me, but perhaps he is on his way to Wisconsin. Lewy, I came through from Washington to New York by day train, 2nd November, had a very pleasant trip, everything went lovely, and I got home in the evening between eight and nine. Next morning I went up to the polls bright and early. I suppose it is not necessary to tell you how I voted. We have gained great victory in the city—it went Union this time, though it went Democratic strong only a year ago, and for many years past. All through the state the election was a very big thing for the Union—I tell you the Copperheads got flaxed out handsomely.

Indeed these late elections are about as great a victory for us as if we had flaxed General Lee himself and all his men. —And as for personal good will, I feel as if I could have more for Lee or any of his fighting men than I have for the Northern Copperheads.

Lewy, I was very glad to get your letter of the 5th—I want you to tell Oscar Cunningham in your ward that I sent him my love, and he must try to keep up good courage while he is confined there with his wounds. Lewy, I want you to give my love to Charley Care and all the boys in Ward K, and to Benton, if he is still there. I wish you would go in Ward C and see James O. Stilwell and also Thomas Carson in same ward, and Chambers that lays next to him, and tell them I sent them my love. Give Carson this letter to read if he wishes it. Tell James Stilwell I have writ from here to his folks in Comac, L.I., and it may be I shall go down there next week on the L.I. railroad; let him have this letter to read if he wishes it. Tell Manvill Winterstein that lays next to him in Ward C that I send him my love, and I hope his wound is healing good.

Lew, I wish you to go in Ward B and tell a young cavalry man (his first name is Edwin; he is wounded in the right arm) that I sent him my love; and on the opposite side a young man wounded in the right knee; and also a young man named Charley, wounded in left hand; and Jennings; and also a young man I love that lays now up by the door just above Jennings—that I sent them all my love. So, Lew, you see I am giving you a good round job, with so many messages; but I want you to do them all, dear son, and leave my letter with each of the boys that wish it, to read for themselves.

Tell Miss Gregg in Ward A that I send my love to Pleasant Barley, if he is still there, and if so, I hope it will be God's will that he will live and get strong to go home yet. I send my love to little Billy, the little Ohio boy in Ward A, and to Miss Gregg herself; and if Miss Doolittle is in Ward B, please ask her to tell the boys in the ward I sent them my love, and to her too, and give her this letter some evening to read to the boys; and one of these days I will come back and read to them myself . . . and the same to Mrs. Southwick in Ward H, if she wishes to read it to the boys for my sake.

Lew, I wish you would go in Ward G and find a very dear friend of mine in Bed 11, Elijah D. Fox, if he is still there. Tell him I sent him my best love and that I made reckoning of meeting him again, and that he must not forget me—though I know he never will. I want to hear how he is, and whether he has got his papers through yet. Lewy, I wish you would go to him first and let him have this letter to read, if he is there. Lewy, I would like you to give my love to a young man named Burns in Ward I, and to all the boys in Ward I—and indeed in every ward, from A to K inclusive, and all through the hospital, as I find I cannot particularize without being tedious. So I send my love to each and all, for every sick and wounded soldier is dear to me as a son or brother; and furthermore, every man that wears the Union uniform and sticks to it like a man is to me a dear comrade, and I will do what I can for him though it may not be much—and I will add that my mother and all my folks feel just the same about it, and would show it by their words too when they can.

Well, dear comrades, what shall I tell you to pass away the time? I am going around quite a great deal, more than I really desire to. Two or three nights ago I went to the New York Academy of Music, to the Italian opera. I suppose you know that is a performance, a play all in music and singing, in the Italian language, very sweet and beautiful. There is a large company of singers and a large band, altogether two or three hundred. It is a splendid great house, four or five tiers high, and a broad parquette on the main floor. The opera here now has some of the greatest singers in the world.

The principal lady singer (her name is Medori) has a voice that would make you hold your breath with wonder and delight—it is like a miracle—no mocking bird or clearest flute can begin with it—and besides she is a tall and handsome lady, and her actions are so graceful as she moves about the stage playing her part.

Boys, I must tell you just one scene in the opera I saw—things have worked so in the piece that this lady is compelled, although she tries very hard to avoid it, to give the cup of poisoned wine to her lover (the king, her husband, forces her to do it). She pleads hard, but her husband threatens to take both their lives (all this is in the singing and music, very fine); so the lover is brought in as a prisoner, and the king pretends to pardon him and make up, and asks the young man to drink a cup of wine, and orders the lady to pour it out. The lover drinks it, then the king gives her and him a look, and walks off the stage.

And now came as good a piece of performance as I ever saw in my life. The lady, as soon as she saw that her husband was really gone, sprang to her lover, clutched him by the arm, and poured out the greatest singing you ever heard—it poured like a raging river more than anything else I could compare it to—she tells him he is poisoned—he tries to inquire, etc., and hardly knows what to make of it—she breaks in, trying to pacify him and explain, etc. —all this goes on very rapid indeed, and the band accompanying. She quickly draws out from her bosom a little vial—to neutralize the poison—then the young man in his desperation abuses her and tells her perhaps it is to poison him still more, as she has already poisoned him once. This puts her in such agony, she begs and pleads with him to take the antidote at once, before it is too late—her voice is so wild and high it goes through him like a knife, yet it is delicious. She holds the little vial to his mouth with one hand, and with the other springs open a secret door in the wall for him to escape from the palace. He swallows the antidote, and, as she pushes him through the door, the husband returns with some armed guards; but she slams the door to, and stands back up against the door, and her arms spread wide open across it, one fist clenched and her eyes glaring like a wildcat, so they dare not touch her—and that ends this scene.

Comrades, recollect all this is in singing and music, and lots of it too, on a big scale; in the band, every instrument you can think and the best players in the world; and sometimes the whole band and the whole men's chorus and the women's chorus all putting on the steam together—and all in a vast house, light as day and with a crowded audience of ladies and men. Such singing and strong rich music always give me the greatest pleasure—and so the opera is the only amusement I have gone to, for my own satisfaction, for last ten years.

But my dear comrades, I will now tell you something about my own folks. Home here there is quite a lot of us. My father is not living; my dear mother is very well indeed for her age, which is sixty-seven. She is cheerful and hearty and still does all her light housework and cooking. She never tires of hearing about the soldiers, and I sometimes think she is the greatest patriot I ever met, one of the old stock. I believe she would cheerfully give her life for the Union, if it would avail anything—and the last mouthful in the house to any Union soldier that needed it. Then I have a very excellent sister-in-law—she has two fine young ones —so I am very happy in the women and family arrangements. Lewy, the brother I mentioned as sick, lives near here; he is very poorly indeed, and I fear will never be much better. He, too, was a soldier; has for several months had throat disease. He is married and has a family—I believe I have told you of still another brother in the army, down in the 9th Army Corps; has been in the service over two years. He is very rugged and healthy—has been in many battles, but only once wounded, at First Fredericksburg. . . .

Dear comrades, I did not finish my letter to you yesterday afternoon, as I had many friends come and see me. I will finish it now. The news this morning is that Meade is shoving Lee back upon Richmond, and that we have already given the Rebs some hard knocks there on the old Rappahannock fighting ground. O I do hope the army of the Potomac will at last gain a first-class victory, for they have had to retreat often enough—and yet I believe a better army never trod the earth than they are and have been for over a year.

Well, dear comrades, it looks so different here in all this

mighty city; everything going with a big rush and so gay, as if there was neither war nor hospitals in the land. New York and Brooklyn appear nothing but prosperity and plenty. Everywhere carts and trucks and carriages and vehicles on the go, loaded with goods; express wagons, omnibuses, cars, etc.—thousands of ships along the wharves, and the piers piled high, where they are loading or unloading the cargoes. All the stores crammed with everything you can think of, and the markets with all sorts of provisions; ten and hundreds of thousands of people everywhere—the population is one million five hundred thousand. Almost everybody well dressed and appearing to have enough.

Then the splendid river and harbor here, full of ships, steamers, sloops, etc.; then the great street Broadway, for four miles one continual jam of people, and the great magnificent stores all along on each side, and the show windows filled with beautiful and costly goods. I never saw the crowd thicker nor such goings-on and such prosperity; and as I passed through Baltimore and Philadelphia it seemed to be the same.

I am quite fond of crossing on the Fulton Ferry, or South Ferry, between Brooklyn and New York, on the big, handsome boats. They run continually day and night. I know most of the pilots, and I go up on deck and stay as long as I choose. The scene is very curious and full of variety. The shipping along the wharves looks like a forest of bare trees. Then there are all classes of sailing vessels and steamers, some of the grandest and most beautiful steamships in the world, going or coming from Europe, or on the California route, all these on the move. As I sit up there in the pilot house, I can see everything—the distant scenery and away down toward the sea and Fort Lafayette, etc. The ferryboat has to pick its way through the crowd. Often they hit each other—then there is a time.

199

My loving comrades, I am scribbling all this in my room in my mother's house. It is Monday forenoon—I have now been home a week in the midst of relations and many friends —many young men, some I have known from childhood, many I love very much. I am out quite a good deal, as we are glad to be with each other—they have entertainments, etc. But truly, my dear comrades, I never sit down, not a single time, to the beautiful dinners and suppers to which I am taken in this land of wealth and plenty without feeling it would be such a comfort to all, if you too, my dear and loving boys, could have each your share of the good things to eat and drink, and of the pleasure and amusement. My friends among the young men make supper parties, after which there is drinking, etc.—everything prodigal and first rate. One Saturday night and another last night—it is much pleasure; yet often in the midst of the profusion, the palatable dishes to eat, and the laughing and talking and liquors, etc., my thoughts silently turn to Washington, to all who lie there sick and wounded, with bread and molasses for supper.

Lewy, dear son, I think I shall remain here ten or twelve days longer and then I will try to be with you once again. If you feel like it, I would like to have you write me soon; tell me about the boys—especially James Stilwell, Pleasant Barley, Cunningham, and the cavalry boy, Edwin, in Ward B. Tell me whether Elijah Fox in Ward G has gone home. Lew, when you write to Tom Sawyer, you know what to say from me. He is one I love in my heart and always shall till death—and afterwards too. I wish you to tell a young man in Ward D, second bed below the middle door (his first name is Isaac; he is wounded in left leg and has had erysipelas) that I sent him my love and I wish him to have this letter to read if he desires it, and I will see him again before long. . . .

Well, Lewy, I must bid you goodbye for present, dear

son, and also to all the rest of my dear comrades, and I
pray God to bless you, my darling boys, and I send you all
my love, and I hope it will be so ordered as to let things go
as easy as possible with all my dear boys wounded or sick,
and I hope it will be God's will that we shall all meet again,
my dear and loving comrades, not only here but hereafter.

No poem sings, nor music sounds those deeds. No formal
generals' report, no newspaper printed, nor letter print, no
book printed for the library, no column in the paper em-
balms our boys, our brave dead and unnamed, my bravest
boys, our darlings, nor proudest warlike deeds. No pictures
give them. None has yet seen them. Their very names are
lost—the bravest of them, like the highest of them, spent
to the last strength—life, nature no more allowing there—
they have fallen in the dark wood unknown—the tide has
swept on and left them to die.

COME UP FROM THE FIELDS FATHER

Come up from the fields father, here's a letter from our Pete,
And come to the front door mother, here's a letter from thy dear
son.

Lo, 'tis autumn,
Lo, where the trees, deeper green, yellower and redder,
Cool and sweeten Ohio's villages with leaves fluttering in the
moderate wind,
Where apples ripe in the orchards hang and grapes on the trellis'd
vines,
(Smell you the smell of the grapes on the vines?
Smell you the buckwheat where the bees were lately buzzing?)

Above all, lo, the sky so calm, so transparent after the rain, and with
wondrous clouds,
Below too, all calm, all vital and beautiful, and the farm prospers
well.

Down in the fields all prospers well,
But now from the fields come father, come at the daughter's call,
And come to the entry mother, to the front door come right away.
Fast as she can she hurries, something ominous, her steps trembling,
She does not tarry to smooth her hair nor adjust her cap.

Open the envelope quickly,
O this is not our son's writing, yet his name is sign'd,
O a strange hand writes for our dear son, O stricken mother's soul!
All swims before her eyes, flashes with black, she catches the main
   words only,
Sentences broken, *gunshot wound in the breast, cavalry skirmish,
   taken to hospital,*
At present low, but will soon be better.

Ah now the single figure to me,
Amid all teeming and wealthy Ohio with all its cities and farms,
Sickly white in the face and dull in the head, very faint,
By the jamb of a door leans.

Grieve not so, dear mother, (the just-grown daughter speaks
   through her sobs,
The little sisters huddle around speechless and dismay'd,)
See, dearest mother, the letter says Pete will soon be better.

Alas poor boy, he will never be better, (nor may-be needs to be
   better, that brave and simple soul,)
While they stand at home at the door he is dead already,
The only son is dead.

But the mother needs to be better,
She with thin form presently drest in black,
By day her meals untouch'd, then at night fitfully sleeping, often
   waking,
In the midnight waking, weeping, longing with one deep longing,
O that she might withdraw unnoticed, silent from life escape and
   withdraw,
To follow, to seek, to be with her dear dead son.

Chapter Nine

'Prisoners and Escapees'

A brief chapter on the horrors of the prison camps and on deserters.

TO THEE OLD CAUSE

To thee old cause!
Thou peerless, passionate, good cause,
Thou stern, remorseless, sweet idea,
Deathless throughout the ages, races, lands,
After a strange sad war, great war for thee,
(I think all war through time was really fought, and ever will be
    really fought, for thee,)
These chants for thee, the eternal march of thee.

(A war O soldiers not for itself alone,
Far, far more stood silently waiting behind, now to advance in this
    book.)

Thou orb of many orbs!
Thou seething principle! thou well-kept, latent germ! thou centre!
Around the idea of thee the war revolving,
With all its angry and vehement play of causes,
(With vast results to come for thrice a thousand years,)
These recitatives for thee,—my book and the war are one,
Merged in its spirit I and mine, as the contest hinged on thee,
As a wheel on its axis turns, this book unwitting to itself,
Around the idea of thee.

'Prisoners and Escapees'

It is generally believed in Washington that the President is in favor of a general exchange but has been for the past year overruled by the head of the War Department and others. The consequences are well known to all who mix much with the people and the soldiers. The Administration has already established a name for bad faith which will [last] for years to come, and the army is far more deeply incensed than appears on the surface.

The Prisoners. To the Editor of the New York Times:
[Tuesday, December 24, 1866]

The public mind is deeply excited, and most righteously so, at the starvation of the United States prisoners of war in the hands of the Secessionists. The dogged sullenness and scoundrelism prevailing everywhere among the prison guards and officials (with, I think, the general exception of the surgeons), the measureless torments of the forty or fifty thousand helpless young men, with all their humiliations, hunger, cold, filth, despair, hope utterly given out, and the more and more frequent mental imbecility I have myself seen the proofs of in so many instances that I know the facts well—and know that the half has not been told, nor the tithe either.

But there is another and full as important side to the story. Whose fault is it at bottom that our men have not been exchanged? To my knowledge it is understood by Colonel Mulford, our capital executive officer of exchange, and also by those among us who have had longest and nearest contact with the Secession exchange officers, that the government of the latter have been and are ready to exchange man for man as far as the prisoners go (certainly all the whites, and, as I understand it, a large proportion of the blacks also).

Under the President (whose humane, conscientious, and fatherly heart I have abiding faith in) the control of exchange has remained with the Secretary of War, and also with Major-General Butler. In my opinion the Secretary has taken and obstinately held a position of cold-blooded policy (that is, he thinks it policy) in this matter more cruel than anything done by the Secessionists. Ostensibly and officially saying he will not exchange at all unless the Secessionist leaders will give us, on average terms, all the blacks they capture in military action, the Secretary has also said (and this is the basis of his course and policy) that it is not for the benefit of the Government of the United States that the power of the Secessionists should be repleted by some fifty thousand men in good condition now in our hands, besides getting relieved of the support of nearly the same number of wrecks and ruins, of no advantage to us, now in theirs.

Major-General Butler, in my opinion, has also incorporated in the question of exchange a needless amount of personal pique and an unbecoming obstinacy. He, too, has taken his stand on the exchange of all black soldiers, has persisted in it without regard to consequences, and has made the whole of the large and complicated question of general exchange turn upon that one item alone, while it is but a drop in the bucket. Then he makes it too much a personal contest and matter of vanity who shall conquer and an occasion to revenge the bad temper and insults of the South toward himself.

This is the spirit in which the faith of the Government of the United States toward fifty thousand of its bravest young men—soldiers faithful to it in its hours of extremest peril—has been for the past year, and is now, handled. Meantime, while the thing has been held in abeyance in this manner, considerably more than one fourth of those helpless and most wretched men (their last hours passed in the thought that they were abandoned by their government and left to their fate) have indeed been exchanged by deaths of starvation (Mr. Editor, or you, reader, do you know what a death by starvation actually is?), leaving half the remainder closely prepared to follow, from mental and physical atrophy; and even then the remnant cannot long tarry behind. So that the Secretary and the Major-General mentioned may find their policy work out more even than they calculated.

In my opinion, the anguish and death of these ten to fifteen thousand American young men, with all the added and incalculable sorrow, long drawn out, amid families at home, rests mainly upon the heads of members of our own government; and if they persist, the death of the remainder of the Union prisoners, and often worse than death, will be added.

. . . While I have been writing this, a very large number of Southern prisoners—I should think one thousand at least—has passed up Pennsylvania Avenue, under a strong guard. I went out in the street, close to them. Poor fellows, many of them mere lads—it brought the tears. They seemed our flesh and blood, too—some wounded, all miserable in clothing, all in dirt and tatters, many of them fine young men. . . . I cannot tell you how I feel to see those prisoners marched. . . .

April 7, 1864.

[A] warmish forenoon, after the storm of the past few days. I see, passing up, in the broad space between the curbs, a big squad of a couple of hundred conscripts, surrounded by a strong cordon of armed guards and others interspersed between the ranks. The government has learned caution from its experiences; there are many hundreds of "bounty jumpers," and already, as I am told, eighty thousand deserters.

Next (also passing up the Avenue), a cavalry company, young but evidently well-drilled and service-hardened men. Mark the upright posture in their saddles, the bronzed and bearded young faces, the easy swaying to the motions of the horses, and the carbines by their right knee; handsome and reckless, some eighty of them riding with rapid gait, clattering along. Then the tinkling bells of passing cars, the many shops (some with large show windows, some with swords and straps for the shoulders of different ranks, hat cords with acorns, or other insignia), the military patrol marching along, with the orderly or second lieutenant stopping different ones to examine passes—the forms, the faces, all sorts crowded together, the worn and pale, the pleased, some on their way to the railroad depot going home, the cripples, the darkies, the long trains of government wagons, or the sad strings of ambulances conveying wounded—the many officers' horses tied in front of the drinking or oyster saloons, or held by black men or boys, or orderlies.

Michael Stansbury, 48 years of age, a seafaring man, a Southerner by birth and raising, formerly captain of *U.S. Lightship Long Shoal*, stationed at Long Shoal Point, Pimlico Sound—though a Southerner, a firm Union man—was captured February 17, 1863, and has been nearly two years in the Confederate prisons; was at one time ordered re-

leased by Governor Vance, but a Rebel officer re-arrested him; then sent on to Richmond for exchange—but instead of being exchanged was sent down (as a Southern citizen, not a soldier) to Salisbury, North Carolina, where he remained until lately, when he escaped among the exchanged by assuming the name of a dead soldier and coming up via Wilmington with the rest. Was about sixteen months in Salisbury.

Subsequent to October, '64, there were about eleven thousand Union prisoners in the stockade; about one hundred of them Southern Unionists, two hundred U.S. deserters. During the past winter, fifteen hundred of these prisoners, to save their lives, joined the Confederacy, on condition of being assigned merely to guard duty. Out of the eleven thousand, not more than twenty-five hundred came out; five hundred of these were pitiable helpless wretches—the rest were in a condition to travel. There were often sixty dead bodies to be buried in the morning; the daily average would be about forty. The regular food was a meal of corn—the cob and husk ground together, and sometimes once a week a ration of sorghum molasses. A diminutive ration of meat might possibly come once a month, not oftener. In the stockade, containing eleven thousand men, there was a partial show of tents, not enough for two thousand. A large proportion of the men lived in holes in the ground, in the utmost wretchedness. Some froze to death, others had their hands and feet frozen. The rebel guards would occasionally, and on the least pretence, fire into the prison from mere demonism and wantonness.

All the horrors that can be named—starvation, lassitude, filth, vermin, despair, swift loss of self-respect, idiocy, insanity, and frequent murder—were there.

Stansbury has a wife and child living in Newbern—has written to them from here—is in the U.S. Lighthouse employ still—had been home to Newbern to see his family, and on his return to the ship was captured in his boat. Has seen men brought there to Salisbury as hearty as you ever see in your life—in a few weeks completely dead gone, much of it from thinking on their condition—hope all gone. Has himself a hard, sad, strangely deadened kind of look, as of one chilled for years in the cold and dark, where his good manly nature had no room to exercise itself.

Deserters. October 24.

Saw a large squad of our own deserters (over three hundred) surrounded with a cordon of armed guards, marching along Pennsylvania Avenue. The most motley collection I ever saw—all sorts of rig, all sorts of hats and caps, many fine-looking young fellows, some of them shame-faced, some sickly, most of them dirty, shirts very dirty and long worn, etc. They tramped along without order, a huge huddling mass, not in ranks.

I saw some of the spectators laughing, but I felt like anything else but laughing. These deserters are far more numerous than would be thought. Almost every day I see squads of them, sometimes two or three at a time, with a small guard, sometimes ten or twelve, under a larger one. (I hear the desertions from the army now in the field have often averaged ten thousand a month. One of the commonest sights in Washington is a squad of deserters.)

Brooklyn, N.Y. December 26, 1864.

I am writing this in the front basement in Portland Avenue, Brooklyn, at home. It is after 9 o'clock at night. We have had a wet day with fog, mud, slush, and the yet unmelted hard-polished ice liberally left in the streets. All sluggish and damp, with a prevailing leaden vapor. Yesterday, Christmas, about the same.

George's trunk came up express early in forenoon today

from City Point, Virginia. Lieutenant Babcock, of the 51st, was kind enough to search it out and send it home. It stood some hours before we felt inclined to open it. Towards evening, Mother and Eddy looked over the things. One could not help feeling depressed. There were his uniform coat, pants, sash, etc. There were many things reminded us of him. Papers, memoranda, books, knick-knacks, a revolver, a small diary, roll of his company, a case of photographs of his comrades (several of them I knew as killed in battle), with other stuff such as a soldier accumulates.

Mother looked everything over, laid out the shirts to be washed, the coats and pants to hang up, and all the rest were carefully put back. It made me feel pretty solemn. We have not heard from him since October 3rd, either living or dead, we know not.

I am aware of the condition of the Union prisoners South through seeing them when brought up, and from lately talking with a friend just returned from taking part in the exchange at Savannah and Charleston—of which we received twelve thousand of our sick. Their situation, as of all our men in prison, is indescribably horrible. Hard, ghastly starvation is the rule. Rags, filth, despair, in large, open stockades; no shelter, no cooking, no clothes—such the condition of masses of men—in some places two or three thousand, and in the largest prison as high as thirty thousand confined. The guards are insufficient in numbers, and they make up by treble severity, shooting the prisoners literally just to keep them under terrorism. . . .

I cannot get any reliable trace of the 51st officers at all. I supposed they were at Columbia, South Carolina, but my friend has brought a list purporting to be a complete record of all in confinement there, and I cannot find any of the 51st among them.

February 23, 1865.

I saw a large procession of young men from the Rebel
Army (deserters they are called, but the usual meaning of
the word does not apply to them) passing the Avenue to-
day. I stood and watched them as they shuffled along in a
slow, tired, worn sort of way; a large proportion of light-
haired, blonde, light-gray-eyed young men among them.
Their costumes had a dirt-stained uniformity; most had
been originally gray; some had articles of our uniform—
pants on one, coat or vest on another; I think they were
mostly Georgia and North Carolina boys. They excited lit-
tle or no attention.

As I stood quite close to them, several good-looking
enough youths (but O what a tale of misery their appear-
ance told!) nodded or just spoke to me, without doubt
divining pity and fatherliness out of my face—for my heart
was full enough of it. Several of the couples trudged along
with their arms about each other, some probably brothers,
as if they were afraid they might somehow get separated.

They nearly all looked what one might call simple, yet
intelligent, too. Some had pieces of old carpet, some blank-
ets, and others old bags around their shoulders. Some of
them here and there had fine faces; still it was a procession
of misery. The two hundred had with them about half-a-
dozen armed guards. Along this week I saw some such up
by the boat. The government does what it can for them,
and sends them north and west.

February 27th, 1865.

Some three or four hundred more escapees from the Con-
federate Army came up on the boat. As the day has been
very pleasant indeed (after a long spell of bad weather),
I have been wandering around a good deal without any
other object than to be outdoors and enjoy it; have met

these escaped men in all directions. I talked with a number of the men. Some are quite bright and stylish, for all their poor clothes—walking with an air, wearing their old head-covering on one side quite saucily.

I find the old, unquestionable proofs, as all along the past four years, of the unscrupulous tyranny exercised by the Secession Government in conscripting the common people by absolute force everywhere and paying no attention to the men's time being up—keeping them in military service just the same.

One gigantic young fellow, a Georgian, at least six feet, three inches high, broad-sized in proportion, attired in the dirtiest, drab, well-smeared rags tied with strings, his trousers at the knees all strips and streamers, was complacently standing eating some meat and bread. He appeared contented enough. It was plain he did not take anything to heart.

February 28.

As I passed the military headquarters of the city, not far from the President's house, I stopped to interview some of the crowd of escapees who were lounging there. In appearance, they were the same as previously mentioned. Two of them, one about seventeen, and the other perhaps twenty-five or twenty-six, I talked with some time. They were from North Carolina and raised there, and had folks there. The elder had been in the Rebel service four years. He was first conscripted for two years. He was then kept arbitrarily in the ranks. This is the case with a large proportion of the Secession Army.

There was nothing downcast in these young men's manners; the younger had been soldiering about a year; there were six brothers (all the boys of the family) in the army—part of them as conscripts, part as volunteers; three had been killed; one had escaped about four months ago, and now this one had got away. He was a pleasant and well-talking lad, with the peculiar North Carolina idiom (not at all disagreeable to my ears). He and the elder one were of the same company, and escaped together—and wished to remain together. They thought of getting transportation back to Missouri and working there; but were not sure it was judicious.

I advised them rather to go to some of the directly Northern states and get farm work for the present. The younger had made six dollars on the boat with some tobacco he brought—he had three-and-a-half left. The elder had nothing; I gave him a trifle.

Soon after met John Wormley, 9th Alabama, a West Tennessee-raised boy, parents both dead; had the look of one for a long time on short allowance; said very little; chewed tobacco at a fearful rate, spitting in proportion; large, clear, dark-brown eyes, very fine; didn't know what to make of me; told me at last he wanted much to get some clean underclothes and a pair of decent pants. Didn't care about coat or hat fixings. Wanted a chance to wash himself well and put on the underclothes. I had the very great pleasure of helping him to accomplish all these wholesome designs.

March 1st.

Plenty more butternut- or clay-colored escapees every day. About one hundred and sixty came in today, a large portion South Carolinians. They generally take the oath of allegiance, and are sent north, west, or extreme southwest, if they wish. Several of them told me that the desertions in their army of men going home, leave or no leave, are far more numerous than their desertions to our side. I saw a very forlorn-looking squad of about a hundred late this afternoon on their way to the Baltimore depot.

. . . The accounts have not been exaggerated; the truth was worse than the stories of it—far worse. [The Southern prisons were] unquestionably [worse than the Northern prisons]. . . . They were poor—but that is no explanation at all; none at all. They starved, maltreated our men, as such things were never known on this side of the water. . . .

. . . I conclude mainly it is better so, better as it is; give these facts to oblivion; let them go; regret nothing in their loss. History has in general been kind to bury the dismalest features of life; somehow it is provided that the darkest spots should be forgotten.

. . . I have no desire to do the South an injustice—far from it; but it looks to me as if this is a damned spot that will not out. . . .

. . . I have in mind . . . a North Carolinian, keeper of North Shore Light there, a magnificent fellow. . . . He was impressed, imprisoned—kept so for years—in some hole like Libby or Andersonville. . . . Put these things together —think of such men—the best sort of men, the plain elect; all their young hopes of life scattered, the blessed joys of camaraderie all crushed out; power, brutality, everywhere, to annul, to destroy; everything crushed out of a man but his resentments—the unutterable memories of barbarisms, the heart's uncompromising revolt.

William Grover Shot for Desertion.
O the horrid contrast and the sarcasm of this sight—to know who they really are that sit on judges' benches and who they [are] who are perched on the criminal's box!

While all this gaud and tinsel shines in people's eyes amid

215

the countless officers' straps, amid all this show of generals' stars and the bars of the captains and lieutenants—amid all the wind and puffing and infidelity—amid the swarms of contractors and their endless contracts and the paper money —and out from all this stalks like a phantom that boy, not yet nineteen years of age, boy who had fought without flinching in twelve battles (no veteran of old wars better or steadier)—stalks forth, I say, that single, simple boy, out of all this huge composite pageant, silently, with a bandage over his eyes—the volley—the smoke—the limpsey falling body and blood streaming in strains and splashes down the breast.

Released Union Prisoners from South.

The released prisoners of war are now coming up from the Southern prisons. I have seen a number of them; the sight is worse than any sight of battlefields or any collection of wounded, even the bloodiest.

There was (as a sample) one large boatload of several hundreds brought about the 25th to Annapolis; and, out of the whole number, only three individuals were able to walk from the boat. The rest were carried ashore and laid down in one place or another.

Can these be *men*—these little, livid brown, ash-streaked, monkey-looking dwarfs? Are they really not mummied, dwindled corpses? They lay there, most of them quite still, but with a horrible look in their eyes and skinny lips— often with not enough flesh to cover their teeth. Probably no more appalling sight was ever seen on this earth.

(There are deeds, crimes, that may be forgiven; but this is not among them. It steeps its perpetrators in blackest, es- capeless, endless damnation. Over fifty thousand have been compelled to die the death of starvation—reader, did you ever try to realize what *starvation* actually is?—in those prisons—and in a land of plenty!) An indescribable meanness, tyranny, aggravating course of insults—almost incredible—was evidently the rule of treatment through all the Southern military prisons. The dead there are not to be pitied as much as some of the living that come from there—if they can be called living—many of them are mentally imbecile and will never recuperate. . . .

I do not think history affords a parallel to some of the methods of these men—the leaders—the dark, low, mean, damnable methods they pursued to break up the country. . . . [In the prisons] words cannot picture the atrocities they inflicted—the horrors—the midnight deeds. I have often thought this is not a subject for the writer but for the artist—these things can only have justice done them by pictorial statement. . . .

ADIEU TO A SOLDIER

Adieu O soldier,
You of the rude campaigning, (which we shared,)
The rapid march, the life of the camp,
The hot contention of opposing fronts, the long manœuvre,
Red battles with their slaughter, the stimulus, the strong terrific game,
Spell of all brave and manly hearts, the trains of time through you and like of you all fill'd,
With war and war's expression.

Adieu dear comrade,
Your mission is fulfill'd—but I, more warlike,
Myself and this contentious soul of mine,
Still on our own campaigning bound,
Through untried roads with ambushes opponents lined,
Through many a sharp defeat and many a crisis, often baffled,
Here marching, ever marching on, a war fight out—aye here,
To fiercer, weightier battles give expression.

Chapter Ten

'Ethiopia Saluting the Colors'

Some observations made by Whitman on the Negro troops in the army.

ETHIOPIA SALUTING THE COLORS

Who are you dusky woman, so ancient hardly human,
With your woolly-white and turban'd head, and bare bony feet?
Why rising by the roadside here, do you the colors greet?

('Tis while our army lines Carolina's sands and pines,
Forth from thy hovel door thou Ethiopia com'st to me,
As under doughty Sherman I march toward the sea.)

Me master years a hundred since from my parents sunder'd,
A little child, they caught me as the savage beast is caught,
Then hither me across the sea the cruel slaver brought.

No further does she say, but lingering all the day,
Her high-borne turban'd head she wags, and rolls her darkling eye,
And courtesies to the regiments, the guidons moving by.

What is it fateful woman, so blear, hardly human?
Why wag your head with turban bound, yellow, red and green?
Are the things so strange and marvelous you see or have seen?

. . . The negro holds firmly the reins of his four horses, the block
    swags underneath on its tied-over chain,
The negro that drives the long dray of the stone-yard, steady and
    tall he stands pois'd on one leg on the string-piece,
His blue shirt exposes his ample neck and breast and loosens over his
    hip-band,

His glance is calm and commanding, he tosses the slouch of his hat
    away from his forehead,
The sun falls on his crispy hair and mustache, falls on the black of
    his polish'd and perfect limbs.

I behold the picturesque giant and love him, and I do not stop there,
I go with the team also. . . .

'Ethiopia Saluting the Colors'

One of my wartime reminiscences comprises the quiet side scene of a visit I made to the 1st Regiment of U.S. Colored Troops, at their encampment, and on the occasion of their first paying off, July 11, 1863. Though there is now no difference of opinion worth mentioning, there was a powerful opposition to enlisting blacks during the earlier years of the Secession War. Even then, however, they had their champions.

"That the colored race," said a good authority, "is capable of military training and efficiency, is demonstrated by the testimony of numberless witnesses, and by the eagerness displayed in the raising, organizing, and drilling of African troops. Few white regiments make a better appearance on parade than the 1st and 2nd Louisiana Native Guards."

The same remark is true of other colored regiments. At Milliken's Bend, at Vicksburg, at Port Hudson, on Morris Island, and wherever tested, they have exhibited determined bravery, and compelled the plaudits alike of the thoughtful and thoughtless soldiery. During the siege of Port Hudson, the question was often asked those who beheld their resolute charges, how the "niggers" behaved under fire; and without exception the answer was complimentary to them. "O, tiptop!" "first rate!" "bully!" were the usual replies. But I did not start out to argue the case—only to give my reminiscence literally, as jotted on the spot at the time.

I write this on Mason's (otherwise Analostan) Island, under the fine shade trees of an old white stucco house with big rooms; the white stucco house, originally a fine country seat (tradition says the famous Virginia Mason, author of the *Fugitive Slave Law*, was born here). I reached the spot from my Washington quarters by ambulance up Pennsylvania Avenue, through Georgetown, across the Aqueduct Bridge, and around through a cut and winding road, with rocks and many bad gullies not lacking. After reaching the island, we get presently in the midst of the camp of the 1st Regiment U.S.C.T. The tents look clean and good; indeed, altogether, in locality especially, the pleasantest camp I have yet seen.

The spot is umbrageous, high, and dry, with distant sounds of the city, and the puffing steamers of the Potomac, up to Georgetown and back again. Birds are singing in the trees, the warmth is endurable here in this moist shade with the fragrance and freshness. A hundred rods across is Georgetown. The river between is swelled and muddy from the late rains up country.

So quiet here, yet full of vitality, all around in the far distance glimpses, as I sweep my eye, of hills, verdure clad and with plenteous trees; right where I sit, locust, sassafras, spice, and many other trees—a few with huge parasitic vines; just at hand the banks sloping to the river, wild with beautiful, free vegetation, superb weeds, better in their natural growth and forms than the best garden. Lots of luxuriant grapevines and trumpet flowers; the river flowing far down in the distance.

Now the paying is to begin. The major (paymaster), with his clerk, seat themselves at a table; the rolls are before them; the money box is opened; there are packages of five, ten, twenty-five cent pieces. Here comes the first company (B), some 82 men, all blacks. Certes, we cannot find fault with the appearance of this crowd—Negroes though they be. They are manly enough, bright enough, look as if they had the soldier stuff in them, look hardy, patient, many of them real handsome fellows.

The paying, I say, has begun. The men are marched up in close proximity. The clerk calls off name after name, and each walks up, receives his money, and passes along out of the way. It is a real study, both to see them come close, and to see them pass away, stand counting their cash (nearly all this company gets $10.03 each). The clerk calls "George Washington." That distinguished personage steps from the ranks, in the shape of a very dark man, good sized and shaped, and aged about thirty, with a military mustache; he takes his "ten three," and goes off, evidently well pleased. (There are about a dozen Washingtons in the company. Let us hope they will do honor to the name.) At the table, how quickly the major handles the bills, counts without trouble, everything going on smoothly and quickly! The regiment numbers today about one thousand men (including twenty officers, the only whites).

Now another company. These get $5.36 each. The men look well. They, too, have great names; besides the Washingtons aforesaid, John Quincy Adams, Daniel Webster, Calhoun, James Madison, Alfred Tennyson, John Brown, Benjamin G. Tucker, Horace Greeley, etc. The men stop off aside, count their money with a pleased, half-puzzled look. Occasionally, but not often, there are some thoroughly African physiognomies—very black in color, large, protruding lips, low forehead, etc. But I have to say that I do not see one revolting face.

Then another company, each man of this getting $10.03 also. The pay proceeds very rapidly (the calculation, roll-signing, etc. having been arranged beforehand). Then some trouble. One company, by the rigid rules of official computation, gets only 23 cents each man. The company (K) is indignant, and after two or three are paid, the refusal to take the paltry sum is universal, and the company marches off to quarters unpaid.

Another company (I) gets only 70 cents. The sullen, lowering, disappointed look is general. Half refuse it in this case. Company G, in full dress, with brass scales on shoulders, looked perhaps as well as any of the companies—the men had an unusually alert look.

These then are the black troops—or the beginning of them. Well, no one can see them, even under these circumstances—their military career in its novitiate—without feeling well pleased with them.

As we entered the island, we saw scores at a little distance, bathing, washing their clothes, etc. The officers, as far as looks go, have a fine appearance, have good faces, and the air military. Altogether it is a significant show, and brings up some "abolition" thoughts. The scene—the porch of an old Virginia's slave-owner's house, the Potomac rippling near, the Capitol just down three or four miles there, seen through the pleasant blue haze of this July day.

After a couple of hours, I get tired and go off for a ramble. I write these concluding lines on a rock—the birds singing, the sluggish, muddy-yellow waters pouring down from the late rains of the upper Potomac; the green heights on the south side of the river before me. The single cannon from a neighboring fort has just been fired to signal high noon. I have walked all around Analostan, enjoying the luxuriant wildness, and stopped in this solitary spot. A water snake wriggles down the bank, disturbed, into the water. The bank nearby is fringed with a dense growth of shrubbery, vines, etc. . . .

. . . As to the Negro question—well, it is a question—a confounded serious question; but who can say the Negro is more likely to get his due from the Republican Party than from the Democratic Party?

I am inclined to repeat what you [1] said . . . the other day here: "The Negro will get his due from the Negro—from no one else." I say so, too; that is the whole story, from beginning, middle and end. . . .

. . . Not the Negro, not the Negro. The Negro was not the chief thing. The chief thing was to stick together. The South was technically right and humanly wrong. . . .

I SING THE BODY ELECTRIC

. . . A man's body at auction,
(For before the war I often go to the slave-mart and watch the sale,)
I help the auctioneer, the sloven does not half know his business.

Gentlemen look on this wonder,
Whatever the bids of the bidders they cannot be high enough for it,
For it the globe lay preparing quintillions of years without one animal or plant,
For it the revolving cycles truly and steadily roll'd.

In this head the all-baffling brain,
In it and below it the makings of heroes.

Examine these limbs, red, black, or white, they are cunning in tendon and nerve,
They shall be stript that you may see them.

Exquisite senses, life-lit eyes, pluck, volition,
Flakes of breast-muscle, pliant backbone and neck, flesh not flabby, good-sized arms and legs,
And wonders within there yet.

Within there runs blood,
The same old blood! the same red-running blood!
There swells and jets a heart, there all passions, desires, reachings, aspirations,
[1] Traubel

(Do you think they are not there because they are not express'd in
parlors and lecture-rooms?)

This is not only one man, this the father of those who shall be fathers
in their turns,
In him the start of populous states and rich republics,
Of him countless immortal lives with countless embodiments and
enjoyments.

How do you know who shall come from the offspring of his off-
spring through the centuries?
(Who might you find you have come from yourself, if you could
trace back through the centuries?)

. . .

A woman's body at auction,
She too is not only herself, she is the teeming mother of mothers,
She is the bearer of them that shall grow and be mates to the moth-
ers.

Have you ever loved the body of a woman?
Have you ever loved the body of a man?

Do you not see that these are exactly the same to all in all nations
and times all over the earth?

* * *

SONG OF MYSELF

. . . The runaway slave came to my house and stopt outside,
I heard his motions crackling the twigs of the woodpile,
Through the swung half-door of the kitchen I saw him limpsy and
weak,
And went where he sat on a log and led him in and assured him,
And brought water and fill'd a tub for his sweated body and bruis'd
feet,
And gave him a room that enter'd from my own, and gave him some
coarse clean clothes,

228

And remember perfectly well his revolving eyes and his awkward-
ness,
And remember putting plasters on the galls of his neck and ankles;
He staid with me a week before he was recuperated and pass'd
north,
I had him sit next me at table, my fire-lock lean'd in the corner. . . .

. . .

I am the hounded slave, I wince at the bite of the dogs,
Hell and despair are upon me, crack and again crack the marksmen,
I clutch the rails of the fence, my gored ribs, thinn'd with the ooze
of my skin,
I fall on the weeds and stones,
The riders spur their unwilling horses, haul close,
Taunt my dizzy ears and beat me violently over the head with
whipstocks.

Agonies are one of my changes of garments.
I do not ask the wounded person how he feels, I myself become the
wounded person,
My hurts turn livid upon me as I lean on a cane and observe. . . .

Chapter Eleven

'O Magnet South'

The poet's observations on the Southern people, the Rebellion, and on Confederate soldiers.

RECONCILIATION

Word over all, beautiful as the sky!

Beautiful that war, and all its deeds of carnage, must in time be
    utterly lost;

That the hands of the sisters Death and Night incessantly
    softly wash again, and ever again, this soil'd world;

. . . For my enemy is dead, a man divine as myself is dead;

I look where he lies white-faced and still in the coffin—I draw near;

Bend down and touch lightly with my lips the white face in the
    coffin.

'O Magnet South'

I am very warmly disposed towards the South; I must admit that my instinct of friendship towards the South is almost more than I like to confess. I have very dear friends there—sacred, precious memories; the people there should be considered, even deferred to, instead of browbeaten. I feel sore, I feel some pain, almost indignation, when I think that yesterday keeps the old brutal idea of subjugation on top.

I would be the last one to confuse moral values—to imagine the South impeccable. I don't condone the South where it has gone wrong—its Negro slavery, I don't condone that—far from it—I hate it. I have always said so, South and North; but there is another spirit dormant there which it must be the purpose of our civilization to bring forth; it cannot, it must not, be killed. It is true that there are a lot of us—like you, me, others—in whom there is developed a new camaraderie, fellowship, love; the farther, truer idea of the race family, of international unity, of making one country of all countries—but the trouble is that we do not hold the whip hand. It is sad, sad to me to face the fact that we have a family here—half the children on one side, half of them opposed, standing in antagonism—the situation does not seem to offer us the brightest prospects. . . .

It is Conway's opinion that the Rebellion was in great part a war that could have been avoided—a war of the politicians. I want Conway to say it all, of course—preach, write, argue, for his point of view—put in his negative in any form he chooses—but still I am forced to dissent. The war was the boil—that was all—not the root.

The war was not the cause of the war—the cause lay deeper—could not have been shifted from its purposes. There are cute historical writers—very cute ones, the best of the whole group—who trace events in modern history back to the Crusades—establish a definite and conclusive connection. So it must be with our Rebellion—to try to consider it without considering what preceded it is only to dally with the truth.

There is one thing I shall always regret for myself—always reproach myself for having neglected. I had some brief experience in the South—an intimate experience while it lasted; was convinced that the "poor white" there, so-called, had never had justice done him in our histories, newspapers, official documents—in our war talk and after-war talk.

Everybody everywhere seems to be interested in crushing him down and keeping him crushed down. If I could undertake the job yet—even yet make some record on this side to show how I hate the tyranny that has oppressed it, pay some tribute to a class so thoroughly, so universally, misunderstood. The horrible patois attributed to the "poor white" there in the South (and not to them only—to Western and Northern classes, also) I never found, never encountered. I discovered courtesy, chivalry, generosity, and by no means such external ugliness as is usually charged to them. In fact, all my experiences South—all my experiences in the hospitals, among the soldiers, in the crowds of the cities, with the masses, in the great centers of population—

allowing for all idiosyncrasies, idiocrasies, passions, what-not—the very worst—have only served to confirm my faith in man—in the average of men.

Take the hospital drill I went through; take the mixtures of men there, men often supposed to be of contrary types —how impressive was the fact of their likeness, their uniformity of essential nature—the same basic traits in them all—in the Northern man, in the Southern man, in the Western man—all of one instinct, one color, addicted to the same vices, ennobled by the same virtues; the dignity, courtesy, openhandedness, radical in all, beautiful in all. When I first went to Washington, I had a great dislike for the typical Yankee—had always had it, years back, from the start—but in my very first contact with the human Yankee, all my prejudices were put to flight.

Confederate Soldiers in the Hospitals.

. . . Some of my best friends in the hospitals were probably Southern boys. I remember one in particular right off—a Kentucky youngster (a mere youngster), illiterate, extremely—I wrote several letters for him to his parents, friends—fine, honest, ardent, chivalrous. I found myself loving him like a son; he used to kiss me good-night—kiss me. He got well, he passed out with the crowd, went home, the war was over. We never met again. Oh! I could tell you a hundred such tales. I don't know, but I've put this case, this Kentucky boy's case, into *Two Rivulets*—maybe not —there's a lot of stuff I never put down anywhere—some of the best of it. I could only give the typical cases.

A Secesh Brave.

The grand soldiers are not comprised in those of one side any more than the other. Here is an example of an unknown Southerner, a lad of seventeen. At the War Department a few days ago I witnessed a presentation of captured flags to the Secretary. Among others, a soldier named Gant, of the 104th Ohio Volunteers, presented a Rebel battle flag, which one of the officers stated to me was borne to the mouth of our cannon and planted there by a boy but seventeen years of age, who actually endeavored to stop the muzzle of the gun with fence rails. He was killed in the effort, and the flagstaff was severed by a shot from one of our men. . . .

Here is a case of a soldier I found among the crowded cots in the Patent Office. He likes to have someone to talk to, and we will listen to him. He got badly hit in his leg and side at Fredericksburg that eventful Saturday, 13th of December. He lay the succeeding two days and nights helpless on the field, between the city and those grim terraces of batteries; his company and regiment had been compelled to leave him to his fate. To make matters worse, it happened he lay with his head slightly downhill, and could not help himself. At the end of some fifty hours he was brought off with other wounded under a flag of truce.

I asked him how the Rebels treated him as he lay during those two days and nights within reach of them—whether they came to him, whether they abused him. He answered that several of the Rebels, soldiers and others, came to him at one time or another. A couple of them, who were together, spoke roughly and sarcastically, but nothing worse. One middle-aged man, however, who seemed to be moving around the field among the dead and wounded for benevolent purposes, came to him in a way he will never forget; treated our soldier kindly, bound up his wounds, cheered him, gave him a couple of biscuits and a drink of whiskey and water; asked him if he could eat some beef. This good Secesh, however, did not change our soldier's position, for it might have caused the blood to burst from the wounds, clotted and stagnated.

Our soldier is from Pennsylvania; has had a pretty severe time; the wounds proved to be bad ones. But he retains a good heart and is at present on the gain. (It is not uncommon for the men to remain on the field this way—one, two, or even four or five days.)

The large ward I am in is used for Secession soldiers exclusively. One man, about forty years of age, emaciated with diarrhoea, I was attracted to, as he lay with his eyes turned up, looking like death. His weakness was so extreme that it took a minute or so every time for him to talk with anything like consecutive meaning; yet he was evidently a man of good intelligence and education. As I said anything, he would lie a moment perfectly still; then, with closed eyes, answer in a low, very slow voice—quiet, correct, and sensible—but in a way and tone that wrung my heart.

He had a mother, wife, and child living (or probably living) in his home in Mississippi. It was a long, long time since he had seen them. Had he caused a letter to be sent them since he got here in Washington? No answer. I repeated the question very slowly and soothingly. He could not tell whether he had or not—things of late seemed to him like a dream. After waiting a moment, I said: "Well, I am going to walk down the ward a moment, and when I come back you can tell me. If you have not written, I will sit down and write." A few minutes after I returned, he said he remembered now that someone had written for him two or three days before.

The presence of this man impressed me profoundly. The flesh was all sunken on face and arms; the eyes low in their sockets and glassy and with purple rings around them. Two or three great tears silently flowed out from the eyes and rolled down his temples (he was doubtless unused to be spoken to as I was speaking to him). Sickness, imprison-

237

ment, exhaustion, etc. had conquered the body, yet the mind held mastery still and called even wandering remembrance back. . . .

Washington, Tuesday morning, June 9, 1863.

It looks from some accounts as though the 9th Army Corps might be going down into East Tennessee (Cumberland Gap, or perhaps bound for Knoxville). It is an important region and has many Southern Unionists.

The staunchest Union man I have ever met is a young Southerner in the 2nd Tennessee (Union regiment)—he was ten months in Southern prisons; came up from Richmond paroled about ten weeks ago; and has been in hospital here sick until lately.

He suffered everything but death (he is [the] one they hung up by the heels, head downwards) and indeed worse than death, but stuck to his convictions like a hero—John Barker, a real manly fellow. I saw much of him and heard much of that country that can be relied on. He is now gone home to his regiment. . . .

Washington, September 15, 1863.

. . . We North don't understand some things about Southerners; it is very strange, the contrast—if I should pick out the most genuine Union and real patriots I have ever met in all my experience, I should pick out two or three Tennessee and Virginia Unionists I have met in the hospitals. . . .

September 22, 1865.

Afternoon and evening at Douglas Hospital, to see a friend belonging to 2nd New York Artillery (Hiram W. Frazee, Sergeant) down with an obstinate compound fracture of left leg received in one of the last battles near Petersburg. After sitting a while with him, went through several neighboring wards. In one of them found an old acquaintance transferred here lately, a Rebel prisoner, in a dying condition. Poor fellow, the look was already on his face. He gazed long at me. I asked him if he knew me. After a moment he uttered something—but inarticulately.

I have seen him off and on for the last five months. He has suffered very much; a bad wound in left leg, severely fractured, several operations, cuttings, extractions of bones, splinters, etc. I remember he seemed to me, as I used to talk to him, a fair specimen of the main strata of the Southerners—those without property or education, but still with the stamp which comes from freedom and equality. I liked him—Jonathan Wallace of Hurd Co., Georgia, age thirty (wife, Susan F. Wallace, Houston, Hurd Co., Georgia. If any good soul of that county should see this, I hope he will send her this word). Had a family; had not heard from them since taken prisoner, now six months.

I had written for him, and done trifles for him before he came here. He made no outward show, was mild in his talk and behavior, but I knew he worried much inwardly. But now all would be over very soon. I half sat upon the little stand near the head of the bed. Wallace was somewhat restless. I placed my hand lightly on his forehead and face, just sliding it over the surface. In a moment or so he fell into a calm, regular-breathing lethargy or sleep, and remained so while I sat there.

It was dark, and the lights were lit. I hardly knew why (death seemed hovering near), but I stayed nearly an hour. A Sister of Charity, dressed in black, with a broad white linen bandage around her head and under her chin, and a black crape overall flowing down from her head in long wide pieces, came to him and moved around the bed. She bowed low and solemn to me. For some time she moved around there noiseless as a ghost, doing little things for the dying man.

I have seen a good deal of the Southern people—know them well, love them well, would not misjudge them. Yet

239

I believe in nationality, too—internationality, for that matter; not the breaking away of peoples but the coming together of peoples—ever more and more the coming together. The war stirs me up—the causes of the war—its consequences; fills me with emotion; possibly because I have been very close to the most painful phases of its tragedies—in the hospitals, in the midst of the most extreme manifestations of its suffering.

You know of Mosby's guerrillas—men who would run a knife through the wounded, the aged, the children, without compunction. . . . In the South, they have what they call a chivalry; a toploftiticality—it is not a real chivalry—not by a damn sight—what men call the moral toplofticality that belongs to the North; here is a distinct difference—they are behind the North—anyone can see it—behind it at least a generation. They will evolve—but will they ever catch up? We must do them justice—not let this obscure the beautiful traits; but you have no idea . . . how really fiendish the disposition of the South towards a foe is likely to be: it's hard lines there to be anybody's enemy. . . .
　　If you had been there, had seen victims who had to endure these cruelties—the maimed, sick, dead, dying—you would not respond to it with a laugh. . . . I know something about those infernalities. You know about the smallpox scare. A great many people down in Washington doubted it—laughed it down, or tried to. The Attorney General sent for me; said he wanted to have the matter looked into; that he thought I was the man; put a good many documents into my hands, some of the funds of the department at my disposal—urging me to investigate, report. I did so—looked closely into all evidence—it was horribly true; true in every iota of evidence. I am sure of it as that we sit here now and talk about it—true, damnably true. It is a foul blot on the fair fame of the country—

those years. By means of infected rags, imported from districts in southern Europe, it was designed to introduce contagion in our big towns—New York, Philadelphia, Boston, Chicago, others. . . .

I had before been very ardent—more ardent than I am about anything these later years—being younger, stronger then—on the subject of allowing drugs to cross the line. I had always contended—I said "Christian" then—that no Christian could afford to refuse medicine to the sick and wounded, wherever found; and when I made my report, the Attorney General asked me if I was now willing to re-assert the same position. I replied ardently, just as I had before: "Yes, even now—at all times! As one in direct contact with these dark facts. . . ."

But I have no feelings . . . detrimental to the honor of the masses South—the great body of people there—worthy toilers, men and women whose share in noble qualifications, in richness of character I cannot, must not, dare not question. No, only a horror of the leaders, the conspirators, the group on top who prepared the way for all these terrors, encouraged, excused, gloried in them. . . .

The Southerners were good at destroying—especially railroads, locomotives; while our boys would put them up again—were rather proud they could do it. Destruction is easy; the Rebels were easy destroying; a few minutes, an hour, would rake up a whole line miles long, demolish everything. It [rebuilding] was, as you say, one of the unique qualities of the Northern soldier; no one had more reason for seeing it, glorying in it, than I. . . .

Calhoun's Real Monument.

In one of the hospital tents for special cases, as I sat today tending a new amputation, I heard a couple of neighboring soldiers talking to each other from their cots. One down with fever, but improving, had come up belated from Charleston not long before. The other was what we now call an "old veteran" (i.e., he was a Connecticut youth, probably of less than the age of twenty-five years, the four last of which he had spent in active service in the war in all parts of the country). The two were chatting of one thing and another. The fever soldier spoke of John C. Calhoun's monument which he had seen, and was describing it.

The veteran said: "I have seen Calhoun's monument. That you saw is not the real monument. But I have seen it. It is the desolated, ruined South; nearly the whole generation of young men between seventeen and thirty destroyed or maimed; all the old families used up; the rich impoverished; the plantations covered with weeds; the slaves unloosed and become the masters; and the name of Southerner blackened with every shame—all that is Calhoun's real monument."

TO THE LEAVEN'D SOIL THEY TROD

To the leaven'd soil they trod calling I sing for the last,
(Forth from my tent emerging for good, loosing, untying the tent-ropes,)
In the freshness the forenoon air, in the far-stretching circuits and vistas again to peace restored,
To the fiery fields emanative and the endless vistas beyond, to the South and the North,
To the leaven'd soil of the general Western world to attest my songs,
To the Alleghanian hills and the tireless Mississippi,
To the rocks I calling sing, and all the trees in the woods,
To the plains of the poems of heroes, to the prairies spreading wide,
To the far-off sea and the unseen winds, and the sane impalpable air;
And responding they answer all, (but not in words,)
The average earth, the witness of war and peace, acknowledges mutely,
The prairie draws me close, as the father to bosom broad the son,
The Northern ice and rain that began me nourish me to the end,
But the hot sun of the South is to fully ripen my songs.

Chapter Twelve

'Of the Corps and Generals'

Whitman's evaluations of some of the Civil War generals and other contemporary public figures.

CAMPS OF GREEN

Not alone those camps of white, old comrades of the wars,
When as order'd forward, after a long march,
Footsore and weary, soon as the light lessens we halt for the night,
Some of us so fatigued carrying the gun and knapsack, dropping
    asleep in our tracks,
Others pitching the little tents, and the fires lit up begin to sparkle,
Outposts of pickets posted surrounding alert through the dark,
And a word provided for countersign, careful for safety,
Till to the call of the drummers at daybreak loudly beating the
    drums,
We rise up refresh'd, the night and sleep pass'd over, and resume
    our journey,
Or proceed to battle.

Lo, the camps of the tents of green,
Which the days of peace keep filling, and the days of war keep
    filling,
With a mystic army, (is it too order'd forward? is it too only halt-
    ing awhile,
Till night and sleep pass over?)

Now in those camps of green, in their tents dotting the world,
In the parents, children, husbands, wives, in them, in the old and
   young,
Sleeping under the sunlight, sleeping under the moonlight, content
   and silent there at last,
Behold the mighty bivouac-field and waiting-camp of all,
Of the corps and generals all, and the President over the corps and
   generals all,
And of each of us O soldiers, and of each and all in the ranks we
   fought,
(There without hatred we all, all meet.)

For presently O soldiers, we too camp in our place in the bivouac-
   camps of green,
But we need not provide for outposts, nor word for the counter-
   sign,
Nor drummer to beat the morning drum.

'Of the Corps and Generals'

Have you ever seen Sherman? It is necessary to see him in order to realize the Norse make-up of the man—the hauteur, noble, yet democratic, a hauteur I have always hoped I, too, might possess. Try to picture Sherman—seamy, sinewy, in style—a bit of stern open air made up in the image of a man. The best of Sherman was best in the war, but has not been destroyed in peace—though peace brought with it military reviews, banquets, bouquets, women, flirtations, flattery.

. . . I can see Sherman now, at the head of the line, on Pennsylvania Avenue, the day the army filed before Lincoln —the silent Sherman riding beyond his aides. Yes, Sherman is all very well! I respect him. But after all, Sheridan was the Napoleonic figure of the war—not subjected to the last tests (though I am sure he would have been equal to them), but adequate, it seemed, to whatever duty arose. That is where I place Sheridan—among Napoleonic things.

Camden, N.J. August 7, 1888.

In the grand constellation of five or six names under Lincoln's Presidency that history will bear for ages in her firmament as marking the last life-throbs of Secession and beaming on its dying gasps, Sheridan's will be bright. One

247

consideration rising out of the now dead soldier's example, as it passes my mind, is worth taking notice of. If the war had continued any long time, these States, in my opinion, would have shown and proved the most conclusive military talents ever evinced by any nation on earth.

That they possessed a rank and file ahead of all other known, in points of quality and limitlessness of number, are easily admitted. But we have, too, the eligibility of organizing, handling, and officering equal to the other. These two, with modern arms, transportation, and inventive American genius, would make the United States, with earnestness, not only able to stand the whole world, but conquer that world united against us.

. . . I met much that instructed me profoundly on that point during the war—among the soldiers, the generals. When something of a major character was to be done—something prompt, decisive, resolute—it was Sheridan they summoned—the Sheridans, the men who sort of recreated circumstances—not McClellan—the McClellans, the inert. . . . In all our history, in all the history of these times—indeed of any time—I never knew a man intrusted with as great responsibilities, opportunities, who was as inert—dead, dead with inertia. . . .

. . . Poor McClellan! Poor McClellan! how they laid it on him! Yet I don't doubt but it is just—that he deserved it. . . .

. . . It would take a great deal to persuade me from my conviction—my old conviction, born at the time and never by any later developments shaken—my old conviction that McClellan straddled. I was on the spot at the time—in the midst of all the controversy, the suspicion, the tension, and the patriotism; and from it all, fairly and sternly, I drew my estimate of McClellan.

248

He thought: the time will come when these sections will be united again (he saw it; we all saw it; knew it was sure to be); then the lucky man, he thought, the man with the most power, will be the man who dealt most gently with the malcontents. . . .

. . . I see no reason for denying or forgetting indubitable facts. Lincoln was not hasty in action—far from it; had almost infinite patience; always waited a long time (an extra long time) before proceeding to extreme measures. He was mighty when aroused. I have seen him both ways—angry as well as calm; more than once seen him when his whole being was shaken up; when his passion was at white heat.

I do not believe he would have taken the position he did towards McClellan except for some reason the logic of which could not be denied—some last reason of all reasons which the most conservative man would find he must obey.

. . . As between Lincoln and McClellan, there is an obvious distinction to be made—their natures were related as higher to lower. Lincoln had a point to make—the Union; McClellan contemplated the prospect of an early end of the war—felt that the man who dealt the softest blows all around would be the great man, the general idol, the savior. So he kept one foot on each side, waiting for the certain sure turn of events which was to give him his immortality.

But events did not turn out the way he expected—McClellan expected. In all that went along with this clash of policies, Lincoln's benignity shone resplendent; the personalism of McClellan was always discouraging, perilous, injurious. Lincoln always stood aside—kept his individual motives in rein—loved, hated, for the common good.

Stanton was another vehement figure there; he had a temper, was touchy, testy, yet also wonderfully patriotic, courageous, farseeing—was the best sort of man at bottom; had been a Democrat; saw trouble coming; was alert, simple-minded; when shock came, was reborn, kindled, into higher, highest interpretations, resolutions; dropped his old partial self away wholly and entirely without a murmur. . . .

Somebody . . . says somewhere that the best saints are those who have been the worst sinners. I consider Mc-Clellan as in some respects a seamed man: he paltered with the army. Yet at Antietam, when pushed to it, he displayed undoubted qualities. They all said, and say now, the battle was well managed to begin with; the fault seems to have been in neglecting to follow out an opportunity—in the loaferly after-hours; in McClellan's "no, no—the army must be rested." A man like Grant would have beaten his way on and on to a positive result.

The real military figure of the war, counting the man in, was Grant, whose homely manners, dislike for military frippery—for every form of ostentation in war and peace—amounted to genius. I was still in Washington while Grant was President. I saw a good deal of him about the city. He went quite freely everywhere alone.

I remember one spot in particular where I often crossed him—a little cottage on the outskirts of Washington; he was frequently there—going there often. I learned that a couple of whom he was very fond lived there. He had met them in Virginia—they received him in a plain democratic way; I would see him leaning on their window sills outside; all would be talking together; they seemed to treat him without deference for place—with dignity, courtesy, appreciation. . . .

. . . Grant was the typical Western man—the plainest, the most efficient; was the least imposed upon by appearances; was most impressive in the severe simplicity of his flannel shirt and his utter disregard for formal military etiquette.

Lee had great qualities of his own, but these [Grant's] were the greatest. I could appreciate such contrasts—I lived in the time, on the spot. I lived in the midst of the life and death vigils of those fearful years—in the camps, in the hospitals, in the fiercest ferment of events. . . .

There are a number of reputations I could prick in that same fashion. It always struck me in the war how honest and direct the private soldiers were—how superior they were, in the main, to their officers. They would freely unbosom to me, tell me of their experiences, perhaps go into minutest details—always, however, as if everything was a matter of fact, was of no value—as if nothing was of enough significance to be bragged of. Their stories justified themselves—did not need to be argued about. My intuitions rarely made a mistake; I believed or did not believe in certain men because—and that was all the reason I had for it. I could always distinguish between a veteran and a tyro—the don't-cry, the calmness, the entire absence of priggishness in the veteran was obvious, conclusive, at once. . . .

. . . I still hold to my opinion formed at that time—[Jeff] Davis was representative, he must bear the onus of that. Besides, Davis is alive; he has perfect freedom; he goes where he wills; every now and then we read accounts of new speeches by him; he is everywhere down South warmly received, applauded to the echo—the echo itself echoed. What more could he have? This has been paralleled nowhere in the world—in any other country on the globe the whole batch of the Confederate leaders would have had their heads cut off. . . .

. . . [As to Stonewall Jackson] there's the story of Lige —Lige Fox. I remember Lige—he was from the Northwest—very free-going, very honest-like. Some day I'll gather all the stories of these books together and give them out—what a jail delivery there will be! There's the story of Lige—it plays the dickens with the character of Stonewall Jackson, taking him down (whipping him off) the pedestal he has decorated by general consent.

Everybody in Washington wanted to think well of Jackson—I with the rest—and we were inclined to the very last to distrust the many stories which seemed to reflect upon his glory. But Lige's tale was so modestly told that I could not doubt it; was told so entirely without brag, bad temper, without any desire for revenge—in fact without any consciousness that Jackson had done anything but what was usual and right.

Lige had been captured. Jackson subjected him to an inquisition; wanted information; would have it—would, would, would—whether or no. Lige only said and kept on saying: "I'm a Union soldier and can't do it." Finding he could get nothing from Lige, Jackson punished him by making him walk the ten miles to Richmond, while the others were conveyed.

I could never think the same of Jackson after hearing that—after seeing how he resented in Lige what was a credit to him—what Lige would not have given and what Jackson could not have taken, and either remain honest. And think of it, too! Jackson was such a praying man— going off into the woods, flopping on his knees everywhere and anywhere to pray!

. . . We must not give too much importance to personalism—it is easy to overcharge it—man moves as man, in all the great achievements—man in the great mass. Yet I, too, think of Lincoln much in that . . . way . . . his poise, his simple, loftiest ability to make an emergency sacred, meet every occasion—never shrinking, never failing, never hurrying—these are things to be remembered and things "providential," if providence ever has a meaning in human affairs.

. . . The radical element in Lincoln was sadness bordering on melancholy, touched by a philosophy, and that philosophy touched again by a humor which saved him from the logical wreck of his powers.

THE ARTILLERYMAN'S VISION

While my wife at my side lies slumbering, and the wars are over
    long,
And my head on the pillow rests at home, and the vacant mid-
    night passes,
And through the stillness, through the dark, I hear, just hear, the
    breath of my infant,
There in the room as I wake from sleep this vision presses upon me;
The engagement opens there and then in fantasy unreal,
The skirmishers begin, they crawl cautiously ahead, I hear the ir-
    regular snap! snap!
I hear the sounds of the different missiles, the short *t-h-t! t-h-t!* of
    the rifle-balls,
I see the shells exploding leaving small white clouds, I hear the great
    shells shrieking as they pass,
The grape like the hum and whirr of wind through the trees,
    (tumultuous now the contest rages,)
All the scenes at the batteries rise in detail before me again,
The crashing and smoking, the pride of the men in their pieces,
The chief-gunner ranges and sights his piece and selects a fuse of the
    right time,
After firing I see him lean aside and look eagerly off to note the
    effect;
Elsewhere I hear the cry of a regiment charging, (the young colo-
    nel leads himself this time with brandish'd sword,)
I see the gaps cut by the enemy's volleys, (quickly fill'd up, no de-
    lay,)
I breathe the suffocating smoke, then the flat clouds hover low
    concealing all;

Now a strange lull for a few seconds, not a shot fired on either side,
Then resumed the chaos louder than ever, with eager calls and
orders of officers,
While from some distant part of the field the wind wafts to my
ears a shout of applause, (some special success,)
And ever the sound of the cannon far or near, (rousing even in
dreams a devilish exultation and all the old mad joy in the depths
of my soul,)
And ever the hastening of infantry shifting positions, batteries,
cavalry, moving hither and thither,
(The falling, dying, I heed not, the wounded dripping and red I
heed not, some to the rear are hobbling,)
Grime, heat, rush, aides-de-camp galloping by or on a full run,
With the patter of small arms, the warning s-s-t of the rifles,
(these in my vision I hear or see,)
And bombs bursting in air, and at night the vari-color'd rockets.

Chapter Thirteen

'Memories of President Lincoln'

Whitman's notes, personal observations, set pieces, etc. on Lincoln, including the final draft of the poet's Lincoln speech.

HUSH'D BE THE CAMPS TO-DAY

[May 4, 1865]

Hush'd be the camps to-day,
And soldiers let us drape our war-worn weapons,
And each with musing soul retire to celebrate,
Our dear commander's death.

No more for him life's stormy conflicts,
Nor victory, nor defeat—no more time's dark events,
Charging like ceaseless clouds across the sky.

But sing poet in our name,
Sing of the love we bore him—because you—dweller in camps,
   know it truly.

As they invault the coffin there,
Sing—as they close the doors of earth upon him—one verse,
For the heavy hearts of soldiers.

'Memories
of President Lincoln'

August 12, 1863.

I see the President almost every day, as I happen to live where he passes to and from his lodgings out of town. He never sleeps at the White House during the hot season, but has quarters at a health location some three miles north of the city—the Soldiers' Home—a United States military establishment.

I saw him this morning about 8:30 coming in to business, riding on Vermont Avenue, near L Street. He always has a company of twenty-five or thirty cavalry, with sabres drawn and held upright over their shoulders. They say the guard was against his personal wish, but he let his counselors have their way.

The party makes no great show in uniform or horses. Mr. Lincoln on the saddle generally rides a good-sized, easy-going, gray horse; is dressed in plain black, somewhat rusty and dusty; wears a stiff black hat; and looks about as ordinary in attire, etc. as the commonest man. A lieutenant with yellow straps rides at his left; and, following behind, two by two, come the cavalry men in their yellow-striped jackets. They are generally going at a slow trot, as that is the pace set them by the one they wait upon. The sabres and accoutrements clank, and the entirely unornamental cortège as it trots toward Lafayette Square arouses no sensation; only some curious stranger stops and gazes.

I see very plainly Abraham Lincoln's dark brown face,

with the deep-cut lines, the eyes always, to me, with a deep latent sadness in the expression. We have got so that we exchange bows, and very cordial ones.

Sometimes the President goes and comes in an open barouche. The cavalry always accompany him, with drawn sabres. Often I notice, as he goes out evenings and sometimes in the morning when he returns early, he turns off and halts at the large and handsome residence of the Secretary of War on K Street and holds conference there. If in his barouche, I can see from my window he does not alight, but sits in his vehicle, and Mr. Stanton comes out to attend him. Sometimes one of his sons, a boy of ten or twelve, accompanies him, riding at his right on a pony.

Earlier in the summer I occasionally saw the President and his wife toward the latter part of the afternoon, out in a barouche on a pleasure ride through the city. Mrs. Lincoln was dressed in complete black, with a long crape veil. The equipage is of the plainest kind—only two horses and they nothing extra.

They passed me once very close, and I saw the President in the face fully, as they were moving slowly; and his look, though abstracted, happened to be directed steadily in my eye. He bowed and smiled, but far beneath the smile I noticed well the expression I have alluded to. None of the artists or pictures have caught the deep though subtle and indirect expression of this man's face. There is something else there. One of the great portrait painters of two or three centuries ago is needed.

The Inauguration, March 4, 1864.

The President very quietly rode down to the Capitol in his own carriage, by himself, on a sharp trot, about noon, either because he wished to be on hand to sign bills, or to get rid of marching in line with the absurd procession— the muslin temple of liberty and pasteboard monitor.

I saw him on his return, at three o'clock, after the performance was over. He was in his plain two-horse barouche, and looked very much worn and tired; the lines, indeed, of vast responsibilities, intricate questions, and demands of life and death cut deeper than ever upon his dark brown face; yet all the old goodness, tenderness, sadness, and canny shrewdness underneath the furrows. (I never see that man without feeling that he is one to become personally attached to for his combination of purest, heartiest tenderness, and native Western form of manliness.)

By his side sat his little boy of ten years. There were no soldiers, only a lot of civilians on horseback, with huge yellow scarves over their shoulders, riding around the carriage. (At the inauguration four years ago he rode down and back again surrounded by a dense mass of armed cavalrymen eight deep, with drawn sabres; and there were sharpshooters stationed at every corner on the route.)

I ought to make mention of the closing levee of Saturday night last. Never before was such a compact jam in front of the White House—all the grounds filled, and away out to the spacious sidewalks. I was there, as I took in a notion to go; was in the rush inside with the crowd; surged along the passageways, the blue and other rooms, and through the great east room. Crowds of country people, some very funny. Fine music from the Marine Band, off in a side place.

I saw Mr. Lincoln, dressed all in black, with white kid gloves and a clawhammer coat, receiving, as in duty bound, shaking hands, looking very disconsolate and as if he would give anything to be somewhere else.

Probably the reader has seen physiognomies (often old farmers, sea captains and such) that, behind their homeliness or even ugliness, held superior points so subtle, yet so palpable, making the real life of their faces almost as impossible to depict as a wild perfume or fruit taste, or a passionate tone of the living voice . . . such was Lincoln's face—the peculiar color, the lines of it, the eyes, mouth, expression. Of technical beauty it had nothing—but to the eye of a great artist it furnished a rare study, a feast, and fascination. The current portraits are all failures—most of them caricatures.

I did not enthuse at the beginning, but I made up what I may call a prophetic judgment from things I heard of him—facts, stories, lights that came in my way. Lincoln's composure was marvellous; he was self-contained, had a thoroughgoing grip on himself. For two or three years he was generally regarded darkly, scornfully, suspiciously in Washington, through the North. . . .

Napoleon didn't study rules first—he first of all studied his task. And there was Lincoln, too—see how he went his own lonely road, disregarding all the usual ways—refusing the guides, accepting no warnings—just keeping his appointment with himself every time. I can hear the advisers saying scornful things to him. They offered him ready-made methods. But Lincoln would only retort: "I want that battle fought—I want that battle won—I don't care how or when—but fought and won!"

. . . But there never has been a portrait of Lincoln—never a real portrait. There were certain ones of us agreed on that. Why? I could not tell; none of us could; all we knew was—it was not there; had we seen it, had it been there, we should have been mighty happy, you can well believe. . . . [Lincoln's] wonderful reserve, restraint of expression, fine nobility staring at you out of all that ruggedness [this had never been] stated pictorially. . . .

Glad am I to give—were anything better lacking—even the most brief and shorn testimony of Abraham Lincoln. Everything I heard about him authentically, and every time I saw him (and it was my fortune through 1862 to '65 to see, or pass a word with or watch him personally, perhaps twenty or thirty times) added to and annealed my respect and love at the moment. And as I dwell on what I myself heard or saw of the mighty Westerner, and blend it with the history and literature of my age, and of what I can get of all ages, and conclude it with his death, it seems like some tragic play, superior to all else I know—vaster and fierier and more convulsionary for this America of ours than Aeschylus and Shakespeare ever drew for Athens or for England. And the Moral permeating, underlying all! the Lesson that none so remote—none so illiterate—no age, no class—but may directly or indirectly read!

Abraham Lincoln's was really one of those characters, the best of which is the result of long trains of cause and effect—needing a certain spaciousness of time, and perhaps even remoteness, to properly enclose them—having un-equalled influence on the shaping of this Republic (and therefore the world) as today, and then far more important in the future. Thus the time has by no means yet come for a thorough measurement of him. Nevertheless, we who live in his era—who have seen him and heard him, face to face, and are in the midst of, or just parting from, the strong and strange events which he and we have had to do with —can in some respects bear valuable, perhaps indispensable, testimony regarding him.

I should like first to give a very fair and characteristic likeness of Lincoln as I saw him and watched him one after-noon in Washington for nearly half an hour, not long be-fore his death. It was as he stood on the balcony of the

National Hotel, Pennsylvania Avenue, making a short speech to the crowd in front on the occasion either of a set of new colors presented to a famous Illinois regiment, or of the daring capture by the Western men of some flags from "the enemy" (which latter phrase, by the by, was not used by him at all in his remarks).

How the picture [I have] happened to be made I do not know, but I bought it a few days afterward in Washington, and it was endorsed by every one to whom I showed it. Though hundreds of portraits have been made by painters and photographers (many to pass on, by copies, to future times), I have never seen one yet that in my opinion deserved to be called a perfectly *good likeness;* nor do I believe there is really such a one in existence. May I not say, too, that, as there is no entirely competent and emblematic likeness of Abraham Lincoln in picture or statue, there is not—perhaps cannot be—any fully appropriate literary statement or summing-up of him yet in existence?

The best way to estimate the value of Lincoln is to think what the condition of America would be today if he had never lived—never been President. His nomination and first election were mainly accidents, experiments. Severely viewed, one cannot think very much of American political parties, from the beginning after the Revolutionary War, down to the present time. Doubtless, while they have had their uses—have been and are "the grass on which the cow feeds" and indispensable economies of growth—it is undeniable that under flippant names they have merely identified temporary passions, or freaks, or sometimes prejudice, ignorance, or hatred. The only thing like a great and worthy idea vitalizing a party and making it heroic was the enthusiasm in 1864 for re-electing Abraham Lincoln and the reason behind that enthusiasm.

How does this man compare with the acknowledged

"Father of his Country"? Washington was modeled on the best Saxon; and Franklin—of the age of the Stuarts (rooted in the Elizabethan period)—was essentially a noble Englishman and just the kind needed for the occasions and the times of 1776–'83. Lincoln, underneath his practicality, was far less European, was quite thoroughly Western, original, essentially non-conventional, and had a certain sort of outdoor or prairie stamp.

One of the best of the late commentators on Shakespeare (Professor Dowden) makes the height and aggregate of his quality to be that he thoroughly blended the ideal with the practical or realistic. If this be so, I should say that what Shakespeare did in poetic expression, Abraham Lincoln essentially did in his personal and official life. I should say the invisible foundations and vertebrae of his character, more than any man's in history, were mystical, abstract, moral, and spiritual—while upon all of them was built, and out of all of them radiated, under the control of the average of circumstances, what the vulgar call *horse sense*, and a life bent by temporary but most urgent materialistic and political reasons.

He seems to have been a man of indomitable firmness (even obstinacy) on rare occasions, involving great points; but he was generally very easy, flexible, tolerant, almost slouchy, respecting minor matters. I note that even those reports and anecdotes intended to level him down all leave the tinge of a favorable impression of him. As to his religious nature, it seems to me to have certainly been of the amplest, deepest-rooted, loftiest kind.

Already a new generation begins to tread the stage, since the persons and events of the Secession War. I have more than once fancied to myself the time when the present century has closed and a new one opened, and the men and deeds of that contest have become somewhat vague and mythical—fancied perhaps in some great Western city, or group collected together, or public festival, where the days of old, of 1863 and '64 and '65 are discussed—some ancient soldier sitting in the background as the talk goes on, and betraying himself by his emotion and moist eyes—like the journeying Ithacan at the banquet of King Alcinoüs, when the bard sings the contending warriors and their battles on the plains of Troy:

> "So from the sluices of Ulysses' eyes
> Fast fell the tears, and sighs succeeded sighs."

I have fancied, I say, some such venerable relic of this time of ours, preserved to the next or still the next generation of America. I have fancied, on such occasion, the young men gathering around; the awe, the eager questions: "What! have you seen Abraham Lincoln—and heard him speak—and touched his hand? Have you, with your own eyes, looked on Grant and Lee and Sherman?"

Dear to Democracy, to the very last! And among the paradoxes generated by America, not the least curious was that spectacle of all the kings and queens and emperors of the earth, many from remote distances, sending tributes of condolence and sorrow in memory of one raised through the commonest average of life—a railsplitter and flatboatman!

Considered from contemporary points of view—who knows what the future may decide?—and from the points of view of current Democracy and the Union (the only thing like passion or infatuation in the man was the passion for the Union of these states), Abraham Lincoln seems to me the grandest figure yet, on all the crowded canvas of the nineteenth century.

A Soldier on Lincoln. May 28, 1865.

As I sat by the bedside of a sick Michigan soldier in hospital today, a convalescent from the adjoining bed rose and came to me, and presently we began talking. He was a middle-aged man belonging to the 2nd Virginia Regiment, but lived in Racine, Ohio, and had a family there.

He spoke of President Lincoln and said: "The war is over, and many are lost. And now we have lost the best, the fairest, the truest man in America. Take him altogether, he was the best man this country ever produced. It was quite a while I thought very different, but some time before the murder that's the way I've seen it."

There was deep earnestness in the soldier. (I found upon further talk he had known Mr. Lincoln personally and quite closely years before.) He was a veteran; was now in the fifth year of his service; was a cavalry man; and had been in a good deal of hard fighting. . . .

Sherman's Army's Jubilation—Its Sudden Stoppage.

When Sherman's armies (long after they had left Atlanta) were marching through South and North Carolina, after leaving Savannah, the news of Lee's capitulation having been received, the men never moved a mile without some part of the line sending up continued, inspiriting shouts. At intervals all day long sounded out the wild music of those peculiar army cries. They would be commenced by one regiment or brigade, immediately taken by others, and at length whole corps and armies would join in these wild triumphant choruses.

It was one of the characteristic expressions of the western troops, and became a habit, serving as a relief and outlet to the men—a vent for their feelings of victory, returning peace, etc. Morning, noon, and afternoon, spontaneous, for occasion and without occasion, these huge, strange cries, differing from any other, echoing through the open air for many a mile, expressing youth, joy, wildness, irrepressible strength, and the ideas of advance and conquest, sounded along the swamps and uplands of the South, floating to the skies. ("There never were men that kept in better spirits in danger or defeat—what then could they do in victory?" said one of the 15th Corps to me afterwards.)

This exuberance continued till the armies arrived at Raleigh. There the news of the President's murder was received. Then no more shouts or yells for a week. All the marching was comparatively muffled. It was very significant—hardly a loud word or laugh in many of the regiments. A hush and silence pervaded all.

Death of President Lincoln. April 16, 1865.

I find in my notes of the time this passage on the death of Abraham Lincoln: He leaves for America's history and biography so far not only its most dramatic reminiscence— he leaves, in my opinion, the greatest, best, most characteristic, artistic, moral personality. Not but that he had faults and showed them in the Presidency; but honesty, goodness, shrewdness, conscience, and (a new virtue, unknown to other lands and hardly yet really known here, but the foundation and tie of all—as the future will grandly develop) UNIONISM, in its truest and amplest sense, formed the hardpan of his character. These he sealed with his life.

The tragic splendor of his death, purging, illuminating all, throws round his form, his head, an aureole that will remain and will grow brighter through time, while history lives and love of country lasts. By many has this Union been helped; but, if one name, one man, must be picked out, he, most of all, is the conservator of it to the future. He was assassinated—but the Union is not assassinated—*ca ira!* One falls and another falls. The soldier drops, sinks like a wave, but the ranks of the ocean eternally press on. Death does its work, obliterates a hundred, a thousand—president, general, captain, private—but the Nation is immortal.

Washington, July 28, 1867.

. . . I suppose you read in the papers about the trial of John S. Surratt for taking part in the murder of President Lincoln. I went down to the trial day before yesterday. Surratt is very young. I sat near him and looked at him a long time. He sits most of the time fanning himself with a big palm leaf fan and watches the witnesses with his sharp eyes; and his brother, a young, farmer-looking man from Texas, sits close by him. The lawyers on both sides are very smart—sometimes the evidence goes strongly against him, and then again for him. It is very interesting to sit and hear the witnesses and the speeches of the lawyers. It has been a tedious trial, and it is hard to tell how it will end. . . .

Death of Abraham Lincoln (The Last Lecture).

Of Abraham Lincoln, bearing testimony twenty-five years after his death, and of that death, I am now, my friends, before you. Few realize the days, the great historic and esthetic personalities, with him as their center, we passed through. Abraham Lincoln, familiar, my own, an Illinoisan, modern yet tallying ancient Moses, Joshua, or later Cromwell—and grander in some respects than any of them—Abraham Lincoln that makes the life of Homer, Plutarch, Shakespeare eligible our day or any day.

My subject this evening for forty or fifty minutes talk is the death of this man, and how that death will finally filter into America. I am not going to tell you anything new; and it is doubtless nearly altogether because I ardently wish to commemorate the hour and martyrdom I now am here. Oft, as the rolling years bring back this hour, let it again, however briefly, be dwelt upon. For my part, I intend until my own dying day, whenever the fourteenth or fifteenth of April comes, to annually gather a few friends and hold its tragic reminiscence.

No narrow or sectional reminiscence. It belongs to these States in their entirety—not the North only, but the South —perhaps belongs most tenderly and devotedly to the South, of all—for there really this man's birthstock; there and then his antecedents stamp. Why should I say that thence his manliest traits, his universality, his canny, easy words upon the surface—his inflexible determination at heart? Have you ever realized it, my friends, that Lincoln, though grafted on the West, is essentially in personality and character a Southern contribution?

And though by no means proposing to resume the Secession War tonight, I would briefly remind you of the public conditions preceding that contest. For twenty years—and especially during the four or five before the war actually began—the aspect of affairs in the United States—though with the flash of military excitement—presents more than the survey of a battle or any extended campaign or series, even, of Nature's convulsions. The hot passions of the South; the strange mixture at the North of inertia, incredulity, and conscious power; the incendiarism of the Abolitionists; the rascality and *grip* of the politicians—unparalleled in any land, any age.

To this I must not omit adding the honesty of the essential bulk of the people everywhere—yet with all the seething fury and contradiction of their natures more aroused than the Atlantic's waves in wildest equinox. In politics what can be more ominous (though generally unappreciated then), what more significant, than the Presidentiads of Fillmore and Buchanan—proving conclusively that the weakness and wickedness of elected rulers are just as likely to afflict us here as in the countries of the Old World under their monarchies, emperors, and aristocracies? In that Old World were everywhere heard underground rumblings that died out only to again surely return. While, in America, the volcano, though civic yet, continued to grow more and more convulsive, more and more stormy and threatening.

In the height of all this excitement and chaos, hovering on the edge at first, and then merged in its very midst and destined to play a leading part, appears a strange and awkward figure.

I shall not easily forget the first time I ever saw Abraham Lincoln. It must have been about the 18th or 19th of February, 1861. It was a rather pleasant afternoon in New York City, as he arrived there from the West, to remain a few hours and then pass on to Washington to prepare for his inauguration. I saw him in Broadway, near the site of the present post office. He came down, I think from Canal Street, to stop at the Astor House.

The broad spaces, sidewalks, and street in that neighborhood and for some distance were crowded with solid masses of people—many thousands. The omnibuses and other vehicles had all been turned off, leaving an unusual hush in that busy part of the city. Presently two or three shabby hack barouches made their way with difficulty through the crowd and drew up at the Astor House entrance.

A tall figure stepped out of the center of these barouches, paused leisurely on the sidewalk, looked up at the granite walls and looming architecture of the grand old hotel—then, after a relieving stretch of arms and legs, turned around for over a minute to slowly and good-humoredly scan the appearance of the vast and silent crowds.

There were no speeches, no compliments, no welcome —as far as I could hear, not a word said. Still, much anxiety was concealed in that quiet. Cautious persons had feared some marked insult or indignity to the president-elect—for he possessed no personal popularity at all in New York City and very little political. But it was evidently tacitly agreed that if the few political supporters of Mr. Lincoln present would entirely abstain from any demonstration on their side, the immense majority—who were anything but supporters—would abstain on their side also. The result was a sulky, unbroken silence, such as certainly never before characterized a New York crowd.

From the top of an omnibus (driven up one side, close by, and blocked by the curbstone and the crowds) I had, I say, a capital view of it all and especially of Mr. Lincoln: his looks and gait; his perfect composure and coolness; his unusual and uncouth height; his dress of complete black, stovepipe hat pushed back on his head; dark-brown complexion; seamed and wrinkled yet canny-looking face; black, bushy head of hair; disproportionately long neck; and his hands held behind, as he stood observing the people.

He looked with curiosity upon that immense sea of faces, and the sea of faces returned the look with similar curiosity. In both there was a dash of comedy, almost farce, such as Shakespeare puts in his blackest tragedies. The crowd that hemmed around consisted, I should think, of thirty to forty thousand men, not a single one his personal friend, while, I have no doubt (so frenzied were the ferments of the time) many an assassin's knife and pistol lurked in hip- or breast-pocket there—ready, soon as break and riot came.

But no break or riot came. The tall figure gave another relieving stretch or two of arms and legs; then, with moderate pace, and accompanied by a few unknown-looking persons, ascended the portico steps of the Astor House, disappeared through its broad entrance—and the dumb-show ended.

I saw Abraham Lincoln often the four years following that date. He changed rapidly and much during his Presidency, but this scene, and him in it, are indelibly stamped upon my recollection. As I sat on the top of my omnibus and had a good view of him, the thought—dim and inchoate then—has since come out clear enough—that four sorts of genius, four mighty and primal hands will be needed to the complete limning of this man's future portrait—the eyes and brains and finger-touch of Plutarch and Aeschylus and Michelangelo, assisted by Rabelais.

And now (Mr. Lincoln passing on from the scene to Washington where he was inaugurated amid armed cavalry and sharpshooters at every point—the first instance of the kind in our history, and I hope it will be the last), now the rapid succession of well-known events (too well known—I believe, these days, we almost hate to hear them mentioned), the National flag fired on at Sumter, the uprising of the North in paroxysms of astonishment and rage, the chaos of divided councils, the call for troops, the First Bull Run, the stunning castdown, shock and dismay of the North—and so, in full flood, the Secession War.

Four years of lurid, bleeding, murky, murderous war. Who paint those years, with all their scenes? The hard-fought engagements; the defeats, plans, failures; the gloomy hours, days, when our Nationality seemed hung in pall of doubt, perhaps death; the Mephistophelean sneers of foreign lands and attachés; the dreaded Scylla of Europe's interference and the Charybdis of the tremendously dangerous latent strata of Secession sympathizers throughout the Free States (far more numerous than is supposed); the long marches in summer; the hot sweat and many a sunstroke, as on the rush to Gettysburg in '63; the night battles in the woods, as under Hooker at Chancellorsville; the camps in winter; the military prisons; the hospitals (alas! alas! the hospitals).

The Secession War? Nay, let me call it the Union War. Though whatever called, it is even yet too near us, too vast and too closely overshadowing, its branches unformed yet (but certain), shooting too far into the future, and the most indicative and mightiest of them yet ungrown.

A great literature will yet arise out of the era of those four years, those scenes—era compressing centuries of na-

tive passion; first-class pictures; tempests of life and death
—and inexhaustible mine for the histories, drama, romance,
and even philosophy of peoples to come—indeed the verte-
ber of poetry and art (of personal character, too) for all
future America—far more grand, in my opinion, to the
hands capable of it, than Homer's siege of Troy, or the
French Wars to Shakespeare.

But I must leave these speculations, and come to the
theme I have assigned and limited myself to. Of the actual
murder of President Lincoln, though so much has been
written, probably the facts are yet very indefinite in most
persons' minds. I read from my memoranda written at the
time and revised frequently and finally since.

The day, April 14, 1865, seems to have been a pleasant
one throughout the whole land—the moral atmosphere
pleasant, too—the long storm, so dark, so fratricidal, full of
blood and doubt and gloom, over and ended at last by the
sunrise of such an absolute National victory and the utter
breakdown of Secessionism—we almost doubted our own
senses! Lee had capitulated beneath the apple tree of Ap-
pomattox. The other armies, the flanges of the revolt,
swiftly followed. And could it really be then? Out of all
the affairs of this world of woe and failure and disorder,
was there really come the confirmed, unerring sign of plan,
like a shaft of pure light—of rightful rule—of God? So the
day, as I say, was propitious. Early herbage, early flowers,
were out. (I remember where I was stopping at the time,
the season being advanced, there were many lilacs in full
bloom. By one of those caprices that enter and give tinge
to events without being at all a part of them, I find myself
always reminded of the great tragedy of that day by the
sight and odor of these blossoms. It never fails.)

But I must not dwell on accessories. The deed hastens.
The popular afternoon paper of Washington, the little
Evening Star, had spattered all over its third page, divided

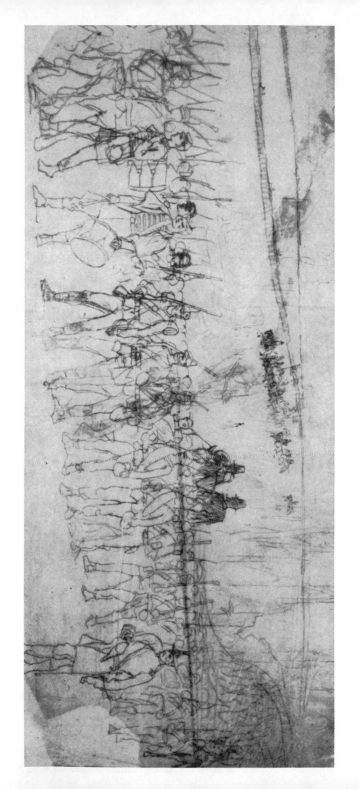

among the advertisements in a sensational manner, in a hundred different places: *The President and his Lady will be at the Theatre this evening*. . . . (Lincoln was fond of the theatre. I have myself seen him there several times. I remember thinking how funny it was that he, in some respects the leading actor in the stormiest drama known to real history's stage through centuries, should sit there and be so completely interested and absorbed in those human jackstraws, moving about with their silly little gestures, foreign spirit, and flatulent text.)

On this occasion the theatre was crowded, many ladies in rich and gay costumes, officers in their uniforms, many well-known citizens, young folks, the usual clusters of gaslights, the usual magnetism of so many people, cheerful, with perfumes, music of violins and flutes (and over all, and saturating all, that vast, vague wonder, *Victory*, the nation's victory, the triumph of the Union, filling the air, the thought, the sense, with exhilaration more than all music and perfumes).

The President came betimes, and, with his wife, witnessed the play from the large stage boxes of the second tier, two thrown into one and profusely draped with the national flag. The acts and scenes of the piece—one of those singularly written compositions which have at least the merit of giving entire relief to an audience engaged in mental action or business excitements and cares during the day, as it makes the slightest call on either the moral, emotional, esthetic, or spiritual nature—a piece ("Our American Cousin") in which, among other characters, so-called, a Yankee (certainly such a one as was never seen, or the least like it ever seen, in North America) is introduced in England, with a varied folderol of talk, plot, scenery, and such phantasmagoria as goes to make up a modern popular drama— had progressed through perhaps a couple of its acts, when, in the midst of this comedy, or nonesuch, or whatever it is to be called; and to offset it, or finish it out (as if in Nature's and the great Muse's mockery of those poor mimes), came interpolated that scene, not really or exactly to be described at all (for on the many hundreds who were there it seems to this hour to have left a passing blur, a dream, a blotch)—and yet partially to be described as I now proceed to give it.

There is a scene in the play representing a modern parlor, in which two unprecedented English ladies are informed by the impossible Yankee that he is not a man of fortune, and therefore undesirable for marriage-catching purposes; after which, the comments being finished, the dramatic trio make exit, leaving the stage clear for a moment. At this period came the murder of Abraham Lincoln.

Great as all its manifold train, circling round it and stretching into the future for many a century, in the politics, history, art, etc. of the New World—in point of fact, the main thing, the actual murder, transpired with the quiet and simplicity of any commonest occurrence—the bursting of a bud or pod in the growth of vegetation, for instance. Through the general hum following the stage pause, with the change of positions, came the muffled sound of a pistol shot, which not one hundredth part of the audience heard at the time—and yet a moment's hush—somehow, surely, a vague, startled thrill—and then through the ornamented, draperied, starred-and-striped spaceway of the President's box, a sudden figure, a man raises himself with hands and feet, stands a moment on the railing, leaps below to the stage (a distance of perhaps fourteen or fifteen feet), falls out of position, catching his boot heel in the copious drapery (the American flag), falls on one knee, quickly recovers himself, rises as if nothing had happened (he really sprains his ankle, but unfelt then)—and so the figure, Booth, the murderer, dressed in plain black broadcloth, bareheaded, with full, glossy, raven hair, and his eyes, like some mad animal's, flashing with light and resolution, and yet with a certain strange calmness, holds aloft in one hand a large knife—walks along not much back from the footlights—turns fully toward the audience his face of statuesque beauty, lit by those basilisk eyes, flashing with desperation, perhaps insanity—launches out in a firm and steady voice the words *sic semper tyrannis*—and then walks with neither slow nor very rapid pace diagonally across to the back of the stage and disappears. (Had not all this terrible scene—making the mimic ones preposterous—had it not all been rehearsed, in blank, by Booth, beforehand?)

A moment's hush—a scream—the cry of *murder*—Mrs. Lincoln leaning out of the box, with ashy cheeks and lips, with involuntary cry, pointing to the retreating figure. *He has killed the President.*

And still a moment's strange, incredulous suspense—and then the deluge!—then that mixture of horror, noises, uncertainty (the sound, somewhere back, of a horse's hoofs clattering with speed)—the people burst through chairs and railings and break them up—there is inextricable confusion and terror—women faint—quite feeble persons fall and are trampled on—many cries of agony are heard—the broad stage suddenly fills to suffocation with a dense and motley crowd, like some horrible carnival—the audience rush generally upon it, at least the strong men do—the actors and actresses are all there in their play costumes and painted faces, with mortal fright showing through the rouge—the screams and calls, confused talk—redoubled, trebled—two or three manage to pass up water from the stage to the President's box—others try to clamber up—etc., etc.

In the midst of all this, the soldiers of the President's guard, with others, suddenly drawn to the scene, burst in (some two hundred altogether), they storm the house, through all the tiers, especially the upper ones, inflamed with fury, literally charging the audience with fixed bayonets, muskets, and pistols, shouting *Clear out! clear out! you sons of. . . .* Such the wild scene, or a suggestion of it rather, inside the playhouse that night.

Outside, too, in the atmosphere of shock and craze, crowds of people filled with frenzy, ready to seize any outlet for it, come near committing murder several times on innocent individuals. One such case was especially exciting. The infuriated crowd, through some chance, got started against one man, either for words he uttered, or perhaps without any cause at all, and were proceeding at once to actually hang him on a neighboring lamppost, when he was rescued by a few heroic policemen, who placed him in their midst and fought their way slowly and amid great peril toward the station house. It was a fitting episode of the whole affair. The crowd rushing and eddying to and fro—the night, the yells, the pale faces, many frightened people trying in vain to extricate themselves—the attacked man, not yet freed from the jaws of death, looking like a corpse—the silent, resolute, half-dozen policemen with no weapons but their little clubs, yet stern and steady through all those eddying swarms—made a fitting side scene to the grand tragedy of the murder. They gained the station house with the protected man, whom they placed in security for the night, and discharged him in the morning.

And in the midst of that pandemonium, infuriated soldiers, the audience, and the crowd, the stage and all its actors and actresses, its paint pots, spangles, and gaslights—the lifeblood from those veins, the best and sweetest in the land, drips slowly down, and death's ooze already begins its little bubbles on the lips.

Thus, the visible incidents and surroundings of Abraham Lincoln's murder, as they really occurred. Thus ended the attempted secession of these States; thus the four years' war. But the main things come subtly and invisibly afterward, perhaps long afterward—neither military, political, nor (great as those are) historical. I say certain secondary and indirect results out of the tragedy of this death are, in my opinion, greatest. Not the event of the murder itself. Not that Mr. Lincoln strings the principal points and personages of the period, like beads, upon the single string of his career. Not that his idiosyncrasy, in its sudden appearance and disappearance, stamps this Republic with a stamp more marked and enduring than any yet given by any one man (more even than Washington's)—but, joined with these, the immeasurable value and meaning of that whole tragedy lies, to me, in senses finally dearest to a nation (and here all our own)—the imaginative and artistic senses—the literary and dramatic ones.

Not in any common or low meaning of those terms, but a meaning precious to the race and to every age. A long and varied series of contradictory events arrives at last at its highest poetic, single, central, pictorial dénouement. The whole involved, baffling, multiform whirl of the Secession period comes to a head, and is gathered in one brief flash of lightning-illumination—one simple, fierce deed. Its sharp culmination and, as it were, solution of so many bloody and angry problems, illustrates those climax-moments on the stage of universal Time, where the historic Muse at one entrance, and the tragic Muse at the other, suddenly ringing down the curtain, close an immense act in the long drama of creative thought, and give it radiation, tableau, stranger than fiction. Fit radiation—fit close! How the imagination, how the student, loves these things! America, too, is to have them. For not in all great deaths, nor far or near—not Caesar in the Roman senate house; or Napoleon passing away in the wild night-storm at St. Helena; not Paleologus, falling, desperately fighting, piled over dozens deep with Grecian corpses; not calm old Socrates drinking the hemlock—outvies that terminus of the Seces-

277

sion War, in one man's life, here in our midst, in our own
time—that seal of the emancipation of three million slaves
—that parturition and delivery of our at last really free
Republic, born again, henceforth to commence its career of
genuine homogeneous Union, compact, consistent with it-
self.

Nor will ever future American patriots and Unionists, in-
differently over the whole land, or North or South, find a
better moral to their lesson. The final use of the greatest
message of a nation is, after all, not with reference to their
deeds in themselves, or their direct bearing on their times
or lands. The final use of a heroic-eminent life—especially
of a heroic-eminent death—is its indirect filtering into the
nation and the race, and to give—often at many removes,
but unerringly—age after age, color and fibre to the per-
sonalism of the youth and maturity of that age, and of man-
kind. Then there is a cement to the whole people, subtler,
more underlying, than anything in written constitution or
courts or armies—namely, the cement of a death identified
thoroughly with that people, at its head and for its sake.
Strange (is it not?) that battles, martyrs, agonies, blood,
even assassination, should so condense—perhaps only really,
lastingly condense—a Nationality.

I repeat it—the grand deaths of the race—the dramatic
deaths of every nationality—are its most important inher-
itance-value—in some respects beyond its literature and art
—as the hero is beyond his finest portrait and the battle it-
self beyond its choicest song or epic. Is not here indeed the
point underlying all tragedy? the famous pieces of the
Grecian masters—and all masters? Why, if the old Greeks
had had this man, what trilogies of plays, what epics, would
have been made out of him! How the rhapsodes would have
recited him! How quickly that quaint tall form would have
entered into the region where men vitalize gods and gods
divinify men! But Lincoln, his times, his death—great as

any, any age—belong altogether to our own, and are autochthonic. (Sometimes indeed I think our American days, our own stage, the actors we know and have shaken hands or talked with—more fateful than anything in Eschylus, more heroic than the fighters around Troy—afford kings of men for our Democracy prouder than Agamemnon, models of character cute and hardy as Ulysses, deaths more pitiful than Priam's.)

When, centuries hence (as it must, in my opinion, be centuries hence before the life of these States, or of Democracy, can be really written and illustrated), the leading historians and dramatists seek for some personage, some special event, incisive enough to mark with deepest cut and mnemonize this turbulent nineteenth century of ours (not only these States, but all over the political and social world), something, perhaps, to close that gorgeous process of European feudalism, with all its pomp and caste prejudices (of whose long train we in America are yet so inextricably the heirs), something to identify with terrible identification by far the greatest revolutionary step in the history of the United States (perhaps the greatest of the world, our century), the absolute extirpation and erasure of slavery from the States—those historians will seek in vain for any point to serve more thoroughly their purpose than Abraham Lincoln's death.

Dear to the Muse—thrice dear to Nationality—to the whole human race—precious to this Union—precious to Democracy—unspeakably and forever precious—their first great Martyr Chief.

O CAPTAIN! MY CAPTAIN!

O Captain! my Captain! our fearful trip is done,
The ship has weather'd every rack, the prize we sought is won;
The port is near, the bells I hear, the people all exulting,
While follow eyes the steady keel, the vessel grim and daring

279

But O heart! heart! heart!
　O the bleeding drops of red,
　　Where on the deck my Captain lies,
　　Fallen cold and dead.

O Captain! my Captain! rise up and hear the bells;
Rise up—for you the flag is flung—for you the bugle trills,
For you bouquets and ribbon'd wreaths—for you the shores
　a-crowding,
For you they call, the swaying mass, their eager faces turning;
　　Here Captain! dear father!
　　　The arm beneath your head!
　　　It is some dream that on the deck,
　　　　You've fallen cold and dead.

My Captain does not answer, his lips are pale and still,
My father does not feel my arm, he has no pulse nor will,
The ship is anchor'd safe and sound, its voyage closed and done,
From fearful trip the victor ship comes in with object won:
　　Exult O shores, and ring O bells!
　　　But I with mournful tread,
　　　　Walk the deck my Captain lies,
　　　　Fallen cold and dead.

Chapter Fourteen

'The Real War Will Never Get in the Books'

Whitman's summing up of the significance of the war—taken from pieces written from 1863–1882.

TURN O LIBERTAD

Turn O Libertad, for the war is over,
From it and all henceforth expanding, doubting no more, resolute,
    sweeping the world,
Turn from lands retrospective recording proofs of the past,
From the singers that sing the trailing glories of the past,
From the chants of the feudal world, the triumphs of kings, slavery,
    caste,
Turn to the world, the triumphs reserv'd and to come—give up
    that backward world,
Leave to the singers of hitherto, give them the trailing past,
But what remains remains for singers for you—wars to come are
    for you,
(Lo, how the wars of the past have duly inured to you, and the
    wars of the present also inure;)
Then turn, and be not alarm'd O Libertad—turn your undying face,
To where the future, greater than all the past,
Is swiftly, surely preparing for you.

'The Real War Will Never Get in the Books'

But what of some of the main premonitions of the war? I may contribute nothing very new on the point, but it is of measureless importance to have the point itself well grounded—which it is not yet—in the understanding of the American people (who still assume the war to have been entirely or mainly the work of the South alone, which it was not at all). . . . What of some of the immediate symptoms and causes of the upheaval? It is an immense topic, which I will but touch upon—seizing the occasion to ventilate one or two notions of my own upon it.

Long, long hence, when the grave has quenched many hot prejudices and vitalities, and an entirely new class of thinkers and writers come to the argument, the complete question, can perhaps be fairly weighed.

The movements of the late Secession War and their results, to any sense that studies well and comprehends them, shows that popular democracy, whatever its faults and dangers, practically justifies itself beyond the proudest claims and wildest hopes of its enthusiasts. Probably no future age can know, but I well know, how the gist of this fiercest and most resolute of the world's warlike contentions resided exclusively in the unnamed, unknown rank and file; and how the brunt of its labor of death was, to all essential purposes, volunteered. The People, of their own choice, fighting, dying for their own idea, insolently attacked by the Secession slave power and its very existence imperiled.

Descending to detail, entering any of the armies, and mixing with the private soldiers, we see and have seen august spectacles. We have seen the alacrity with which the American-born populace, the peaceablest and most good-natured race in the world, and the most personally independent and intelligent, and the least fitted to submit to the irksomeness and exasperation of regimental discipline, sprang, at the first tap of drum, to arms—not for gain, not for glory, nor to repel invasion—but for an emblem, a mere abstraction—for the life, *the safety, of the flag.* We have seen the unequalled docility and obedience of these soldiers. We have seen them tried long and long by hopelessness, mismanagement, and by defeat; have seen the incredible slaughter toward or through which the armies (as at First Fredericksburg, and afterward at the Wilderness) still unhesitatingly obeyed orders to advance.

We have seen them in trench, or crouching behind breastwork, or tramping in deep mud, or amid pouring rain or thick-falling snow, or under forced marches in hottest summer (as on the road to get to Gettysburg)—vast suffocating swarms, divisions, corps, with every man so grimed and black with sweat and dust, his own mother would not have known him—his clothes all dirty, stained, and torn, with sour, accumulated sweat for perfume—many a comrade, perhaps a brother, sunstruck, staggering out, dying by the roadside of exhaustion—yet the great bulk bearing steadily on, cheery enough, hollow-bellied from hunger, but sinewy with unconquerable resolution.

We have seen this race proved by wholesale by drearier yet more fearful tests—the wound, the amputation, the shattered face or limb; the slow, hot fever; long impatient anchorage in bed; and all the forms of maiming, operation, and disease.

284

Alas! America we have seen, though only in her early youth, already to hospital brought. There have we watched these soldiers, many of them only boys in years—marked their decorum, their religious nature and fortitude, and their sweet affection. Wholesale, truly. For at the front and through the camps, in countless tents, stood the regimental, brigade, and division hospitals; while everywhere amid the land, in or near cities, rose clusters of huge, white-washed, crowded, one-story wooden barracks; and there ruled agony with bitter scourge, yet seldom brought a cry; and there stalked death by day and night along the narrow aisles between the rows of cots or by the blankets on the ground, and touched lightly many a poor sufferer, often with blessed, welcome touch.

I know not whether I shall be understood, but I realize that it is finally from what I learned personally mixing in such scenes that I am now penning these pages.

One night in the gloomiest period of the war, in the Patent Office Hospital in Washington City, as I stood by the bedside of a Pennsylvania soldier who lay, conscious of quick approaching death, yet perfectly calm and with noble, spiritual manner, the veteran surgeon, turning aside, said to me that though he had witnessed many, many deaths of soldiers and had been a worker at Bull Run, Antietam, Fredericksburg, etc., he had not seen yet the first case of man or boy that met the approach of dissolution with cowardly qualms or terror. My own observation fully bears out these remarks.

What have we here if not, towering above all talk and argument, the plentifully supplied, last-needed proof of democracy, in its personalities? Curiously enough, too, the proof on this point comes, I should say, every bit as much from the South as from the North. Although I have spoken only of the latter, yet I deliberately include all. Grand, common stock! To me the accomplished and convincing growth, prophetic of the future; proof, undeniable to sharpest sense, of perfect beauty; tenderness and pluck that never feudal lord nor Greek nor Roman breed yet rivaled.

Let no tongue ever speak in disparagement of the American races, north or south, to one who has been through the war in the great army hospitals.

Origins of Attempted Secession.

I consider the War of Attempted Secession . . . not as a struggle of two distinct and separate peoples, but a conflict (often happening and very fierce) between the passions and paradoxes of one and the same identity—perhaps the only terms on which that identity could really become fused, homogeneous and lasting. The origin and conditions out of which it arose are full of lessons, full of warnings yet to the Republic, and always will be. The underlying and principal of those origins are yet singularly ignored. The Northern States were really just as responsible for that war (in its precedents, foundations, instigations) as the South.

Let me try to give my view. From the age of 21 to 40 (1840–'60) I was interested in the political movements of the land, not so much as a participant but as an observer and a regular voter of the elections. I think I was conversant with the springs of action and their workings not only in New York City and Brooklyn, but understood them in the whole country, as I have made leisurely tours through all the Middle States and partially through the Western and Southern, and down to New Orleans, in which city I resided for some time. (I was there at the close of the Mexican War—saw and talked with General Taylor and the other generals and officers who were fêted and detained several days on their return victorious from that expedition.)

Of course, many and very contradictory things, specialties, developments, constitutional views, etc. went to make up the origin of the war, but the most significant general fact can be best indicated and stated as follows: For twenty-five years previous to the outbreak, the controlling "democratic" nominating conventions of our Republic—starting from their primaries in wards and districts, and so expanding to counties, powerful cities, states, and to the great presidential nominating conventions—were getting to represent and be composed of more and more putrid and dangerous materials.

Let me give a schedule or list of one of these representative conventions for a long time before, and inclusive of, that which nominated Buchanan. (Remember they had come to be the fountains and tissues of the American body politic, forming, as it were, the whole blood, legislation, office-holding, etc.) One of these conventions, from 1840 to '60, exhibited a spectacle such as could never be seen except in our own age and in these states. The members who composed it were, seven eighths of them, the meanest kind of bawling and blowing officeholders, office seekers, pimps, malignants, conspirators, murderers, fancy-men, custom-house clerks, contractors, kept editors, spaniels well trained to carry and fetch, jobbers, infidels, disunionists, terrorists, mail-riflers, slave-catchers, pushers of slavery, creatures of the president, creatures of would-be presidents, spies, bribers, compromisers, lobbyers, sponges, ruined sports, expelled gamblers, policy backers, monte dealers, duellists, carriers of concealed weapons, deaf men, pimpled men scarred inside with vile disease, gaudy outside with gold chains made from the people's money and harlots' money twisted together—crawling, serpentine men—the lousy combings and born freedom-sellers of the earth.

And whence came they? From backyards and barrooms; from out of the custom houses, marshals' offices, post offices and gambling hells; from the President's house, the jail, the stationhouse; from unnamed byplaces where devilish disunion was hatched at midnight; from political hearses, and from the coffins inside, and from the shrouds inside of the coffins; from the tumors and abscesses of the land; from the skeletons and skulls in the vaults of the federal almshouses; and from the running sores of the great cities.

Such I say, formed, or absolutely controlled the forming of, the entire personnel, the atmosphere, nutriment and chyle of our municipal, state, and national politics—substantially permeating, handling, deciding, and wielding everything—legislation, nominations, elections, "public sentiment," etc.—while the great masses of the people—farmers, mechanics, and traders—were helpless in their grip. These conditions were mostly prevalent in the north and west and especially in New York and Philadelphia cities; and the Southern leaders (bad enough, but of a far higher order) struck hands and affiliated with, and used them. Is it strange that a thunderstorm followed such morbid and stifling cloud strata?

I say then that what, as just outlined, heralded and made the ground ready for Secession revolt, ought to be held up, through all the future, as the most instructive lesson in American political history—the most significant warning and beacon-light to coming generations. I say that the sixteenth, seventeenth, and eighteenth terms of the American Presidency have shown that the villainy and shallowness of rulers (backed by the machinery of great parties) are just as eligible to these States as to any foreign despotism, kingdom, or empire—there is not a bit of difference.

History is to record those three Presidentiads, and especially the administrations of Fillmore and Buchanan, as so far our topmost warning and shame. Never were publicly displayed more deformed, mediocre, snivelling, unreliable, false-hearted men. Never were these States so insulted and attempted to be betrayed. All the main purposes for which the government was established were openly denied. The

288

perfect equality of slavery with freedom was flauntingly preached in the North—nay, the superiority of slavery. The slave trade was proposed to be renewed. Everywhere frowns and misunderstandings—everywhere exasperations and humiliations.

(The slavery contest is settled—and the war is long over —yet do not those putrid conditions, too many of them, still exist? still result in diseases, fevers, wounds—not of war and army hospitals—but the wounds and diseases of peace?)

Out of those generic influences, mainly in New York, Pennsylvania, Ohio, etc., arose the attempt at disunion. To philosophical examination, the malignant fever of that war shows its embryonic sources, and the original nourishment of its life and growth, in the North. I say, Secession, below the surface, originated and was brought to maturity in the Free States. I allude to the score of years preceding 1860. My deliberate opinion is now that if at the opening of the contest the abstract duality-question of *slavery and quiet* could have been submitted to a direct popular vote, as against their opposite, they would have triumphantly carried the day in a majority of the Northern States—in the large cities, leading off with New York and Philadelphia, by tremendous majorities.

The events of '61 amazed everybody North and South, and burst all prophecies and calculations like bubbles. But even then, and during the whole war, the stern fact remains that *not only did the North put it down, but the Secession cause had numerically just as many sympathizers in the Free, as in the Rebel, States.*

As to slavery, abstractly and practically (its idea and the determination to establish and expand it, especially in the new territories, the future America), it is too common, I repeat, to identify it exclusively with the South. In fact, down to the opening of the war, the whole country had about an equal hand in it. The North had at least been just as guilty, if not more guilty; and the East and West had. The former presidents and congresses had been guilty; the governors and legislatures of every Northern State had been guilty; their hands were all stained. And as the conflict took decided shape, it is hard to tell which class, the leading Southern or Northern disunionists, was more stunned and disappointed at the non-action of the Free State secession element, so largely existing and counted on by those leaders—both sections.

So much for that point and for the North. As to the inception and direct instigation of the war in the South itself, I shall not attempt interiors or complications. Behind all, the idea that it was from a resolute and arrogant determination on the part of the extreme slaveholders, the Calhounites, to carry the States' Rights portion of the constitutional compact to its farthest verge, and nationalize slavery—or else disrupt the Union and found a new empire with slavery for its cornerstone, was and is undoubtedly the true theory. (If successful, this attempt might—I am not sure, but it might—have destroyed not only our American Republic in anything like first-class proportions, in itself and its prestige, but for ages, at least, the cause of liberty and equality everywhere—and would have been the greatest triumph of reaction and the severest blow to political and every other freedom possible to conceive. Its worst result would have inured to the Southern States themselves.)

That our national democratic experiment, principle, and machinery could triumphantly sustain such a shock, and that the Constitution could weather it, like a ship a storm, and come out of it as sound and whole as before, is by far the most signal proof yet of the stability of that experiment—Democracy—and of those principles and that Constitution.

Of the war itself, we know in the ostent what has been done. The numbers of the dead and wounded can be told or approximated, the debt posted and put on record, the material events narrated, etc. Meantime, elections go on, laws are passed, political parties struggle, issue their platforms, etc., just the same as before. But immensest results, not only in politics but in literature, poems, and sociology, are doubtless waiting yet unformed in the future. How long they will wait I cannot tell.

The pageant of history's retrospect shows us, ages since, all Europe marching on the Crusades, those armed uprisings of the people, stirred by a mere idea to grandest attempt— and, when once baffled in it, returning at intervals, twice, thrice, and again. An unsurpassed series of revolutionary events, influences. Yet it took over two hundred years for the seeds of the Crusades to germinate before beginning even to sprout.

Two hundred years they lay—sleeping, not dead—but dormant in the ground. Then, out of them, unerringly, arts, travel, navigation, politics, literature, freedom, the spirit of adventure, inquiry, all arose, grew and steadily sped on to what we see at present. Far back there that huge agitation struggle of the Crusades stands as undoubtedly the embryo, the start, of the high preëminence of experiment, civilization, and enterprise, which the European nations have since sustained and of which these States are the heirs.

Another illustration (history is full of them, although the war itself, the victory of the Union, and the relations of our equal States, present features of which there are no precedents in the past): The conquest of England eight centuries ago by the Franco-Normans—the obliteration of the old (in many respects so needing obliteration), the Domesday Book, and the repartition of the land—the old impedimenta removed, even by blood and ruthless violence, and a new progressive genesis established, new seeds sown —time has proved plain enough that, bitter as they were,

291

all these were the most salutary series of revolutions that could possibly have happened. Out of them, and by them mainly, have come, out of Albic, Roman, and Saxon England—and without them could not have come—not only the England of the five hundred years down to the present and of the present, but these States. Nor, except for that terrible dislocation and overturn, would these States, as they are, exist today.

It is certain to me that the United States, by virtue of that war and its results—and through that and them only—are now ready to enter, and most certainly enter, upon their genuine career in history, as no more torn and divided in their spinal requisites, but a great homogeneous Nation—free states all—a moral and political unity in variety, such as Nature shows in her grandest physical works, and as much greater than the merely physical.

Out of that war not only has the Nationality of the States escaped from being strangled, but, more than any of the rest and in my opinion more than the North itself, the vital heart and breath of the South have escaped as from the pressure of a general nightmare, and are henceforth to enter on a life, development, and active freedom whose realities are certain in the future, notwithstanding all the Southern vexations of the hour—a development which could not possibly have been achieved on any less terms or by any other means than that grim lesson or something equivalent to it. And I predict that the South is yet to outstrip the North.

And so good-bye to the war. I know not how it may have been or may be to others—to me the main interest I found (and still, on recollection, find) in the rank and file of the armies, both sides, and in those specimens amid the hospitals and even the dead on the field. To me, the points illustrating the latent personal character and eligibilities of these States in the two or three millions of American young and middle-aged men, North and South, embodied in those armies—and especially the one third or one fourth of their number stricken by wounds or disease at some time in the course of the contest—were of more significance even than the political interests involved. (As so much of a race depends on how it faces death, and how it stands personal anguish and sickness; as, in the glints of emotions under emergencies, and the indirect traits and asides in Plutarch, we get far profounder clues to the antique world than all its more formal history.)

Future years will never know the seething hell and the black infernal background of countless minor scenes and interiors (not the official surface courteousness of the generals, not the few great battles) of the Secession War; and it is best they should not. The real war will never get in the books.

In the mushy influences of current times, too, the fervid atmosphere and typical events of those years are in danger of being totally forgotten. I have at night watched by the side of a sick man in the hospital, one who could not live many hours. I have seen his eyes flash and burn as he raised himself and recurred to the cruelties on his surrendered brother and mutilation of the corpse afterward. (See in the preceding pages the incident at Upperville—the 17 killed as in the description were left there on the ground. After they dropped dead, no one touched them—all were made sure of, however. The carcasses were left for the citizens to bury or not, as they chose.)

Such was the war. It was not a quadrille in a ballroom. Its interior history will not only never be written—its practicality, minutiae of dead and passions, will never even be suggested. The actual soldier of 1862–'65, North and South, with all his ways, his incredible dauntlessness, habits, practices, tastes, language, his fierce friendship, his appetite, rankness, his superb strength and animality, lawless gait, and a hundred unnamed lights and shades of same, I say, will never be written—perhaps must not and should not be.

The preceding notes may furnish a few stray glimpses into that life and into those lurid interiors, never to be fully conveyed to the future. The hospital part of the drama from '61 to '65, deserves indeed to be recorded. Of that many-threaded drama with its sudden and strange surprises, its confounding of prophecies, its moments of despair, the dread of foreign interference, the interminable campaigns, the bloody battles, the mighty and cumbrous and green armies, the drafts and bounties—the immense money expenditure like a heavy-pouring constant rain—with, over the whole land the last three years of the struggle, an unending, universal mourning wall of women, parents, orphans—the marrow of the tragedy concentrated in those army hospitals (it seemed sometimes as if the whole interest of the land, North and South, was one vast central hospital, and all the rest of the affair but flanges)—those forming the untold and unwritten history of the war—infinitely greater (like life's) than the few scraps and distortions that are ever told or written. Think how much, and of importance, will be—how much, civic and military, has already been buried in the grave, in eternal darkness.

Sources, Bibliography, Notes, and Appendix

Sources

Published and unpublished sources from which *Walt Whitman's Civil War* was compiled and edited

Abbreviations used in Notes

Collections

BERG	Henry W. and Albert A. Berg Collection, New York Public Library.
FEINBERG	Private collection of Charles E. Feinberg, Detroit, Mich.
LION	Oscar Lion Collection, New York Public Library
MORGAN	Whitman Collection, Pierpont Morgan Library, New York City
TRENT	Josiah Trent Collection, Duke University Library, Durham, N.C.
VIRGINIA	Barrett Literary Manuscript Collection, Alderman Library, University of Virginia, Charlottesville.
WASHINGTON	Manuscript Collection, Library of Congress, Washington, D.C.
YALE	Adrian van Sinderen Collection, Yale University Library, New Haven.
PENNSYLVANIA	Rare Book Collection, University of Pennsylvania, Philadelphia.

Abbreviations

Books

CLEWS	*Faint Clews and Indirections*, edited by Clarence Gohdes and Rollo G. Silver, Duke University Press, Durham, N.C.

DRESSER | *The Wound Dresser, A Series of Letters Written from the Hospitals in Washington during the War of the Rebellion by Walt Whitman;* edited by Richard Maurice Bucke, M.D., Boston: Small, Maynard & Co., 1898.

FORCES | *The Gathering of the Forces,* edited by Rodgers & Black, New York & London; G. P. Putnam's Sons, 1920.

GLICKSBERG | *Walt Whitman and the Civil War,* A Collection of Original Articles and Manuscripts, edited by Charles I. Glicksberg, Philadelphia: University of Pennsylvania Press, 1933.

LEAVES | *Leaves of Grass,* edited by Emory Holloway, Garden City: Doubleday, Doran & Co., 1929.

LINCOLN | *Abraham Lincoln and Walt Whitman,* by William E. Barton, Indianapolis: the Bobbs-Merrill Co., 1928.

PROSE | *Complete Prose Works: Specimen Days and Collect, November Boughs and Good-Bye My Fancy,* London: Nonesuch Press, 1938.

TRAUBEL | *With Walt Whitman in Camden,* by Horace L. Traubel; *Vol. 1, March 8–July 14, 1888,* Boston: Small, Maynard & Co., 1906; *Vol. 2, July 16–Oct. 31, 1888,* New York: D. Appleton & Co., 1908; *Vol. 3, March 28–July 14, 1888 and Nov. 1, 1888–Jan. 20, 1889;* New York: Mitchell Kennerly, 1914; *Vol. 4, Jan. 2–April 7, 1889;* Philadelphia: University of Pennsylvania Press, 1953.

UNCOLLECTED | *The Uncollected Poetry and Prose of Walt Whitman,* collected and edited by Emory Holloway, 2 vols., New York: Doubleday, Doran & Co., 1921.

WORKSHOP | *Walt Whitman's Workshop,* edited by Clifton Joseph Furness, Cambridge: Harvard University Press, 1928.

The editor has gone to original sources for newspaper dispatches, letters [1] and manuscripts appearing in *Walt Whitman's Civil War.*

[1] An invaluable checklist, *Walt Whitman's Correspondence,* compiled by Edwin H. and Rosalind S. Miller, is published by the New York Public Library (1957).

Wherever this material exists in book form, it is so identified.

<small>PASSAGES FROM UNPUBLISHED SOURCES ARE LISTED BELOW.</small>

Page

Chapter One

7 From "Under the Southern sun" to "this union should be lost."   FEINBERG

9 From "Brooklyn, N.Y., December 26, 1864" to "unalterable determination on the other."   YALE

10 From "The way to bring" to "in the future."   YALE

12 From "I have entertained" to "artistic and literary relations."   WASHINGTON

13 From "The long, long solemn trenches" to "ever written or chanted."   FEINBERG

Chapter Four

63 From "Went with Mrs. O'Connor" to "perfect manipulation."   FEINBERG

64 From "This is the last day" to "vestments of majesty."   FEINBERG

78 From "Brooklyn, April 7, 1865. Dear friend" to "whole of mankind."   BERG

Chapter Eight

177 From "April 21, 1863. I thought" to "God bless you."   BERG

201 From "No poem sings" to "left them to die."   FEINBERG

Chapter Nine

205 From "It is generally believed" to "it appears on the surface."   TRENT

210 From "Brooklyn, N.Y., December 26, 1864" to "among them."   YALE

Chapter Thirteen

267 From "I suppose you read" to "it will end."   FEINBERG

Page

Chapter Fourteen

Selected Bibliography

Partial list of works consulted in the preparation of *Walt Whitman's Civil War*

Allen, G. W.: *Walt Whitman Handbook*. Chicago: Packard & Co.; 1946.

———: *The Solitary Singer*. New York: Macmillan Co.; 1938.

Arvin, Newton: *Whitman*. New York: Macmillan Co.; 1938.

Barrus, Clara: *Whitman and Burroughs, Comrades*. New York: Houghton Mifflin Co.; 1931.

Bazalgette, L.: *Walt Whitman, L'homme et son oeuvre*. Paris: Mercure de France; 1908.

Binns, H. B.: *A Life of Walt Whitman*. London: Methuen & Co.; 1905.

Brooks, Van Wyck: *The Times of Melville and Whitman*. New York: E. P. Dutton; 1947.

Bucke, R. M. (*ed.*): *Calamus*. Boston: Laurens Maynard; 1897.

———: *Walt Whitman*. Philadelphia: David McKay; 1883.

———, T. B. Harned, & H. L. Traubel (*eds.*): *The Complete Writings of Walt Whitman*. 10 vols., New York: G. P. Putnam's Sons; 1902.

Burroughs, J.: *Notes on Walt Whitman as Poet and Person*. New York: American News Co.; 1867.

———: *Whitman: A Study*. Boston: Houghton Mifflin Co.; 1943.

Canby, H. S.: *Walt Whitman, An American*. Boston: Houghton Mifflin Co.; 1943.

Capek, Abe (*ed.*): *Walt Whitman*. Berlin: Seven Seas Publishers; 1958.

Catel, Jean: *La Naissance du poète*. Paris: Les Editions Rieder; 1929.

Carpenter, E.: *Days with Walt Whitman*. London: George Allen; 1906.

Faner, R. D.: *Walt Whitman and Opera*. Philadelphia: University of Pennsylvania Press; 1928.

Holloway, Emory & V. Schwartz (*eds.*): *I Sit and Look Out*. New York: Columbia University Press; 1932.

—— & R. Adimari (*eds.*): *New York Dissected*. New York: Rufus Rockwell Wilson; 1936.

——: *Whitman: An Interpretation in Narrative*. New York, Alfred A. Knopf; 1926.

Kennedy, W. S. (*ed.*): *Walt Whitman's Diary in Canada*. Boston: Small, Maynard; 1904.

—— (*ed.*): *Reminiscences of Walt Whitman*. London: Alexander Gardner; 1896.

——: *The Fight of a Book for the World*. West Yarmouth, Mass.: Stonecraft Press; 1926.

Perry, Bliss: *Walt Whitman, His Life and Work*. Boston: Houghton Mifflin Co.; 1906.

Rivers, W. C.: *Walt Whitman's Anomaly*. London: George Allen; 1913.

Schyberg, F.: *Walt Whitman* (trans. E. A. Allen). New York: Columbia University Press; 1951.

Sillen, S. (*ed.*): *Walt Whitman, Poet of American Democracy*. New York: International Publishers; 1955.

Symonds, J. A.: *Walt Whitman, A Study*. London: George Routledge; 1893.

Traubel, H. L., R. M. Bucke, & T. B. Harned: *In Re Walt Whitman*. Philadelphia: David McKay; 1893.

Trowbridge, J. T.: *My Own Story: with Recollections of Noted Persons*. Boston: Houghton Mifflin Co.; 1903.

Notes

EDITORIAL NOTE: The editor feels that the title "Notes" for the section that follows may require a bit of explanation. After having identified here the sources of each chapter, the people closest to Whitman, and other matters referred to in the text, it seemed desirable to include certain passages, documents and poems (many of them previously unpublished), placing them under the chapter heading that seemed most relevant. If the choice and position of these items appear somewhat arbitrary, the treatment was dictated by the fragmentary and widely dispersed nature of the original material.

Whitman's Own Chronology of His Life [1]

1819—May 31
Born at West Hills, Long Island, State of New York—second child of Walter and Louisa (born Van Velsor) Whitman. 1820, '21, '22, '23 continued at West Hills.

1824
Moved to Brooklyn. Went to Public School. 1831, tended in Lawyer's office. Then in doctor's. In 1834 went into printing office to learn typesetting.

1838
Teaching country schools in Suffolk county. Continued at it partly in Queens county for three years. Then starts a weekly paper "The Long Islander" at Huntington, L. I.

1840
Back in New York City. Working at printing and journalistic writing. In 1846 and '7 edits the "Eagle" newspaper in Brooklyn.

1848
Goes to New Orleans as an editor on the staff of "The Crescent" newspaper. Afterward travels south and south west.

1850
Returns north. Publishes "the Freeman" newspaper in Brooklyn. Then works at building houses and selling them.

[1] From the facsimile of a handwritten document in *Leaves of Grass*, Philadelphia: David McKay; 1900.

1855

Issues "Leaves of Grass," first edition, small quarto, 95 pages. In 1856, 2d edition, 16 mo. 384 pages. 1860, third edition, 456 pages, 12 mo. Boston.

1862

Goes down to the Secession War Fields. Begins his ministrations to the wounded in the hospitals and after battles, and continues at them steadily for three years. In 1865 gets an appointment as Department Clerk.

1867

Publishes 4th edition of "Leaves of Grass" including "Drum Taps." In 1871 fifth edition.

1873

Prostrated by paralysis at Washington. Starts for Atlantic seashore by order of the physician. Breaks down badly at Philadelphia and takes up quarters in Camden, New Jersey; where he has remained up to date; for over fifteen years.

1876

Sixth or Centennial issue of L. of G. with another Volume, "Two Rivulets" of prose and poems alternately. In 1881, seventh edition of L. of G. published by Osgood & Co., Boston.

1882

Eighth issue of "Leaves of Grass" pub'd by David McKay, Philadelphia. Also "Specimen Days" a prose and autobiographic Volume.

1888

Mr. Whitman is now in his 70th year. He is almost entirely disabled physically, through the paralysis from his persistent army labors in 1863 and '64, but is now just printing, we hear, a little volume of additional prose and verse called "November Boughs." He resides in Mickle St., Camden, N.J.[1]

Notes on Editor's Foreword

Sources: Quotations appearing in the foreword from letters and original manuscripts used in the text are identified elsewhere in the notes. The veteran's letter quoted is in BERG.[2]

[1] On March 26, 1892, four years after this last entry, Walt Whitman died in the Mickle Street house.

[2] For key to abbreviations used in notes, see *Sources,* pp. 297–8.

Leaves of Grass: The first edition, published by Whitman in 1855, contained twelve poems. By the time of the Civil War *Leaves* had grown, in a third edition, to 415 pages with 156 poems. The 1892, "Deathbed," edition contained hundreds of additional poems.

Mrs. Abby Price: A family friend with whom Whitman maintained a lifelong friendship and correspondence. A woman of warmth and keen intelligence, Mrs. Price was active in such reform movements as anti-slavery, woman's rights, and dress reform.

William Douglas O'Connor: Author of the abolitionist novel *Harrington.* One of Whitman's closest friends. His pamphlet *The Good Gray Poet* defended Whitman when he was dismissed from his government post because of his *Calamus* poems.

James Redpath: Editor, journalist, reformer, and abolitionist; author of *The Public Life of John Brown;* editor for a time of the *North American Review.* Remained Whitman's friend and ally through many years of the poet's life.

Horace L. Traubel: Devoted friend and aide of Whitman's in the poet's later years. In 1888, Traubel, who visited the ailing Whitman at this period sometimes two or three times a day, began making the voluminous verbatim record of their conversations that appears in *With Walt Whitman in Camden.* Four volumes of this work are now available; three more are in preparation. Traubel was one of Whitman's literary executors.

Louisa Van Velsor Whitman (1795–1873): Whitman's mother. His extraordinary devotion is manifested in the letters he wrote her throughout his life—far more than to any other correspondent. He would often use her own unlettered language to convey the intimate communion between them. In his poem, "As at Thy Portals Also Death," he writes: ". . . memories of my mother, to the divine blending, maternity."

George Washington Whitman (1829–1901): Whitman's younger brother, the seventh of Louisa Whitman's children. George enlisted in the Brooklyn 13th Regiment in April 1861, and, after the expiration of his hundred-day term, joined the 51st New York Volunteers, then commanded by Colonel Edward Ferrero, who made him a sergeant major. He was later promoted several times—to captain after First Fredericksburg. On September 30, 1864, George, who was acting lieutenant colonel of his regiment, was captured and imprisoned. He was exchanged in February, 1865.

Notes on Chapter One

Sources: "Pivotal to the Rest" brings together a number of passages from various sources to serve as Whitman's own introduction to this book. The letter to Redpath (YALE, published in TRAUBEL 4) and unpublished manuscripts (YALE and WASHINGTON) reveal Whitman's plans for a Civil War volume of his own. "The long, long solemn trenches," an unpublished poem, is in FEINBERG. The rest of this chapter will be found in PROSE and in TRAUBEL 2 and 3.

James Redpath: An unpublished memo [1] in Whitman's handwriting reads:

"To James Redpath   Oct. 12, 1863

. . . Do you want to print a little 30 or 50¢ book about the scenes, war camps, hospitals, etc . . . (especially these, etc.). . . ."

Redpath's reply to Whitman's proposal for a Civil War Book [2] reads:

Boston, October 28, 1863

Friend W.

I have taken your proposition into consideration.

There is a lion in the way—$

I could easily publish a small Book, but the one you propose—to stereotype, advertise and push it implies an expenditure that may be beyond my means. But if I can get credit, I may try. Whether I will or no depends somewhat on the printer's notion as to whether the book would sell.

Suppose you finish it and send it on: if I cannot publish it, I will see if some other person won't.

This is the best I can safely promise you. If I can get one or two jobbers to read and like it, and they will make an advance order, or give a favorable trade opinion, the way is clear.

What say?

James Redpath.

A draft prospectus for the book Whitman proposed to Redpath [3] reads:

[1] FEINBERG.   [2] TRAUBEL 2.
[3] YALE.

"MEMORANDA OF A YEAR (1863) by Walt Whitman
Walt Whitman's publisher's announcement. A new book. Memoranda of a Year. Probably no greater year has ever sped to its close, in the world's history, than the one now terminating. At all events, the year 1863 is by far the most important in the hitherto history of America. And this book, with its framework jotted down on the battlefield, in the shelter tent, by the wayside amid the rubble of passing artillery trains, or the moving of cavalry in the streets of Washington, in the gorgeous halls of gold where the national representatives meet, and above all in the great military hospitals, amid the children of every one of the United States, the representatives of every battle, amid the ashy face, the bloody bandage, with death and suffering on every side. An ardent book arresting many of the most significant things; flashes, stormy, and quick, that characterize the time and spirit and fact of the events all are passing through—a book indeed full of *these* vehement, these tremendous days—full of incidents, full of the blood and vitality of the American people—a book, antedating from a mentality gestated amid the ocean life and cosmopolitanism of New York, with all the proclivities of *Nationality, Freedom,* and real *Democracy.*

Such is the new volume the publishers offer to the public, confident it will prove all that the foregoing description claims for it."

Notes on Chapter Two

Sources: In *Specimen Days,* from which the material in "Beat! Beat! Drums!" is selected, Whitman—after fifteen pages of autobiography—begins to record his impressions on the day war was declared. The passages in this chapter will be found in PROSE.

Copy of a Whitman pass to a military district: [1]

HEADQUARTERS MILITARY DISTRICT

Washington, D.C., March 25, 1864

No. 238

Pass the Bearer *Walter Whitman* within the limits of the fortifications to *Arlington* and return. This pass will expire on *return* trip

By order of John H. Martindale
Brig. Gen. and Military Governor
A. S. Gummee, Capt. Ast. Adj. Gen.

[1] Reproduced in LINCOLN.

[On the reverse, the oath of allegiance and description of Whit-
man, as follows:]

Age *45*

Height *6 ft.*   Hair *Gray*

Complexion *Ruddy*   Eyes *Blue*

(*Italicized words* are in handwriting in the facsimile of this pass)

Notes on Chapter Three

Sources: "The Dense Brigades Press On" is made up
of paragraphs and passages in PROSE; let-
ters to Whitman's mother (FEINBERG, pub-
lished in DRESSER); and manuscript material
in WASHINGTON (collected and first pub-
lished in GLICKSBERG).

Hannah Whitman Hyde ("*Han*"): Whitman's younger sister
(1823–1908). "It was Hannah alone of all the Whitman family that
liked *Leaves* and found them 'fascinating.' "[1]
Thomas Jefferson Whitman ("*Jeff*"): Whitman's younger brother
(1833–90). When Whitman went to New Orleans in 1848, Jeff,
then fifteen, accompanied him.

Notes on Chapter Four

Sources: "By Broad Potomac's Shore" fits together
certain aspects of Whitman's wartime life
in Washington. The material is selected
from letters to his mother (DRESSER); other
letters (FEINBERG); a paragraph from a let-
ter to O'Connor (BERG); a letter to his
mother in the Whitman House collection
(printed in SELECTED); and passages from
PROSE.

Major Lyman Hapgood: Army paymaster in whose office Whit-
man worked two or three hours a day as copyist. The rest of the
day the poet had the freedom of the office for his own work and
correspondence.
Charles W. Eldridge: A clerk in Major Hapgood's office. Before
coming to Washington, he had been associated with the Boston

[1] H. S. Canby, in *Walt Whitman, An American.* Boston: Houghton
Mifflin Co., 1943.

publishers, Thayer and Eldridge, who published the third edition of *Leaves* (1860).

Ellen O'Connor ("Nellie"): Mrs. William Douglas O'Connor, later Mrs. Calder. A constant friend and ally of Whitman's throughout his life.

Notes on Chapter Five

Sources: "The Great Army of the Wounded" uses dispatches to the *New York Times* and the *Brooklyn Eagle* (collected in DRESSER); a letter appearing in CLUES (manuscript in TRENT); and a letter to Mrs. Abby Price (MORGAN), originally printed in the posthumously published COMPLETE PROSE, Vol. 4 (1902).

Dr. B. B. Bliss: A physician whom Whitman met in the course of his visits to Washington hospitals. He became a warm friend and admirer of the poet.

Dr. LeBaron Russell: Boston physician who collected and contributed money for the comforts Whitman brought to the wounded soldiers.

Notes on Chapter Six

Sources: "Dear Love of Comrades" is selected from PROSE and from a Whitman conversation in TRAUBEL 3. The passage *Christmas Night* is in manuscript (TRENT).

Notes on Chapter Seven

Sources: "Dearest Mother" opens with introductory paragraphs from TRAUBEL 2 and 3. The rest of the chapter is selected from letters Whitman wrote to his mother from Washington (DRESSER). *The Wound Dresser*, published posthumously by his executors, contains the entire correspondence. One of the letters tells of the first symptoms of ill health that culminated in Whitman's paralytic stroke in 1873.

Whitman on Women: "I don't think our Northern women have ever been given sufficient credit; we have heard of the women of the South—of their fortitude, patriotism; we have heard them cheered, lauded to the echo—which is all right, too—but the women up here who stayed at home, watched, worked, worried; who prayed for our soldiers, armies—their self-control, their sacrifice, has never been recognized for what it is or means. . . ."[1]

Moses Lane: Superintendent of Brooklyn Water Works, where Jeff, Whitman's brother, was employed. He contributed to Whitman's fund for his wounded soldiers.

Wager Swayne: Entered Union Army as major, 1861; awarded medal of honor for bravery at Battle of Corinth.

U.S. Sanitary Commission: When Whitman arrived in Washington, conditions in the military hospitals were arousing grave concern among many citizens. The government had been caught unprepared for the tremendous number of casualties. By the end of 1862, however, a Sanitary Commission was set up and effected some reforms and improvements.

The Christian Commission: A civilian organization set up by the churches to give some aid and comfort to the wounded. Whitman, who applied to the Commission as a volunteer, received the following authorization, dated January 20, 1863:

"The Commission is given to Walt Whitman of Brooklyn, N.Y. His services [as a delegate] will be rendered without remuneration. . . . His work will be that of . . . visiting the sick and wounded, to instruct, comfort, and cheer them. . . ."[2]

Whitman did not remain long with the Christian Commission; he was concerned with a broader, more personal service to the wounded—as the text of the present book reveals. (The many groups who now render volunteer hospital service did not exist in Whitman's day.)

Elias Hicks: The great Quaker leader whose lectures Whitman had heard in his early youth. Whitman was greatly influenced by him; later wrote a piece about him.[3] On July 25, 1888, Whitman remarked to Traubel, in their discussion of Whitman's long delay in finishing his essay on Hicks: "My internal laziness, neglect, inanition, for thirty years of fifty or more, has put this off and off till now it is no longer possible. My fatal procrastination has tripped me up at last."[4]

---

[1] TRAUBEL 2.
[2] FEINBERG.
[3] PROSE.
[4] TRAUBEL 2.

Notes on Chapter Eight

Sources: "O My Soldiers, My Veterans" opens with a short paragraph from TRAUBEL 3, in which Whitman recalls the letters he wrote to and for his soldier friends. The rest of the chapter consists of selections from the following letters: to Nat and Fred Gray (manuscript in VIRGINIA, published in UNCOLLECTED); to Tom Sawyer (BERG); the Haskell letter (manuscript in FEINBERG, published in TRAUBEL 3); two letters to Hugo Fritsch, one of which is in FEINBERG (both published in TRAUBEL 3); two letters to Lewis Brown, one dated August 1, 1863 (WASHINGTON, printed in GLICKSBERG), and the other dated November 8, 1863 (manuscript in FEINBERG, printed in TRAUBEL 3). The closing passage of this chapter is from an unpublished manuscript in FEINBERG.

Soldiers' Letters: A manuscript collection of soldiers' letters to Whitman is contained in a folder entitled "A Series of 94 soldiers' letters addressed to Walt Whitman, 1863, etc." [1] The following extracts from these letters are typical in reflecting the love of the soldiers for Whitman.
"I will never forget you as long as life should last. . . . I can't find words to tell you the love thier is in me for you. . . ."—William H. Miller, Ward M, January 12, 1865.
". . . You seemed like a father, why it was so I am unable to say . . . but such has been the case with thousands of fellow soldiers. . . ."—C. L. Scott, August 31, 1863.
In a similar vein, a mother wrote: "You have been more than a brother to James . . . and I still ask you to be a Father and Mother to him."

Tom Sawyer: Sergeant Thomas P. Sawyer, 11th Massachusetts Volunteers, one of Whitman's close friends and correspondents.

---

[1] BERG.

Lewis Kirk Brown (*"Lewy"*): Enlisted when eighteen; received severe leg wounds at Cedar Mountain; leg amputated at Armory-Square Hospital, where Whitman met him. The poet looked upon Lewy as an adopted son.

Hugo Fritsch (*"Fritschy"*): Son of the Austrian consul-general, with whom Whitman often went to the opera.

Pfaff's: A restaurant frequented by Whitman and his friends. It was located above Bleecker Street on Broadway, in New York. Around 1854, Pfaff's began building up a clientele of writers and artists. The food and drink were excellent, the atmosphere Bohemian.

Horatio Stone: Sculptor and physician who served as contract surgeon with the Union forces at various hospitals.

Notes on Chapter Nine

Sources: The opening passage in "Prisoners and Escapees" is from an unpublished manuscript (FEINBERG). The *New York Times* item is a letter to the editor—not one of Whitman's formal dispatches. A short passage from a letter to his mother (DRESSER) is followed by an important manuscript dated December 26 (YALE), which throws light on Whitman's hope of doing a history of his brother's regiment. (Another part of this manuscript appears in Chapter One.) The "William Grover" passage (WASHINGTON) is published in GLICKSBERG. The rest of this chapter is from PROSE and TRAUBEL.

Manuscript note on "The Good Old Cause": "The good old cause is that, in all its diversities, at all times, under all circumstances, which promulges liberty, justice, the cause of the people as against infidels and tyrants." [1]

William Grover: Company A, 46th Pennsylvania. When eighteen or nineteen, he was shot at Leesburg for desertion. He had been in the service for two years, and was reputed to be a good soldier.

[1] PENNSYLVANIA.

Notes on Chapter Ten

Sources: "Ethiopia Saluting the Colors" uses material from a piece Whitman published in *November Boughs* (PROSE), entitled "Paying the First U. S. C. T." (United States Colored Troops). The closing paragraphs are from TRAUBEL I.

For an account of Whitman's many varied utterances as poet, prose writer, citizen, and editorialist, on Negroes and slavery, see Newton Arvin's *WHITMAN*, Chapter Two; also Clara Barrus's *WHITMAN AND BURROUGHS, Comrades*, which describes his quarrel with William O'Connor on the question of Negro suffrage after the war—a quarrel that kept the friends apart for ten years.

Comments made by Whitman on this subject at various times are quoted below:

"I say where liberty draws not the blood out of slavery, there slavery draws the blood out of liberty." [1]

"After all, I may have been tainted a bit, just a little bit, with the New York feeling with regard to anti-slavery. . . ." [2]

"The horror of slavery always had a strong hold on me. . . ." [3]

". . . slavery and the tremendous spreading of hands to protect it and the stern opposition to it which shall never cease, or the speaking of tongues and the moving of lips ceases." [4]

"I observe the slights and degradations cast by arrogant persons upon laborers, the poor, and upon Negroes, and the like. . . ." [5]

"Or I guess the grass itself is a child . . . a uniform hieroglyphic . . . growing among black folks as among white. . . ." [6]

"You dim-descended, black, divine-souled African, large, fine-headed, nobly formed, superbly destined, on equal terms with me!" [7]

"Everyone who speaks his word for slavery is himself the worst slave—the spirit of a freeman is not light enough in him to show that all the fatness of the earth were bitter to a bondaged neck. —When of a feast I eat corn and roast potatoes for my dinner through my own voluntary choice, it is very well and I much con-

[1] From "Says," a poem later discarded.
[2] TRAUBEL.
[3] Ibid.
[4] PROSE (1855 Preface).
[5] LEAVES.
[6] Ibid.
[7] Ibid.

tent; but if some arrogant head of the table prevent me by force from touching anything but corn and potatoes, then is my anger aroused. . . ." [1]
"I was a decided and outspoken anti-slavery believer myself then and always, but steered from the extremest, the red hot fellows of these times. . . ." [2]

Whitman's attitude on slavery was expressed in a dispatch to the *Brooklyn Daily Eagle,* dated March 18, 1856:

Public attention within the last few days has been naturally turned to the slave trade—that most abominable of all man's schemes for making money without regard to the character of the means used for the purpose. Four vessels have, in about as many days, been brought to the American territory for being engaged in this monstrous business! It is a disgrace and a blot on the character of our Republic and on our boasted humanity!

Though we hear less nowadays of this trade—of the atrocious slave hunt—of the crowding of a mass of compact human flesh into little more than its own equal in space—we are not to suppose that such horrors have ceased to exist. The great nations of the earth—our own first of all—have passed stringent laws against the slave traffic. But Brazil encourages it still. And many citizens of Europe and America pursue it notwithstanding its illegality. Still the Negro is torn from his simple hut—from his children, his brethren, his parents and friends—to be carried far away and made the bondsman of a stranger. Still the black-hearted traitors who ply this work go forth with their armed bands and swoop down on the defenseless villages, and bring their loads of human trophy, chained and gagged, and sell them as so much merchandise!

The slave-ship! How few of our readers know the beginning of the horrors involved in that term! Imagine a vessel of the fourth or fifth class, built more for speed than space, and therefore with narrow accommodations even for a few passengers; a space between decks divided into two compartments, three feet, three inches from floor to ceiling—one of these compartments sixteen feet by eight, the other forty by twenty-one—the first holding two hundred and twenty-six children and youth of both sexes; the second, *three hundred and thirty-six men and women*—and all this in a latitude where the thermometer is at eighty degrees in the shade.

[1] WORKSHOP.   [2] TRAUBEL.

Are you sick of the description? O, this is not all, by a good sight. Imagine neither food nor water given these hapless prisoners—except a little of the latter, at long intervals, which they spill in their mad eagerness to get it; many of the women advanced in pregnancy—the motion of the seas sickening those who have never before felt it—dozens of the poor wretches dying, and others already dead (and they are most to be envied!)—the very air so thick that the lungs cannot perform their office—and all this for filthy lucre! Pah! we are almost a misanthrope to our kind when we think they will do such things!

Of the nine hundred Negroes (there were doubtless more) originally on board the Pons, not six hundred and fifty remained when she arrived back and landed her inmates at Monrovia! It is enough to make the heart pause its pulsation to read the scene presented at the liberation of these sons of misery. —Most of them were boys, of from twelve to twenty years. What woe must have spread through many a Negro mother's heart from this wicked business!

It is not ours to find an excuse for slaving in the benighted condition of the African. Has not God seen fit to make him and leave him so? Nor is it any less our fault because the chiefs of that barbarous land fight with each other and take slave-prisoners. The whites encourage them and afford them a market. Were that market destroyed, there would soon be no supply.

We would hardly so insult our countrymen as to suppose that any among them yet countenance a system only a little portion of whose horrors we have been describing—did not facts prove the contrary. The "middle passage" is yet going on with all its deadly crime and cruelty. The slave trade yet exists. Why? The laws are sharp enough —too sharp. But who ever heard of their being put in force, further than to confiscate the vessel, and perhaps imprison the crews a few days? But the laws should pry out every man who helps the slave-trade—not merely the sailor on the sea, but the *cowardly rich villain and speculator on the land*—and punish *him*. It cannot be effectually stopped until that is done—and Brazil forced by the black muzzles of American and European men-of-war cannot to stop her part of the business, too.

Another essay on slavery,[1] addressed to the young men of America in 1856, follows:

[1] FORCES.

Voice of Walt Whitman to each Young Man in the Nation, North, South, East and West.

To the American young men, mechanics, farmers, etc.: How much longer do you intend to submit to the espionage and terrorism of the three hundred and fifty thousand owners of slaves? Are you too their slaves and their most obedient slaves? Shall no one among you dare open his mouth to say he is opposed to slavery, as a man should be on account of the whites, and want it abolished for their sake? Is not a writer, speaker, teacher to be left alive but those who lick the spit that drops from the mouths of the three hundred and fifty thousand masters? Is there hardly one free, courageous soul left in fifteen large and populous states? Do the ranks of the owners of slaves themselves contain no men desperate and tired of that service and sweat of the mind, worse than any of that service in sugar fields or cornfields, under the eyes of overseers? Do the three hundred and fifty thousand expect to bar off forever all preachers, poets, philosophers—all that makes the brain of these States: free literature, free thought, the good old cause of liberty? Are they blind? Do they not see those unrelaxed circles of death narrowing and narrowing every hour around them?

You young men of the Southern States! Is the word abolitionist so hateful to you, then? Do you know that Washington, Jefferson, Madison, and all the great Presidents and primal warriors and sages were declared abolitionists?

You young men! American mechanics, farmers, boatmen, manufacturers, and all work-people of the South, the same as the North! you are either to abolish slavery, or it will abolish you.

To the three hundred and fifty thousand owners of slaves: Suppose you get Kansas, do you think it would be ended? Suppose you and the politicians put Buchanan into the Eighteenth Presidency, or Fillmore into the Presidency, do you think it would be ended? I know nothing more desirable for those who contend against you than that you should get Kansas. Then would the melt begin in these States that would not cool till Kansas should be redeemed as of course it would be.

O gentlemen, you do not know whom Liberty has nursed in these States, and depends on in time of need. You have not received any report of the Free States, but have received only the reports of the trustees who have betrayed a few men like you? Raised on plantations or in towns full of menial workmen and workwomen, you do not know, as I know, those fierce and turbulent races that fill the

Northeast, the East, the West and Northwest, the Pacific Shores, the great cities, Manhattan Island, Brooklyn, Newark, Boston, Worcester, Hartford, New Haven, Providence, Portland, Bangor, Augusta, Albany, Buffalo, Rochester, Syracuse, Lockport, Cleveland, Detroit, Milwaukee, Racine, Sheboygan, Madison, Galena, Burlington, Iowa City, Chicago, St. Louis, Cincinnati, Columbus, Pittsburgh, Philadelphia, San Francisco, Sacramento, and many more. From my mouth hear the will of these States taking form in the great cities.

Where slavery is, there it is. The American compacts, common sense, all things unite to make it the affair of the States diseased with it, to cherish the same as long as they see fit, and to apply the remedy when they see fit. But not one square mile of continental territory shall henceforth be given to slavery, to slaves or to the masters of slaves—not one square foot. If any laws are passed giving up such territory, those laws will be repealed. In organizing the territories, what laws are good enough for the American freeman must be good enough for you; if you come in under the said laws, well and good; if not, stay away. What is done, is done; henceforth there is no further compromise. All this is now being cast in the stuff that makes the tough national resolves of these States, that every hour only anneals tougher. It is not putty that you see in Congress and in the Presidency; it is iron—it is the undissuadable swift metal of death . . .

The times are full of great portents in these States and in the whole world. Freedom against slavery is not issuing here alone, but is issuing everywhere. The horizon rises, it divides, I perceive, for a more august drama than any of the past. Old men have played their parts; the act suitable to them is closed; and if they will not withdraw voluntarily, must be bid to do so with unmistakable voice. Landmarks of masters, slaves, kings, aristocracies, are motheaten, and the peoples of the earth are planting new vast landmarks for themselves. Frontiers and boundaries are less and less able to divide men. The modern inventions, the wholesale engines of war, the world-spreading instruments of peace, the steamship, the locomotive, the electric telegraph, the common newspaper, the cheap book, the ocean mail, are interlinking the inhabitants of the earth together as groups of one family—America standing, and for ages to stand, as the host and champion of the same, the most welcome spectacle ever presented among nations.

Everything indicates unparalleled reforms. Races are marching

317

and countermarching by swift millions and tens of millions. Never was justice so mighty amid injustice; never did the idea of equality itself erect itself so haughty and uncompromising amid inequality, as today. Never were such sharp questions asked as today. Never was there more eagerness to know. Never was the representative man more energetic, more like a god, than today. He urges on the myriads before him, he crowds them aside, his daring step approaches the arctic and antarctic poles, he colonizes the islands of the Pacific, the Asiatic Indias, the birthplace of languages and of races, the archipelagoes, Australia; he explores Africa, he unearths Assyria and Egypt, he restates history, he enlarges morality, he speculates anew upon the soul, upon original premises; nothing is left quiet, nothing but he will settle by demonstrations for himself.

What whispers are running through the eastern continents and crossing the Atlantic and Pacific? What historic dénouements are these that are approaching? On all sides tyrants tremble, crowns are unsteady, the human race restive, on the watch for some better era, some divine war. No man knows what will happen next, but all know that some such things are to happen as mark the greatest moral convulsions of the earth. Who shall play the band for America in these tremendous games? A pretty time for two dead corpses to go walking up and down the earth, to guide by feebleness and ashes a proud, young, friendly, fresh, heroic nation of thirty millions of live and electric men!

Notes on Chapter Eleven

Sources: "O Magnet South" contains some of Whitman's observations on the South, most of them made during conversations with Traubel. These extracts (TRAUBEL 1, 2, and 3) are scattered through this chapter. The two letters to his mother are in FEINBERG (printed in DRESSER). The remaining passages are in PROSE.

Moncure D. Conway: Former Methodist minister turned author. One of the earliest admirers of Whitman's work and his lifelong friend and interpreter. A personal sketch that he wrote on Whitman appeared in the *Fortnightly Review* (Oct. 15, 1866).

On Southern Rulers: "Why do not the Free States grow a powerful compact set of leaders representing the theory of American freedom, the theory of the founders, the crown and glory of political science and of the Christian religion—as they have in the Slave

States—under all aristocratic forms, the thing that is admirable. (And this will deserve and take the mead of historic applause for ages.) There is great personal force in the ruling class, the planters, the central figures—while the mass of the people are either little or nothing, or at best serve as the body, the entourage which the ruling class vivifies and makes move or stand still, as the strong will makes the body. When the South is spoken of, no one means the people, the mass of the freemen." [1]

Notes on Chapter Twelve

Sources: "Of the Corps and Generals" is made up of reminiscences and opinions concerning various public figures. Although most of Whitman's wartime writings (with the exception of his Lincoln essays) were about rank-and-file soldiers, in talks with Traubel he voiced his estimates and impressions of political and military leaders. The passages selected are from TRAUBEL 1, 2, and 3.

Notes on Chapter Thirteen

Sources: "Memories of Lincoln" comprises material from unpublished manuscripts, set pieces, and extracts from letters. Although Whitman frequently saw Lincoln, they never actually met—except perhaps to bow to each other in passing. The poet was in New York when Lincoln was assassinated. The text of the Lincoln lecture (which Whitman delivered on many occasions) is found in PROSE. The chapter opens with an introductory passage Whitman used when he delivered the lecture for the last time (in Boston). This appeared in the *Boston Transcript* and was later printed in LINCOLN. Other passages are from TRAUBEL 2, 3, and 4, and from PROSE. The extract from the July 8, 1867 letter is the only evidence the editor has found that Whitman attended the Surratt trial. (The complete letter is in FEINBERG.)

[1] YALE.

John Harrison Surratt: Son of Mary Eugenia Surratt, one of the suspected conspirators in the Lincoln assassination. Mrs. Surratt was hanged; John Surratt was tried, imprisoned for a year, and later released.

In addition to Whitman's utterances and speeches in the text, he is quoted as having remarked: "Lincoln is particularly my man—particularly belongs to me; yes, and by the same token, I am Lincoln's man; I guess I particularly belong to him; we are afloat on the same stream—we are rooted in the same ground." [1]

Notes on Chapter Fourteen

Sources: The opening passage of "The Real War Will Never Get In the Books" is an outline in manuscript (YALE) for a speech Whitman proposed to make but never completed. The balance of the chapter is from *Democratic Vistas, Origins of Attempted Secession,* and other sections of PROSE.

Some general comments made by Whitman on the nature of war, and two unpublished poems, are given here to amplify the poet's conception of the "real war."

"Our land and history are so full of spinal subjects. To take only one siege—what the ancient war of Ilium and the puissance of the respective Greek and Trojan warriors proved to Hellenic poetry and art, and onward indeed to all poetry and art since, so it has been predicted by more than one shrewd thinker and prophet, will prove the War of Attempted Secession of 1861–5 to the future esthetic of the United States." [2]

"The Wars of Peace":

"I guess that the war eras are about or nearly past: we will have more wars, wars more important, men more warriorlike, than any recorded in history; but the new wars, the new warriors, will be spiritual wars, spiritual warriors. The fiercest wars are yet to be fought—the wars of peace: the wars of classes that honor labor with castes that don't; the wars of the arts demanding admission to common life or of the common life to be admitted to and to

---

[1] LINCOLN.   [2] YALE.

vivify the arts; and these wars will require the strongest men—
the restrained, the self-contained, the self-mastered men." [1]

"*Agitations, Dangers in America.*"

"In the main, wars, as fought down to the present ages, have ceased
for the civilized world, and are to cease. —Wars have always done
a work that they only could do; but greater wars will yet arouse
men. —Pitched battles will be fought—and are fought in these
States today. On less terms, no strong nation is made.

I will at once admit there is something in us as a race, as races, that,
against peace, against solidity, against enjoyment, restless, hungry,
offensive, full of danger, full of death, often unable to account for
itself, will allow nothing long to remain established, for all we have
done it well, or it has been done well for us. —But heedless of risks,
deaf to the warnings of the good, the orthodox, the experienced—
deaf to majorities, deaf to ridicule—this something, more resolute
in the hour of defeat than in the hour of triumph, urges us onward
to never be content with what we have, but always advance, initiat-
ing others we have not.

I think that agitation awaits us, relentless, continually. Our destiny
doubtless is to walk out more and more amid strong questions—to
enter combats—not like the old combats but more exhilarating,
more spiritual. Face to face meeting many a rude shock, many a low
reality of life—hardening the muscle of our young men—forcing
them to acquire the quick eye and the supple joint—passing through
bitterness to attain what is attained only through bitterness. Our
pride to see ourselves at last, not what was told in false prophecies
—a fat, respectable, abiding tempered, unwarlike race—but a
race of warrior-brothers, armed for such conflicts, trained to cope
with danger—race owning no law but the law of ourselves—true to
that law forever—fearless, independent, haughty—race of passion
and the storm." [2]

*An undated version in manuscript of some lines from "Return of the
Heroes":* [3]

Yet the dead mar not—they also fit well in nature,
They fit very well in the landscape
      Under the trees and the grasses

[1] FEINBERG.
[2] *The Artsman,* edited by Traubel (FEINBERG).
[3] VIRGINIA.

And along the edge of the sky in the horizon's far margin
Nor do I forget you, departed,
Nor in winter or summer,
    My lost ones,
But must trace you in the open air as now, when my soul is rapt & at
    peace like passing phantoms
You dear memories rising, glide silently by me
I saw the return of the heroes
(Yet the heroes never surpassed, shall never return—them that day,
    I saw not)
I saw the great corps with divisions approach defiling by
And each at its head, riding in the midst of his staff, the General,
I saw the procession of armies
Streaming northward, their work done, in clusters of mighty camps
No holiday soldiers—youthful but veterans,
Worn, swart, strong, of the stock of homestead, and workshop
Men, hardened of many a long campaign & sweaty march
Figured in maps in a hard-fought bloody field.
Exult indeed—O lands!
    Victorious lands!
Not there your victory on those red-studded fields—
    but here and hence your victory!
Melt, melt away ye armies! Disperse ye blue-clad heroes!
Resolve ye back again—give up for good your deadly arms
Other the arms, the fields henceforth for you, or South or North,
    or West, or East
With calmer, saner wars—sweet wars—life-giving wars.

FROM A MSS POEM:

There rises in my brain the thought of graves—
to my lips a word for dead soldiers
The Dead we left behind—there they lie, embedded low,
    already fused by Nature
Through broad Virginia's soil, through Tennessee—
The Southern states cluttered with cemeteries
the borders dotted with their graves—the Nation's dead.
Silent they lie—the passionate hot tears have ceased to flow—
time has assuaged the anguish of the living.[1]

[1] FEINBERG.

322

Appendix

Whitman's Civil War Poems
in Addition to Those Used in Text

BY BROAD POTOMAC'S SHORE

By broad Potomac's shore, again old tongue,
(Still uttering, still ejaculating, canst never cease this babble?)
Again old heart so gay, again to you, your sense, the full flush
    spring returning,
Again the freshness and the odors, again Virginia's summer sky,
    pellucid blue and silver,
Again the forenoon purple of the hills,
Again the deathless grass, so noiseless soft and green,
Again the blood-red roses blooming.

Perfume this book of mine O blood-red roses!
Lave subtly with your waters every line Potomac!
Give me of you O spring, before I close, to put between its pages!
O forenoon purple of the hills, before I close, of you!
O deathless grass, of you!

HOW SOLEMN AS ONE BY ONE

How solemn as one by one,
As the ranks returning worn and sweaty, as the men file by where
    I stand,
As the faces the masks appear, as I glance at the faces studying the
    masks,
(As I glance upward out of this page studying you, dear friend,
    whoever you are,)
How solemn the thought of my whispering soul to each in the
    ranks, and to you!
I see behind each mask that wonder a kindred soul,
O the bullet could never kill what you really are, dear friend,
Nor the bayonet stab what you really are;
The soul! yourself I see, great as any, good as the best,

Waiting secure and content, which the bullet could never kill,
Nor the bayonet stab O friend.

I SAW OLD GENERAL AT BAY

I saw old General at bay,
(Old as he was, his gray eyes yet shone out in battle like stars,)
His small force was now completely hemm'd in, in his works,
He call'd for volunteers to run the enemy's lines, a desperate
emergency,
I saw a hundred and more step forth from the ranks, but two or
three were selected,
I saw them receive their orders aside, they listen'd with care, the
adjutant was very grave,
I saw them depart with cheerfulness, freely risking their lives.

LONG, TOO LONG AMERICA

Long, too long America,
Traveling roads all even and peaceful you learn'd from joys and
prosperity only,
But now, ah now, to learn from crises of anguish, advancing, grap-
pling with direst fate and recoiling not,
And now to conceive and show to the world what your children
en-masse really are,
(For who except myself has yet conceiv'd what your children en-
masse really are?)

LOOK DOWN FAIR MOON

Look down fair moon and bathe this scene,
Pour softly down night's nimbus floods on faces ghastly, swollen,
purple,
On the dead on their backs with arms toss'd wide,
Pour down your unstinted nimbus sacred moon.

LO, VICTRESS ON THE PEAKS

Lo, Victress on the peaks,
Where thou with mighty brow regarding the world,
(The world O Libertad, that vainly conspired against thee,)
Out of its countless beleaguering toils, after thwarting them all,
Dominant, with the dazzling sun around thee,

Flauntest now unharm'd in immortal soundness and bloom—lo, in
these hours supreme,
No poem proud, I chanting bring to thee, nor mastery's rapturous
verse,
But a cluster containing night's darkness and blood-dripping
wounds,
And psalms of the dead.

OLD WAR-DREAMS

In midnight sleep of many a face of anguish,
Of the look at first of the mortally wounded, (of that indescribable
look,)
Of the dead on their backs with arms extended wide,
    I dream, I dream, I dream.

Of scenes of Nature, fields and mountains,
Of skies so beauteous after a storm, and at night the moon so un-
earthly bright,
Shining sweetly, shining down, where we dig the trenches and
gather the heaps,
    I dream, I dream, I dream.

Long have they pass'd, faces and trenches and fields,
Where through the carnage I moved with a callous composure, or
away from the fallen,
Onward I sped at the time—but now of their forms at night,
    I dream, I dream, I dream.

RISE O DAYS FROM YOUR FATHOMLESS DEEPS

. . . Thunder on! stride on, Democracy! strike with vengeful
stroke!
And do you rise higher than ever yet O days, O cities!
Crash heavier, heavier yet O storms! you have done me good,
My soul prepared in the mountains absorbs your immortal strong
nutriment,
Long had I walk'd my cities, my country roads through farms,
only half satisfied,
One doubt nauseous undulating like a snake, crawl'd on the ground
before me
Continually preceding my steps, turning upon me oft, ironically
hissing low;

The cities I loved so well I abandon'd and left, I sped to the certainties suitable to me,
Hungering, hungering, hungering, for primal energies and Nature's dauntlessness,
I refresh'd myself with it only, I could relish it only,
I waited the bursting forth of the pent fire—on the water and air I waited long;
But now I no longer wait, I am fully satisfied, I am glutted,
I have witness'd the true lightning, I have witness'd my cities electric,
I have lived to behold man burst forth and warlike America rise,
Hence I will seek no more the food of the northern solitary wilds,
No more the mountains roam or sail the stormy sea.

THE RETURN OF THE HEROES

. . . (Pass, pass, ye proud brigades, with your tramping sinewy legs,
With your shoulders young and strong, with your knapsacks and your muskets;
How elate I stood and watch'd you, where starting off you march'd. . . .

Melt, melt away ye armies—disperse ye blue-clad soldiers,
Resolve ye back again, give up for good your deadly arms,
Other the arms the fields henceforth for you, or South or North,
With saner wars, sweet wars, life-giving wars.

THIS DUST WAS ONCE THE MAN

This dust was once the man,
Gentle, plain, just and resolute, under whose cautious hand,
Against the foulest crime in history known in any land or age,
Was saved the Union of these States.

WHEN LILACS LAST IN THE DOORYARD BLOOM'D

I

When lilacs last in the dooryard bloom'd,
And the great star early droop'd in the western sky in the night,
I mourn'd, and yet shall mourn with ever-returning spring.

Ever-returning spring, trinity sure to me you bring,
Lilac blooming perennial and drooping star in the west,
And thought of him I love.

2

O powerful western fallen star!
O shades of night—O moody, tearful night!
O great star disappear'd—O the black murk that hides the star!
O cruel hands that hold me powerless—O helpless soul of me!
O harsh surrounding cloud that will not free my soul.

3

In the dooryard fronting an old farm-house near the white-wash'd
    palings,
Stands the lilac-bush tall-growing with heart-shaped leaves of rich
    green,
With many a pointed blossom rising delicate, with the perfume
    strong I love,
With every leaf a miracle—and from this bush in the dooryard,
With delicate-color'd blossoms and heart-shaped leaves of rich
    green,
A sprig with its flower I break.

4

In the swamp in secluded recesses,
A shy and hidden bird is warbling a song.

Solitary the thrush,
The hermit withdrawn to himself, avoiding the settlements,
Sings by himself a song.

Song of the bleeding throat,
Death's outlet song of life, (for well dear brother I know,
If thou wast not granted to sing thou would'st surely die.)

5

Over the breast of the spring, the land, amid cities,
Amid lanes and through old woods, where lately the violets peep'd
    from the ground, spotting the gray debris,
Amid the grass in the fields each side of the lanes, passing the end-
    less grass,
Passing the yellow-spear'd wheat, every grain from its shroud in the
    dark-brown fields uprisen,
Passing the apple-tree blows of white and pink in the orchards,
Carrying a corpse to where it shall rest in the grave,
Night and day journeys a coffin.

6

Coffin that passes through lanes and streets,
Through day and night with the great cloud darkening the land,
With the pomp of the inloop'd flags with the cities draped in black,
With the show of the States themselves as of crape-veil'd women
    standing,
With processions long and winding and the flambeaus of the night,
With the countless torches lit, with the silent sea of faces and the
    unbared heads,
With the waiting depot, the arriving coffin, and the sombre faces,
With dirges through the night, with the thousand voices rising
    strong and solemn,
With all the mournful voices of the dirges pour'd around the coffin,
The dim-lit churches and the shuddering organs—where amid these
    you journey,
With the tolling tolling bells' perpetual clang,
Here, coffin that slowly passes,
I give you my sprig of lilac.

7

(Nor for you, for one alone,
Blossoms and branches green to coffins all I bring,
For fresh as the morning, thus would I chant a song for you O sane
    and sacred death.

All over bouquets of roses,
O death, I cover you over with roses and early lilies,
But mostly and now the lilac that blooms the first,
Copious I break, I break the sprigs from the bushes,
With loaded arms I come, pouring for you,
For you and the coffins all of you O death.)

8

O western orb sailing the heaven,
Now I know what you must have meant as a month since I walk'd,
As I walk'd in silence the transparent shadowy night,
As I saw you had something to tell as you bent to me night after
    night,
As you droop'd from the sky low down as if to my side, (while the
    other stars all look'd on,)
As we wander'd together the solemn night, (for something I know
    not what kept me from sleep,)
As the night advanced, and I saw on the rim of the west how full
    you were of woe,

As I stood on the rising ground in the breeze in the cool transparent
    night,
As I watch'd where you pass'd and was lost in the netherward black
    of the night,
As my soul in its trouble dissatisfied sank, as where you sad orb,
Concluded, dropt in the night, and was gone.

9

Sing on there in the swamp,
O singer bashful and tender, I hear your notes, I hear your call,
I hear, I come presently, I understand you,
But a moment I linger, for the lustrous star has detain'd me,
The star my departing comrade holds and detains me.

10

O how shall I warble myself for the dead one there I loved?
And how shall I deck my song for the large sweet soul that has
    gone?
And what shall my perfume be for the grave of him I love?

Sea-winds blown from east and west,
Blown from the Eastern sea and blown from the Western sea, till
    there on the prairies meeting,
These and with these and the breath of my chant,
I'll perfume the grave of him I love.

11

O what shall I hang on the chamber walls?
And what shall the pictures be that I hang on the walls,
To adorn the burial-house of him I love?

Pictures of growing spring and farms and homes,
With the Fourth-month eve at sundown, and the gray smoke lucid
    and bright,
With floods of the yellow gold of the gorgeous, indolent, sinking
    sun, burning, expanding the air,
With the fresh sweet herbage under foot, and the pale green leaves
    of the trees prolific,
In the distance the flowing glaze, the breast of the river, with a
    wind-dapple here and there,
With ranging hills on the banks, with many a line against the sky,
    and shadows,
And the city at hand with dwellings so dense, and stacks of
    chimneys,

And all the scenes of life and the workshops, and the workmen
homeward returning.

12

Lo, body and soul—this land,
My own Manhattan with spires, and the sparkling and hurrying
tides, and the ships,
The varied and ample land, the South and the North in the light,
Ohio's shores and flashing Missouri,
And ever the far-spreading prairies cover'd with grass and corn.

Lo, the most excellent sun so calm and haughty,
The violet and purple morn with just-felt breezes,
The gentle soft-born measureless light,
The miracle spreading bathing all, the fulfill'd noon,
The coming eve delicious, the welcome night and the stars,
Over my cities shining all, enveloping man and land.

13

Sing on, sing on you gray-brown bird,
Sing from the swamps, the recesses, pour your chant from the
bushes,
Limitless out of the dusk, out of the cedars and pines.

Sing on dearest brother, warble your reedy song,
Loud human song, with voice of uttermost woe.

O liquid and free and tender!
O wild and loose to my soul—O wondrous singer!
You only I hear—yet the star holds me, (but will soon depart,)
Yet the lilac with mastering odor holds me.

14

Now while I sat in the day and look'd forth,
In the close of the day with its light and the fields of spring, and the
farmers preparing their crops,
In the large unconscious scenery of my land with its lakes and
forests,
In the heavenly aerial beauty, (after the perturb'd winds and the
storms,)
Under the arching heavens of the afternoon swift passing, and the
voices of children and women,

The many-moving sea-tides, and I saw the ships how they sail'd,
And the summer approaching with richness, and the fields all busy
 with labor,
And the infinite separate houses, how they all went on, each with its
 meals and minutia of daily usages,
And the streets how their throbbings throbb'd, and the cities pent
 —lo, then and there,
Falling upon them all and among them all, enveloping me with the
 rest,
Appear'd the cloud, appear'd the long black trail,
And I knew death, its thought, and the sacred knowledge of death.

Then with the knowledge of death as walking one side of me,
And the thought of death close-walking the other side of me,
And I in the middle as with companions, and as holding the hands
 of companions,
I fled forth to the hiding receiving night that talks not,
Down to the shores of the water, the path by the swamp in the
 dimness,
To the solemn shadowy cedars and ghostly pines so still.

And the singer so shy to the rest receiv'd me,
The gray-brown bird I know receiv'd us comrades three,
And he sang the carol of death, and a verse for him I love.

From deep secluded recesses,
From the fragrant cedars and the ghostly pines so still,
Came the carol of the bird.

And the charm of the carol rapt me,
As I held as if by their hands my comrades in the night,
And the voice of my spirit tallied the song of the bird.

Come lovely and soothing death,
Undulate round the world, serenely arriving, arriving,
In the day, in the night, to all, to each,
Sooner or later delicate death.

Prais'd be the fathomless universe,
For life and joy, and for objects and knowledge curious,
And for love, sweet love—but praise! praise! praise!
For the sure-enwinding arms of cool-enfolding death.

Dark mother always gliding near with soft feet,
Have none chanted for thee a chant of fullest welcome?
Then I chant it for thee, I glorify thee above all,

331

I bring thee a song that when thou must indeed come, come un-falteringly.

Approach strong deliveress,
When it is so, when thou hast taken them I joyously sing the dead,
Lost in the loving floating ocean of thee,
Laved in the flood of thy bliss O death.

From me to thee glad serenades,
Dances for thee I propose saluting thee, adornments and feastings for thee,
And the sights of the open landscape and the high-spread sky are fitting,
And life and the fields, and the huge and thoughtful night.

The night in silence under many a star,
The ocean shore and the husky whispering wave whose voice I know,
And the soul turning to thee O vast and well-veil'd death,
And the body gratefully nestling close to thee.

Over the tree-tops I float thee a song,
Over the rising and sinking waves, over the myriad fields and the prairies wide,
Over the dense-pack'd cities all and the teeming wharves and ways,
I float this carol with joy, with joy to thee O death.

15

To the tally of my soul,
Loud and strong kept up the gray-brown bird,
With pure deliberate notes spreading filling the night.

Loud in the pines and cedars dim,
Clear in the freshness moist and the swamp-perfume,
And I with my comrades there in the night.

While my sight that was bound in my eyes unclosed,
As to long panoramas of visions.

And I saw askant the armies,
I saw as in noiseless dreams hundreds of battle-flags,
Borne through the smoke of the battles and pierc'd with missiles I saw them,
And carried hither and yon through the smoke, and torn and bloody,

And at last but a few shreds left on the staffs, (and all in silence,)
And the staffs all splinter'd and broken.

I saw battle-corpses, myriads of them,
And the white skeletons of young men, I saw them,
I saw the debris and debris of all the slain soldiers of the war,
But I saw they were not as was thought,
They themselves were fully at rest, they suffer'd not,
The living remain'd and suffer'd, the mother suffer'd,
And the wife and the child and the musing comrade suffer'd,
And the armies that remain'd suffer'd.

16

Passing the visions, passing the night,
Passing, unloosing the hold of my comrades' hands,
Passing the song of the hermit bird and the tallying song of my
    soul,
Victorious song, death's outlet song, yet varying ever-altering song,
As low and wailing, yet clear the notes, rising and falling, flooding
    the night,
Sadly sinking and fainting, as warning and warning, and yet again
    bursting with joy,
Covering the earth and filling the spread of the heaven,
As that powerful psalm in the night I heard from recesses,
Passing, I leave thee lilac with heart-shaped leaves,
I leave thee there in the dooryard, blooming, returning with spring.

I cease from my song for thee,
From my gaze on thee in the west, fronting the west, communing
    with thee,
O comrade lustrous with silver face in the night.

Yet each to keep and all, retrievements out of the night,
The song, the wondrous chant of the gray-brown bird,
And the tallying chant, the echo arous'd in my soul,
With the lustrous and drooping star with the countenance full of
    woe,
With the holders holding my hand nearing the call of the bird,
Comrades mine and I in the midst, and their memory ever to keep,
    for the dead I loved so well,
For the sweetest, wisest soul of all my days and lands—and this for
    his dear sake,
Lilac and star and bird twined with the chant of my soul,
There in the fragrant pines and the cedars dusk and dim.

Index of Poems

A Note about the Editor

WALTER LOWENFELS, himself a poet and critic, has been a long-time admirer and student of Walt Whitman. So this book is not merely a Civil War Centennial collection, but springs from years of reading of Whitman's poetry and prose and from a growing sense of the importance of Whitman's war writings to our own times. Mr. Lowenfels, New York City born, has lived for extended periods in Europe, and four of his books were published first in Paris or London. He now resides in Mays Landing, New Jersey. His poetry has appeared in many magazines, big and little; in 1930 he shared with E. E. Cummings the Richard Aldington Award for American Poets; in 1954 he received the Mainstream Award and in 1959 the Longview Foundation Award.

September 1960